Praise for *A Guide to SE...*
the Early Years

'*A Guide to SEND in the Early Years* is a must-read for all working across the EYFS, whether directly or indirectly. Informed, practical, down to earth and thought provoking.'
Dr Sue Allingham, independent Early Years consultant, @DrSue22

'This book offers a uniquely honest, actually useful, critical yet relatable toolkit for Early Years educators who remain committed to taking care of and educating *all* babies and young children in our current educational system.'
David Cahn, Early Years teacher and carer, and author, @DavidN_Cahn

'*A Guide to SEND in the Early Years* is a book that highlights the importance of a child-centred approach and being in tune with the children in your care. It highlights the importance of training and dispelling urban myths about supporting SEND. *A Guide to SEND in the Early Years* shatters outdated views on SEND that may incite labelling. Kerry has skilfully collated case studies and a plethora of contributions, from parents, Early Years educators and specialists promoting advocacy, agency and activism. This book gives a view of supporting SEND not only from a policy-driven perspective but from a trained, experienced and neurodiverse one.'
Jamel Carly Campbell, Early Years SEND specialist and Men in the Early Years Ambassador, @JamelCarly

'A book of real integrity, a celebration of uniqueness, championing the rights of children with SEND and their families. A game changer, which will reframe thinking and perspectives; from difficulties to differences, problems to possibilities, with tangible strategies to impact practice and ultimately, the lives of children. An essential read for practitioners and parents alike.'
Sarah Doyle, Early Years and SEND advisor, and proud parent to an autistic boy

'A clear, helpful and refreshingly honest book which explains SEND from top to bottom. I would highly recommend this book to anyone trying to navigate SEND in the UK.'
Kim Griffin, Occupational Therapist, GriffinOT, @Griffin_OT

'An accurate synopsis of the dedication and practice of the Early Years workforce to support children and families with SEND despite the barriers and limitations of current government policies.'
Maria Goncalves, London Early Years Foundation SEND Manager

'This is a book that every educator needs to read. It will transform how we think about SEND! Kerry Murphy's words will be music to the ears of professionals and parents. We need this book in every school.'
Dr Gavin Reid, independent educational psychologist, @drgavinreid

'Kerry invites us to consider a child-centred, rights-based and celebratory view of special needs, with intelligent, engaging writing, passion, vulnerability, challenge and a focus on practical application. A must-read.'
David Wright, owner of Paint Pots Nursery, @Mr_PaintPots

A Guide to SEND in the Early Years

A Guide to SEND in the Early Years

Kerry Murphy

FEATHERSTONE

LONDON   OXFORD   NEW YORK   NEW DELHI   SYDNEY

FEATHERSTONE
Bloomsbury Publishing Plc
50 Bedford Square, London, WC1B 3DP, UK
29 Earlsfort Terrace, Dublin 2, Ireland

BLOOMSBURY, FEATHERSTONE and the Feather logo are trademarks of
Bloomsbury Publishing Plc

First published in Great Britain, 2022 by Bloomsbury Publishing Plc

A catalogue record for this book is available from the British Library

ISBN: PB: 978-1-4729-8101-1; ePDF: 978-1-4729-8091-5; ePub: 978-1-4729-8092-2

4 6 8 10 9 7 5

Typeset by Newgen KnowledgeWorks Pvt. Ltd., Chennai, India
Printed and bound in the UK by CPI Group Ltd, Croydon CR0 4YY

MIX
Paper | Supporting
responsible forestry
FSC
www.fsc.org   FSC® C013604

To find out more about our authors and books visit www.bloomsbury.com
and sign up for our newsletters

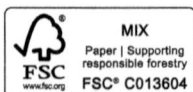

For Olivia & June x

Acknowledgements

Firstly, this book would not have been possible without the many experiences I have had with the children and families I have worked with throughout my career. Olivia, Daniel and Hermione will have no idea of their impact. The Early Years team I worked with in local authority provided a safe and brave space to challenge, debate and expand my understanding of SEND and always held me accountable, so thank you Shelley, Lizzie, Samira, Sarah, Alice and June. Without their endless encouragement and belief, I would not have gotten to do half the things that I dared ask to do – they are literally the best team that I have ever worked with. Thank you to the nurseries and practitioners who were always open to finding solutions amidst many challenges, including Dalia, an amazing nursery manager who let me test out all my ideas at her nursery.

I also have to acknowledge my husband, Nick, and my two dogs, who were never far from my feet as I typed away. The proofreading, sounding board and putting up with my ideas late into the night were much appreciated. My mum and sister, Hayley, also spotted my skills as a SENDCo way before I did and helped me to find my place in the Early Years.

And thank you to all the contributors to this book: the willing parents, specialists and practitioners who shared their stories, advice and guidance, including:

Sarah Doyle
Liz Pemberton
David Cahn
Fifi Benham
Dalia Hamid
Emma Davis
James Tunnell
Rosie Davies
Kate Moxley
Melissa Blignaut
Lianna Wilding

Please note that some of the contributors wished to remain anonymous.

Contents

Author's note

While this book has special educational needs and disability (SEND) in the title, there is an increasing dialogue that the term SEN is becoming outdated. Many people with developmental differences and disabilities believe that defining children as 'special needs' further perpetuates stereotyping, labeling and exclusion through a process known as 'othering'. I have used the term SEN because it is one which is known and used nationally to describe children who learn differently. Professionally, I believe that all children have needs, and our role is to meet them in the best way we can, and so while SEN is used, I fully agree that it is a term that has an expiration date.

In addition, the 0-25 SEND code of practice (DfE, 2015) predominately refers to SEN support. For inclusion of all children, I tend to use SEND support because many settings will be supporting children with a range of disabilities also.

Introduction

'Call it a clan, call it a network, call it a tribe, call it a family. Whatever you call it, whoever you are, you need one. You need one because you are human.'
                                        (Jane Howard, 1998, as cited in Murthy, 2020, pg. 53)

I first read the above quote in Vivek Murthy's book, *Together: Loneliness, Health and What Happens When We Find Connection* (2020). It resonated with me because togetherness and connection are at the heart of inclusion. I decided to write this book because I wanted to demonstrate how our togetherness can have the most significant influence on children, and so it is not just a book for Special Educational Needs and Disabilities Coordinators (SENDCos) but is for anyone who is invested in advocating the rights of *all* children. Much of what I hear about inclusion comes from the higher echelons. Still, it is the work of inclusion from the ground up where most of our lessons can be learned. Being on the 'shop floor' as an Early Years practitioner can often feel like being thrown into the deep end of a pool while you are still learning how to swim. The things that you pick up on the job are invaluable, yet we can still feel very much out of our depth. There is no denying that inclusion in practice is complex, challenging and, at times, very frustrating. We are often the ones standing side by side with a child and their family at the beginning of a significant journey. We are the ones navigating the trickiest of systems and conversations. We are the ones who show up every day, still curious and eager to do better. While this book acknowledges the challenges and the ways in which we don't get it right, it also recognises that we always give it a good go. This is often without consistent support, encouragement or access to training.

You have to be a somewhat optimistic human when working in the Early Years sector because it can take an emotional and physical toll. I intentionally start with a bit of doom and gloom because I do not want you as the reader to think that I am not acutely aware of the challenges. However, this is not a book that aims to tell you everything that is wrong with you or the sector, followed by a bullet-point list of solutions (although there is some of that). I aim to unpick the things that you are likely already doing and to think about how we can realistically build on the wealth of good practice to become even better. Most of the things that I have come to know as a specialist have come from unwavering Early Years practitioners, who dedicate so much time to providing the right support. This is a space for me to share all the practical knowledge that I have collated and picked up along the way.

But before we dive into the book, I would like to dispel a couple of *'SENDisms'* – those typical clichés that we hear when we are already under a great deal of pressure and which can sometimes feel unhelpful.

'Smooth running'

I would like to note that inclusion is not a 'smooth running' process. It is messy, complicated and, at times, disorientating. Still, it is also a rewarding, joyous and crucial part of our everyday work. It should be easier than it is, but it is not always on us to carry the weight of the things that are not going to plan. Think of inclusion as taking 'snakes and ladders' movements rather than straightforward steps. Sometimes we breeze through, and at other times we have to work harder and climb our way around.

'Every teacher is a teacher of SEND'

This is quite controversial, but this is the dream in the Early Years, and not the current reality. We must challenge any policy-maker who thinks that this blanket statement helps our sector. How can we all be teachers of SEND if we haven't had adequate support or training? Also, there are huge tensions around the concept of an Early Years practitioner being viewed as a teacher. While I believe it to be a fundamental principle of inclusion, it can feel tokenistic when we aren't equipped to support SEND. I'm changing it: **If you believe in children's rights, this must include the rights of *all* children including those with SEND**.

The aim of early intervention is to 'fix' or cure a child's SEND

This book prescribes to a pro-neurodiversity approach, which means that I do not see SEND purely through the deficit lens of delays and impairments. While children may have difficulties, this only describes certain aspects of their development, and so we must understand their overall profile of strengths, interests, differences and needs. Some children will also be neurodivergent, meaning that they will have lifelong developmental differences. We need to understand these differences rather than focusing on 'fixing', correcting or training children to behave neurotypically.

The work of inclusion is ongoing and continuous, as we will see throughout the book. While we may not all be super skilled within SEND, we can all build on our current knowledge base and everyday practice. I often find that the biggest reluctance to engage in this specific area of inclusion is that it requires us to understand both the child and the SEND system. This simultaneous body of work on top of everything else that we are expected to do can be hard to navigate. However, over time, I have realised that we must not be flattened by the weight of the 'rule books' and systems that can often feel separate from our daily work. Instead, those 'rule books' have to work for us and be flexible enough to allow us to overcome the barriers to SEND & inclusion. I will venture into policy and procedure throughout this book, but merely to demonstrate how it can work for us – the child, family and setting.

At the heart of what I write is the importance of upholding the rights of the child. Many of you who have picked this book up will have done so because you have a child in mind. The child whom you have sought to understand but fell short. The child who made you see things differently. The child who tested every fibre of your resilience. The child who made you beam with pride. The child who broke your heart, and the child who keeps you here today doing this role. And this brings me back to the original quote: we need each other. The Early Years sector needs to recognise that our togetherness with each other, child and family, is the best form of advocacy that we can offer.

So, while I know that this book cannot change the world, I hope the practitioner who reads it knows that they can…

1 'I think he has autism':
Developing a rights- and strengths-based approach to inclusion

Starting points

Do you believe…
… that every child has a right to belong?
… that every child has a right to be loved and nurtured?
… that every child has a right to education?
… that the purpose of education is for children and young people to find out what they are good at?
… that no child should be discriminated against on the basis of their disability, race, gender, ethnicity, culture or background?

Inclusion! What is it all about anyway?

It is likely that you automatically answered 'yes' to the questions in the box above. Why on earth would we answer otherwise? In truth, my own immediate reaction would be to answer 'yes', but if I stop and think for a moment, there is actually a lot to unpick in those above statements. I can think of examples where my practice and my actions have contradicted those very rights. I did not land in the Early Years sector as a pre-packaged and perfect practitioner, so I have often had to reflect that my practice has not always matched up to my well-meaning intentions.

Contrary to how it should be, we do not always normalise growth within our sector. Our bad bits, our weaknesses and our humanness are not always welcome. We are often told to leave our baggage at the door. But to be in active pursuit of an inclusive pedagogy, we must cultivate spaces in which we challenge and expand our ideas of what it means to be inclusive.

When I started to map out this chapter, I looked for a definition of inclusion. I felt disappointed by the lack of nuance or creativity in an incredibly important concept. Many of the descriptions felt almost tokenistic, too theoretical or quite narrow. I realised that inclusion cannot be neatly summed up because it's undergoing constant change, and it is as much about unlearning as it is about learning. For example, the first time I supported an autistic child was the first time that I had to challenge some of the stereotypes I had about autism, and I had to unlearn my 'one-size-fits-all' mindset. I also had to learn to let go of my own preconceived judgements about 'typical spectrum' behaviours and venture more deeply into understanding the child.

I have learned that inclusion is driven by an openness to engage with complex, sometimes uncomfortable and not always straightforward situations. This requires a continuous 'personal interrogation of our own views and prejudices around differences and difficulties' (Nutbrown et al., 2013, pg. 3). Supporting children with SEND is not always easy. It can often throw up many challenging feelings, especially when we do not possess a deep understanding of the child's unique development. We have all been in situations where we have felt 'inconvenienced' by a child with SEND, and then felt the dull thud of shame and guilt. I recall spending time setting up a fantastic activity and it immediately being 'destroyed' and bulldozed by a child. The way it looked seemed to be more important to me than how it was played with, so I placed the issue within the child, rather than consider that my rigid thinking and learning was interfering with the child's style of play. A helpful and more experienced colleague mentioned that I wouldn't last very long in the field if my expectation was that all children should behave or be the same. She reminded me that my own experience of being taught wasn't necessarily the best blueprint because it was likely rooted in principles of conformity and control, what I now often refer to as the 'conveyor belt curriculum'. Our education system, at least within the Early Years, embraces a much more open and creative process nowadays, and one which acknowledges learning as personal to the child. Early on in my career as a practitioner, I was told to relinquish some of my outdated beliefs about what education is supposed to do and to let go of the need to control children. By being more flexible in my own thinking, I was able to learn to value individual children's natural pace of learning. We might feel shame looking back on our previous selves, but it is an integral part of the learning process as practitioners. We don't just suddenly become inclusive, but instead, it is what we are always becoming (Nutbrown, 2013). Our deeply embedded views and behaviours take time to shift especially in a society that has not always valued developmental differences and disability. If we think of ourselves as the complete package within our professional roles, we are essentially communicating that we don't really believe we still have room to grow. It always reminds me of the evaluations that I receive on training courses where, when asked what they have learned, a self-assured practitioner will write 'confirmed what I already know and do'. There is almost a reluctance to acknowledge that new learning can occur.

Becoming a reflective practitioner

All practitioners should be empowered to develop skills and knowledge within SEND and inclusion. There is still a tendency to view SEND support as separate or additional to the everyday role, so practitioners do not always feel equipped or skilled to support children and often lack confidence. When I was a local authority consultant, my work's burden was that I was expected to be a critical eye, so I became a bit of a faultfinder and action-setter which quickly deterred practitioners from engaging with me. I picked up that a balance needed to be found between constructive and positive feedback especially if I wanted more honest and reflective discussions further down the line. To normalise growth, we need to allow practitioners time to reflect upon the different aspects of their practice and to come to terms with the more difficult experiences of the role. The work of an Early Years practitioner is emotionally complex, physically demanding and time-consuming, and so maintaining consistent high-quality practice can be difficult if these issues go unexplored. Most of our good practice is, if we are honest, born out of the trial and error of bad practice – for example, when I thought that shouting 'Be quiet' was the right way of commanding silence, or when I thought repeating a complicated sequence of instructions to a child with attention differences would work, rather than breaking those instructions down. To paraphrase Maya Angelou, 'it is only when we know better, that we can do better'. But when, as a team or as a childminder, do we get time to unpick these little moments so that we can do better? As a team or as a personal reflective activity, have a think about the following.

Activity: Inclusion process

- List three strong features of your inclusive practice.
- List three things that you feel you do less well in inclusive practice.
- List three ways in which you would like to develop.
- Look at the lists that you have just created. What changes could you realistically make in the short term, and what could you add as a long-term goal?

The inclusion jigsaw

One of the most significant issues with Early Years and inclusion is that we are largely expected to be good at every aspect of the role. Dare I admit as a practitioner that I detest outdoor play when it's raining, or that the 'rinse and repeat' routine of circle time often felt arduous? If I want to teach children about the weather, surely, I get them to go outside rather than look at a picture of the sun? (Except when it is raining!) If you compare the above reflections with your colleagues or within your networks, the answers are likely to differ significantly but together create a jigsaw of good and developing practice.

For many years, I worked at my mum's nursery. She would always be active and often refer to herself as the 'boss, cook and bottle washer', an idiom to describe a job that includes many roles. My mum is a phenomenal childcare practitioner. Everywhere she goes she is known for sprinkling 'fairy dust', because she genuinely loves being around children. She cannot, however, do anything that involves administration or technology, and she often felt overwhelmed by the SEND processes. She recognised this and utilised her team's skills to ensure that, holistically, we were able to deliver a high standard of education for children. Early on in my career, I learned that we do not need to like and be good at everything. We certainly need to be 'good enough', but we must also recognise we have a variety of skills that fit together like jigsaw pieces. This applies to the childminder as well, in that they will each have their 'selling points' that will make their setting the right choice for parents and children.

And so, rather than work ourselves into exhaustion and defeat, we need to direct our energy where it can make the most difference. We need to acknowledge that we are one piece of a gigantic jigsaw, and as the African proverb goes, 'it takes a village to raise a child'. If you look at your fellow villagers, they each will be adding something different. Your villagers include your colleagues, the families for whom you work, the community and the local services. The following case study further demonstrates how these different skillsets can work effectively for inclusion within your setting.

Case study: Building on strengths

Kate had worked in the toddler room for three years and loved working with this age group because she loved the types of play associated with children of this age. She embraced messy play and was always coming up with ideas for sensory activities. One day, her manager asked her to run a workshop for parents because they were always commenting that their children requested similar activities at home. This was Kate's worst nightmare because it was the one aspect of her practice about which she still felt anxious. Talking with parents, especially fathers, made her feel nauseous and she felt like she always said the wrong things. Kate approached her manager and shared this vulnerability, to which her manager suggested that, rather than not do it all, she do it alongside a practitioner who felt confident with parents. And so Eugene and Kate hosted the workshop together. Eugene talked through the slides and Kate did the demonstrations, meaning that she didn't need to lead, but instead could do something within her comfort zone. As the session went on, Kate found that she felt braver to narrate what she was doing, and together Kate and Eugene were able to work to each other's strengths, both building on new skills.

- **What do you consider your strengths in practice? And how are these strengths reinforced?** Kate knew very clearly that her strength was sensory play, and this was further reinforced by the feedback from children, parents and the manager who suggested the workshop.

- **What are the challenges? And how do you feel when you need to go beyond your comfort zone?** Sensory play enabled Kate to believe in herself and her abilities, but engaging with parents was a challenge that hadn't eased over a long period. It was only when faced with going out of her comfort zone that she had to acknowledge this as an issue.

- **Do you feel comfortable when sharing your vulnerabilities? And are you open to problem-solving your way forward with these?** When Kate shared her vulnerabilities with her manager, together they were able to think of a practical solution that still enabled the workshop to go ahead. By stepping outside of her comfort zone, she was able to begin to make steps to increased engagement. Though this might never be her strongest point, she was still able to strengthen her practice.

- **In what ways are you supported when you do this?** In this case, Kate was supported by her manager to find a solution, but this is not always the case. It is important that there is some flexibility in our expectations of each other's skill sets. If we do not acknowledge this, it can be hard for a practitioner to have a good level of self-belief and purpose.

You are enough, but we deserve better…

Despite best efforts, I commonly hear practitioners say that they don't feel knowledgeable, skilled or confident enough when it comes to inclusion. Feeling de-skilled within this role can be frustrating, and it is often those experiences with SEND children where we most commonly fall off-kilter. So often, practitioners will know quite quickly whether there is a developmental difference, and yet so often they are restricted with time, capacity and resources to respond quickly. Early Years providers have a statutory duty to have systems to ensure high-quality provision and approaches in SEND support. While a Special Educational Needs and Disabilities Coordinator (SENDCo) oversees these systems, it is the key person's responsibility to carry out this support (DfE, 2015). In principle, key people *should* be well-equipped, skilled and knowledgeable. However, continued austerity measures and funding cuts to SEND services have limited capacity and access to professional development for the Early Years workforce (House of Commons Committee, 2019). We exist within a sector that also has an assortment of qualifications, making high-quality, consistent and sustainable support problematic (Nutbrown, 2013). It appears that neither qualification level nor access to relevant specialist training is thoughtfully considered. Even when looking for books for practitioners, I found myself feeling really frustrated that we seem to be, in the most part, expected to just knuckle down and self-teach. Research has also found that Early Years practitioners are not supported to be adequately equipped or specifically prepared for SEND support (Nicholson & Palaiologou, 2016). The lack of training does put us at a significant disadvantage. Despite these challenges, we can take some matters into our own hands. There are several ways in which we can reduce the bureaucracy of SEND, especially since the SEND code of practice: 0 to 25 years (DfE & DoH, 2015) does allow for flexibility in how we implement support. I would also like us to consider two important points before we move on.

Challenge 'tickboxery' approaches

The starting point for any setting, whether nursery, school or childminder, is to say no to inclusion's *tickboxery*. Envisage SEND like the layers in a trifle: the bottom layer is what you must do, the second layer represents what you would like to do, the third layer is what you actually do and the toppings are those practical tasks that can become needlessly complicated by leadership teams or local services. These often prohibit our ability to get the right support at the right time. As a disclaimer, I have a lot of time for local authorities and their work, but they are often subject to bureaucracy as much as we are, and become cogs in the wheel of outdated practice. For example, when I became an inclusion consultant, I was asked to help lead the SENDCo training, and it was odd to me that they only allow one person per setting to attend, and that it also had to be someone who intended to be the SENDCo. Coming back to the point about us all being SEND teachers, why don't we all get fair access to the training then? Oh yes – budget cuts. This was inexcusable to me, and eventually I developed two courses, one based on leadership practices and one specifically targeted at key people. The amount of talent and skill that you find within the workforce when you actually enable them to come out to training is incredible. The point that I am making is that we often get told about 'rules', but these rules need to be challenged more frequently because quite often they just do not make sense. If someone were to ask me to do something beyond my statutory duty, I would want to ensure that it was not just another way to slow me down – for example, asking me to fill in a 20-page statutory request when I have the information all clearly completed in another format. My day job is littered with these examples of needless expectations that actually take us away from children. We will keep coming back to this bureaucracy throughout the book, but as a starting point, I would advise that you clarify why you are being required to tick boxes or follow arbitrary rules.

Recognising that caregiving is not a dirty word

Activity

- Note down all the tasks and skills associated with caregiving.
- What impact do you think these have on a child?
- Do you agree that caregiving is a form of education?
- What positive and negative perceptions have you experienced as the result of being an Early Years practitioner?

Practitioner's voice

I'm *just* a childminder.

Contrary to outdated but still very much existing beliefs, working with children doesn't just come naturally. Sure, people might be good with children, but it is not enough to like them; we have to be invested in understanding them collectively and individually. We are too often perceived as 'low-skilled' and therefore unimportant, but you will immediately recognise the complex skills within caregiving when you come across a good practitioner. To tune in to a child or group of children and synchronously meet all their needs is an excellent skill to develop.

Caregiving is education; it is the teaching of attachment, trust, dignity and empathy, and eventually independence. It is crucial that children with SEND first and foremost experience caregivers invested in their wellbeing. Before strategies, interventions, therapies and programmes, they need professional love and acceptance, cultivated through caregiving. I often receive frantic phone calls from practitioners asking for ideas and strategies when they have a child with SEND start at their setting, because they have become conditioned so deeply to think that what they currently have to offer is not of value. So, your power is to know that the practitioner as a caregiver is one of the most critical responsibilities that exists across any form of education.

'In the past, caring may have been viewed as a minimum standard of keeping a child safe and clean, or as something anyone could do. In the emerging future, care is viewed as the intentional teaching practice that connects us to one another, and requires specialised knowledge about children, about learning and human development.' (Garboden Murray, 2021, pg. 17)

It is in part why I wanted this book to appeal to more than just the SENDCo. Practitioners as key people and caregivers forms the foundations for healthy development. We have to know that the foundations for the procedures, systems and support must be built on a solid and steady set of relationships.

What do we mean by SEND and inclusion?

In the 14 years that I have worked in Early Years education, I cannot count the number of times that I have heard 'I think he has...' which is the very title of this first chapter. 'I think he has autism' was inspired by this premature labelling mindset that still permeates the education sector and is potentially very harmful to the child and their family. I certainly did it myself early on when I was a SENDCo: 'Hmm, he is always lining things up, and he doesn't give me eye contact; it must be autism.' It may seem harmless and is often well intended because we seek to understand the developmental differences. Still, I am always eager to remind a practitioner that this speculation can have a far-reaching impact. The following case study, which is adapted from a real example, should outline why.

Case study: Speculating about diagnosis

Adam is three years old (38 months) and has been attending his local pre-school for three months. He is an energetic and curious child, and is very interested in spinning, running and emptying containers. He is using quite a few single words and is keen to connect with others through different forms of communication. On occasion, he will hold onto the face of peers to gain their attention, and this is his way of indicating that he wants to play. Recently he has enjoyed lining up different items and will engage in this for a sustained period of time. His key person has formed a strong bond with him, and he goes to her with ease.

The key person is concerned about Adam's development, and in her most recent progress summary has identified that he is below his expected stage of development. She had recently read an article about the signs of autism and believes that Adam fits into this category. She has shared these concerns with colleagues and has suggested to parents that they take him for an autism assessment. The parents were extremely distressed, as they knew little about this condition and they did not understand why the key person would speculate about this, having known him for only three short months.

- In discussions about children's development, do you ever speculate about a potential diagnosis?
- What are the benefits of discussing potential diagnoses?
- Why might it be harmful for a practitioner to openly speculate on diagnosis?

Parents and diagnosis

Q: What if the parent asks for my opinion?

A: The most important thing here is that the parent feels listened to and heard. You can validate those concerns, and even agree, but that should ideally be initiated by the parent. You should also emphasise that it is the qualified specialists that will help the parent to find that answer with the support of you, the practitioner.

Q: What if the parents ask which services are best to refer to and this is a 'give away' of what I think it could be?

A: It is important that we are transparent about the types of referral and potential outcomes, but we should explain that their child's needs must be explored by the appropriate professional. It is also important to emphasise that a diagnosis is an important signpost to the right support. Diagnosis is not a dirty word and is not negative, although it may sometimes feel this way.

Q: What if a specialist asks for our perspective?

A: A qualified specialist will ask for your perspective so that they can build a clear picture of the child's developmental profile. If it gets to this stage, you can be honest with your professional view to both the specialist and parent.

Q: What should I do if a key person speculates and labels children?

A: Firstly, ensure that no harm has been caused by the practitioner doing this. But also view it as a learning opportunity, and speak to the key person about their thinking and ideas. You can set supportive guidelines, and help the key person to think about how they describe children.

It is essential to recognise that our role requires us to make observations and judgments about children's development, to be alert to emerging concerns, discuss them and support children and families on a potential diagnosis pathway. It is never, however, our role to guess or to suggest a diagnosis. It is important to clarify that this is not because receiving a diagnosis is bad, or that developmental conditions are bad, but as practitioners, we are simply not qualified to do so. To fully understand why this can be harmful, we need to start with the basics. What do we even mean by SEND?

Defining special educational needs and disability (SEND)

There are key points to remember when we think about the definition of SEN as given in the SEND code of practice (2015):

- It is not a **diagnosis**.
- It is not a **fixed label**.
- It should not be a **deficit** term focused on delays but is a way to understand **areas of need** and **differences**.
- It is **anticipatory** in the Early Years.
- It differs from the definition given in the Equality Act (UK Government, 2010), which addresses more broadly the defining **characteristics of a disability**. We will explore this further in Chapter 2.

Definition: SEN

'A child of compulsory school age or a young person has a learning difficulty or disability if he or she:
- has a significantly greater difficulty in learning than the majority of others of the same age, or
- has a disability which prevents or hinders him or her from making use of facilities of a kind generally provided for others of the same age in mainstream schools or mainstream post-16 institutions.

A child under compulsory school age has special educational needs if he or she is likely to fall within the above definition when they reach compulsory school age or would do so if special educational provision was not made for them.'
(SEND code of practice: 0–25, 2015, pg. 16)

> ### Definition: Disability
>
> The definition of a disability, which also covers special educational needs (SEN), is given as 'a physical or mental impairment and the impairment has a substantial and long-term adverse effect on their ability to carry out normal day-to-day activities.'
> (Equality Act, 2010)
>
> 'A physical or mental impairment includes learning difficulties, mental health conditions, medical conditions and hidden impairments such as specific learning difficulties, autism, and speech, language and communication impairments.'
> (Meggitt et al., 2016, pg. 19)

Practitioners need to be aware of both definitions so that you are clear on children's protection against discriminatory practices. Practitioners should also be aware of emerging terminology within the sector that describes SEND more holistically such as neurodiversity and neurodivergence.

Defining neurodiversity, neurodivergence and neurotypical

It is important to be aware of the language of neurodiversity for neurodevelopmental conditions such as autism and attention deficit hyperactivity disorder (ADHD). It is believed that the term 'neurodiversity' was coined by autism activist Judy Singer in the 1990s and is short for neurological diversity – or differences in the brain. It is an approach and movement you may have heard of, particularly within the autistic community, which challenges the idea that neurodevelopmental differences are abnormal and need to be cured (see Understood.org for more information). Individuals with neurodevelopmental conditions often define themselves as neurodivergent because their differences diverge from neurotypical development. Embracing neurodiversity is important in the Early Years because we know that some children will go on to be diagnosed with lifelong differences. We have an important responsibility to ensure that children view their identity positively when this occurs.

SEN is not a diagnosis

One of the most significant challenges with the current definition of SEN is that it is quite often confused with a diagnosis. Many of the practitioners with whom I work with are reluctant to use the term because they feel that they are applying a diagnosis that cannot be changed, and this is not the case. One of the critical things to remember is that the identification of SEN is an important and positive step towards putting in the right support. If you recognise that a child needs help or you suspect that a child may need a formal diagnosis, you should use the definition of SEN to guide you, not restrict you.

'I think he has autism'

SEND is not a fixed label

As stated in the author disclaimer, the term SEND is becoming outdated because of the way it 'others' children and reinforces a deficit approach. However, it is important to recognise that identifying developmental needs is not in itself negative. The ability to do so can help children to make progress. As an Early Years SENDCo, I would always try to consider the definition as a help and not a hindrance to myself or the child. Knowledge is power, and by knowing and understanding a child's development needs, I was able to plan support more clearly. It is not uncommon for children to develop emerging needs or have minor difficulties, and as a result of support, they no longer have those difficulties. Similarly, there will be children whose SEND is indicative of a lifelong learning difference, and our support can help a child to understand their differences and to build upon their learning strengths. One of the other issues with seeing SEND as a fixed label is that parents can worry about how their child will be viewed, as outlined in the case study below.

Case study: SEND and transition

David is due to turn four soon and will begin his transition into Reception. He is energetic and is very lively in his superhero play. He also loves vehicles, especially if they are outdoors where he can run them through mud, stones and rocks. During his time at nursery, his key person, Viktoria, has supported his speech and pronunciation. He had some difficulties in being understood and became frustrated when his friends were not responsive to his requests. Viktoria partnered with his parents to arrange an assessment for speech and language therapy, and for a period of time he was on the setting's SEND register. However, he has made significant progress and usually only struggles when he is tired or has lots that he wants to say. David's dad is very worried about the transition, as he feels that sharing his previous experience of SEND will lead to him being viewed differently on his transition to school. He doesn't want his son or his parenting skills to be judged.

Activity: Team meeting reflection

- What might you do in the specific situation outlined in the case study?
- How do you ensure that parents understand key terminology and systems so that these worries do not escalate?
- What might you do if the child continues to have SEND on the transition?

Identified needs should not be viewed as a deficit

In deciding whether a child has SEND, we are often referring to different milestone documents that outline 'typical' development, such as the EYFS 'Development matters' guidance (Early Education, 2012, 2021d) or the Birth to Five Matters (Early Years Coalition, 2021). The issue with these types of documents is that they can encourage a deficit mindset about those children who do not fit neatly into the development statements. Although the documents were never designed to encourage this, they have been adapted ten times over to become a checklist rather than a guidance tool. Whenever we begin to use these tools to standardise children, we begin to promote exclusion. The implications of exclusionary practices are felt very acutely by children and families, who often have to battle for their right to a fair and equitable education.

While we must be alert to development needs and provide the appropriate support, children with SEND should not be viewed purely in terms of what they cannot do. Children with SEND are not a sum of faults. SEND is an identification of needs but, as with any child, we should be describing those with SEND first and foremost by their characteristics and their strengths.

It is also vital that we don't become fixated on the term 'delay'. For example, an autistic child will learn differently rather than being delayed. Autism is lifelong, so we need to be mindful of how our language can insinuate that those differences are bad. Similarly, I often hear practitioners say, 'The child is suffering from…'. At times, yes, they may suffer due to difficulties they experience, but to assume that the very existence of SEND equates with suffering is unhelpful.

SEND is anticipatory in the Early Years

Reflection

You may work in a setting that does not have many or any children with SEND, and unfortunately, this can sometimes lead to non-anticipatory practice. For example, you may decide not to attend SEND-based training because you don't currently have children that require support, and therefore you may not feel equipped when the time does come to offer support. As the saying goes, fail to prepare, prepare to fail.

An important factor to consider when thinking about applying the definition of SEND to a child is whether you **anticipate** that, without support, the child would fall under this definition by the time they reach compulsory school age. Some children have minor difficulties with certain aspects of their development and are responsive to the high-quality teaching and SEND support that you provide, so you may find that they no longer fall under the definition of SEND over time. Equally, there may be children who have more complex or diverse needs, and you anticipate that, even with support, they will still fall under the definition by the time they start school.

The moment that you find out a child will be attending your setting, you can begin to anticipate and prepare for their arrival. This will not only reduce your own anxiety about your adaptations, but it will also ease the worries of the child and family. Being proactive saves time along the way.

Labelling

Labels stick

Labelling is difficult to avoid, and we need to consider how labels can be helpful and harmful. As the saying goes, 'labels stick', and they are often used to negatively describe children. Children also pick up on our perceptions of these labels, and often we can accidentally use labels in front of children to describe them. In her book *The Book You Wish Your Parents Had Read*, psychotherapist Phillipa Perry (2019) reminds us that it is not helpful to judge someone as 'good' or 'bad' or indeed judge them as anything at all. She explains that it can very difficult for a child to thrive under the restrictions of a label, particularly if we view that label through a negative lens.

When we are labelling a child, we are more often describing the feelings that they invoke in us – for example, saying that a child is disruptive because it disrupts us, rather than seeing the child as movement-driven, energetic, bored, overloaded or just not yet ready to manage the expectations that we have placed on them. Labels can put a full stop on our understanding, and so we must always check and challenge when we become quick to label.

Of course, we can embrace positive labels and use them to empower children. As we grow older, labels can also help us to process our learning needs as individuals and define key aspects of our identity. The critical thing to remember is that the label has to propel you and not hold you or the child back.

Diagnosis labels

Activity: Labelling

Write 'attention deficit hyperactivity disorder' (ADHD) on a piece of paper. Now write all the words that spring to mind. When you look at the words, are they predominantly positive or negative? How easy would you find generating a positive list?

The most important thing we must remember when supporting SEND children is that we directly influence how they think about themselves. We have a responsibility to support the development of self-esteem and a strong sense of identity. Without these things, children will struggle to self-advocate. The way we think and talk about a child including their SEND can have crucial implications, and so we must make the effort to understand firstly the child as an individual, and if they have a diagnosis, to understand how this defines them. It is common for neurotypical people to say that disability does not define a person, but this suggests that the developmental difference or disability is a bad thing. It isn't. Seek to understand more holistically different types of SEND.

Worst days

I was speaking to a colleague and friend whose child has a diagnosis, and she explained that part of the emotional toll is that she is always talking about her child on his worst days. The battle for SEND support can be so tough on a parent that they become accustomed to only ever talking about the SEND challenges rather than the celebratory aspects. As well as understanding a child's personality, if there is a diagnosis, we should also know about the positive aspects of their condition. For example, children with ADHD may struggle to regulate their attention, but they can also become hyper-focused when something is interesting to them and they can have creative tendencies. Build upon those positive labels as much as you can.

Practitioner's voice

Formal diagnoses do give us an insight into a child's needs, but this doesn't make an individual assessment of needs any less important. An ongoing effort needs to be made to recognise where a child needs support, where they are making progress, what is interesting to them and what their vehicle for learning is. This is the only way in which we can truly centre the individual: through gaining as much insight as we can into who they are as a person and how their additional needs fit into that.

The language of labels

Table 1: Key definitions

Key term	Defintion
Ableism	Discrimination in favour of able-bodied and neurotypical people.
Identity-first language	A way of recognising a person's neurodivergence as a core part of their identity, e.g. by saying 'an autistic person' as opposed to 'a person with autism'. This is an area of debate and often argued against despite repeated emphasis that it is the disabled community's preference.
Masking	The conscious or unconscious act of suppressing SEND behaviours to 'fit in'; also referred to as 'camouflaging'. It can have a range of negative implications such as stress, trauma, burnout and meltdowns.
Neurodivergent	A person whose neurotype (brain wiring) is divergent of the majority of society. This includes those with autism, ADHD, dyslexia, dyspraxia and others.
Neurodiversity	Neurodiversity is the viewpoint that brain differences are normal, rather than deficits.
Neurotypical	A person whose neurotype is typical of the majority of society.
Stimming	Any type of repetition using the different senses. They help a child to regulate, express emotion, or communicate or they may do it for pleasure. Examples include hand clapping, spinning, using fidgets.

When I first became an inclusion consultant, I referred to someone as an autistic person. A colleague looked at me, horrified, and explained how offensive it was to see the disability before the person. And from that moment on, I used what is known as person-first language. This is a way of communicating the fact that you see the person before the disability. When I look back, I realise that I had been so badly shamed that I had no courage to question whether it was really that straightforward. As time has gone on, I have become much more informed around the concept of identity-first language, which communicates that the disability forms part of the person's identity. You will often hear neurotypical people arguing about which terminology to use, rarely stopping to take the time to just ask the person in question. As a neurodivergent person myself, I really don't mind how I am addressed, so long as my ADHD is not viewed negatively, and I am not treated as 'less than' because of its existence. However, the reality is that we, as practitioners, should make it our responsibility to ask. This is mirrored by the practitioner's voice below.

Practitioner's voice

Person-first language relating to disability (e.g. 'child with autism' rather than 'autistic child') is often emphasised in educational settings. In reality, centring the individual over the diagnosis cannot fully be achieved by switching words around. Of course, there are some people who do want person-first language in relation to them and that needs to be respected. However, this isn't the macro-solution to disabled people being seen as individuals. Often, people will use lovely person-first language while introducing someone only by their disability and offering no other information about them. Language isn't unimportant, but the use of specific language allows people to feel like they're being inclusive without putting the work in. Labels can be informative and empowering, but we must remember that people's identities contain a fairly limitless set of labels, and disabilities aren't always the most important or relevant introduction. Therefore, when talking about children with SEND, it is crucial to cultivate conversation and action that genuinely centres the child and which means doing an awful lot more than just enforcing person-first language.

Top tip: Name calling

Mum's the word: Parents can feel offended when we just refer to them as 'mum' or 'dad'. Ask them specifically how they would like to be referred to, because a lot of parents want to be recognised equally by their names as well as their parental roles.

Ask: This is a really simple one, but talk to the parent if you are unsure about how to use SEND terminology. Parents will often share if they have a preference for person-first or identity-first language. As the child gets older, they can make that decision for themselves.

What labels can be helpful?

All that talk of labelling can leave us wondering 'What *can* we say?' As I said earlier, discussions are inevitable, and we need to navigate the tricky aspects. In Chapter 5, we will unpick the four broad areas of need in much greater detail, but for now, make yourself familiar with the headings. The SEND code of practice: 0–25 (DfE & DoH, 2015) recognises that we must categorise our concerns somehow; otherwise, we may find it extremely difficult to navigate the right support.

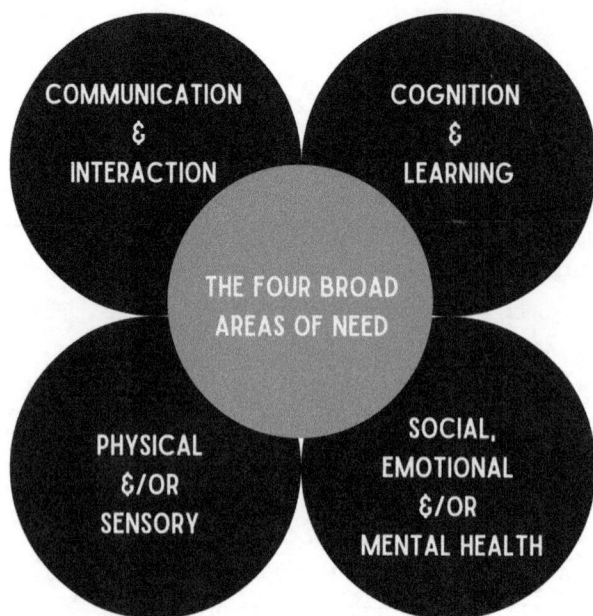

Figure 1: *The four broad areas of need (DfE, 2015)*

A word on acronyms

Sometimes it can be the smallest of things that creates the most powerful feelings of isolation for parents and key people. In our everyday practice, we become accustomed to terminology, acronyms and processes.

In one way, the use of jargon is simply a demonstration of our expertise. Still, when we use too much technical language, we risk miscommunication, which is a big no-no in inclusion. So much of what we discuss is sensitive and crucial for connection, and so we need to ensure that our language is accessible and non-discriminatory. Review the statements in Table 2 and think about the benefits of reframing language.

Table 2: Reframing language

What you might hear	What you should hear	Explanation
'suffers from…'	'is neurodivergent'	To say 'suffers' suggests that the condition is a disease. It is not. It is a neurodevelopmental difference. We should not assume suffering within SEND.
'a person with autism'	'autistic person'	Many people prescribe to identity-first language because their SEND is part of their identity and cannot be cured. Always ask the person's preference.
'disorder'	'neurological difference'	Disorder is biased towards the difficulties of a condition and perpetuates the view that developmental differences and disabilities are wholly negative. For many types of SEND, there is a holistic profile of strengths and needs.
'handicapped' 'mong' 'differently abled'	'disabled'	Disability is a lived reality for many people and forms part of their identity. It is not considered a negative word, and so should be used and embraced.
'aggressive'	'unsettled or unmet needs'	SEND behaviours such as difficulties with self-regulation are often labelled as aggression, but in most cases, the child is communicating distress and a need for help.
'high-functioning autism' 'low-functioning autism'	'autism'	Functioning labels suggest that there are good and bad types of autism and create further discrimination. Autism exists on a non-linear spectrum and each person presents uniquely.
'severely autistic'	'autistic'	See above! Also consider how non-autistic people are usually the ones who define what is severe and what is not. This is not appropriate.
'impaired'	'learns differently'	While many types of SEND can impact development, defining everything as impaired is incorrect. It is a difference or variation.

How do we start to think about inclusion in practice?

To be inclusive doesn't always mean to 'include'…

Often when we are developing inclusive approaches, we can fall into habits that still exclude children from full participation. The following descriptions provide some key considerations when we think about meaningful inclusion, and when we might fall out of sync with inclusive practices.

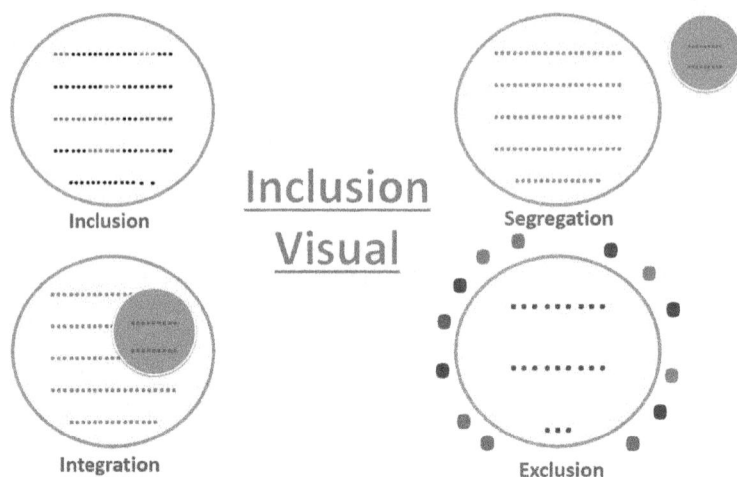

Inclusion Visual

Inclusion

Segregation

Integration

Exclusion

Figure 2: *Working towards inclusion*

Reflection

Take a look at Figure 2. What is your current understanding of these terms and does it match the visual?

Educational inclusion

Parent's voice

I can't even put into words how it felt to walk into a nursery and to not be glared at. My child's disability gains attention, and these practitioners came over wide-eyed and eager to welcome us. You get so used to living a life of feeling out of place, but this nursery was our absolute place.

Child's voice

My Becky puts my special shoes on so I can go play. She let me put stickers on them because I love the sparkles.

Educational inclusion is a child-centred approach that recognises that *all* children have an innate drive to learn. Their learning is unique and often propelled by their interests, intrinsic motivation and freedom to explore. It is an approach dependent on knowledgeable practitioners who seek to understand differences and who actively work to provide fair and equitable opportunities for equal participation. By striving for inclusion, networks of trust are formed between the child, family and setting, and collaborative experiences ensure optimal growth and development (Greenfield & Suzuki, 1998). It is essential to understand that educational inclusion refers not only to children with SEND but also to other marginalised groups and so we must consider intersectional identities including race, gender and class.

Inclusion is well-suited to the Early Years because we so often deliver play-rich and child-led approaches, meeting the child where they are in our daily interactions. I think that, as a source of knowledge, we are often overlooked by other education phases. The divide between Early Years and primary education looms large but we could learn a lot from each other due to wealth of expertise, and this could lead to more meaningful inclusion. Opportunities to work together, particularly during transition points could offer us an insight into how children are best supported as they progress through their education.

Educational exclusion

Educational exclusion is the practice of directly or indirectly preventing a child from participating in their education. According to the Independent Provider of Special Educational Needs (IPSEA) website, 'informal' exclusions in a school can include removal from the mainstream environment for short periods, sending children home to 'cool off' or calm down, or reducing a child's hours because of their SEND. However, exclusion within an Early Years provider can become complicated. As a sector, we support children who are not yet at compulsory school age, so we often think that we have more wriggle room to exclude. However, children defined as having a disability, including special educational needs, are protected by the Equality Act (2010). The reality is that no practitioner wants to be in the position of having to exclude, but you must talk to someone when you think that this could be a possibility. Acting without guidance is dangerous territory.

When I was a consultant, there were three exclusions in the Early Years settings that I supported. While the immediate reaction was one of shock, when I ran a focus group with the three practitioners, I found that there is often much more to a story, and sometimes, the decisions are made in the child's best interests. If you feel backed into this type of corner, contact your local authority and ask for mediated support. (We will discuss when exclusion becomes discriminatory in Chapter 2.)

Educational segregation

Practitioner's voice

I felt very uncomfortable taking children off to engage in separate activities from the main group, especially when we could have used strategies within the main environment so that children were included. However, I have found that some experiences suit a different environment – for example, I run an activity called 'Calm Creatures' for children with sensory differences, and they benefit from going to the sensory room that I have set up.

Educational segregation occurs when children appear to be included but not in an inclusive way. It is important to recognise that segregated practice elements can be inclusive and have 'a time and a place', mainly when an activity or experience is designed to enhance a child's learning and wellbeing. We often see this when children access sensory spaces or rooms, or when they may become overloaded by specific transitional points.

Another common form of segregation relates to those children who receive part of their education away from the main groups of children or spaces. This practice can take away opportunities for the child to play, build peer connections and develop independence. Imagine, for example, that the children will take part in a messy paint activity, but the child with SEND is taken off for a one-to-one because his messy play style is considered 'too messy'. Further still, children are often segregated for out-of-class interventions. While there are times at which a child needs a more focused level of support, if they are segregated because their SEND is considered problematic, this can be viewed as discriminatory.

It is sometimes useful for children of differing abilities to have space to learn without the pressure of 'typically developing' peers. McCoy and Banks (2012) suggest that marked differences in ability can negatively impact the self-image of children with SEND, and this needs to be supported sensitively. This is not to be entirely avoided, however, because practitioners can play a crucial role in guiding children through these social dynamics by mirroring, modelling, engaging in discussion and developing parallel play (Trawick-Smith, 2019).

Educational segregation becomes an issue when we become inconvenienced by the child's needs and try to pacify them away from the main group. In her book *Special Needs in the Early Years*, Crutchley (2017) refers to how children are organised into cohorts or groups as per their ability or needs. While this may seem like a good way to manage children, it creates a clear divide and can place limits on learning and the way in which we perceive learning and development.

Educational integration

Educational integration is the expectation that the child needs to adapt their learning and behaviour to fit in. Therefore, the child's SEND is considered problematic, and the focus is on management rather than effective differentiation and inclusion. Differentiation is the ability to adapt teaching to meet individual children's unique needs within a group (Taylor, 2017). Imagine that you had six children engaged in a painting activity; they are likely to have different interests and needs. For example, one child may be developing turn-taking, while another is interested in colour-mixing, and another is learning to use more than single words. Differentiation occurs when a practitioner can optimise these unique learning needs and opportunities. It is highly relevant in an early childhood curriculum that promotes children developing at different rates, but often differentiation falls victim to 'one size fits all' teaching, thus further promoting integrative practices.

Educational integration can also lead to practitioners prescribing to intervention approaches that are designed to train children to behave or learn more neurotypically. The interventions become based on teaching skills that fall in line with general classroom expectations, such as sitting still, listening and paying attention. While these skills are important, they are demonstrated in different ways. For example, sitting still isn't always a sign of paying attention, and many children need to be able to move to focus.

To inclusion and beyond…

As a starting point, you are hopefully beginning to see that while inclusion is indeed complex in practice, it is not impossible. There are actions that we can be taking to develop more inclusive approaches, remembering that it is a process of becoming, not being. Developing good inclusive foundations provides us with a springboard to action, and we can now consider the different ways in which to build our own unique inclusive pedagogy.

Inclusion is a state of becoming, not being

It is important to recognise that practitioners need safe and brave spaces to explore what inclusion means personally, professionally, in theory and in practice.

Developing a celebratory framework for SEND

At the very heart of inclusion is the respect that we have for people's differences. This includes how practitioners differ in their skillsets. It is crucial to recognise practitioners' strengths and build upon them, rather than expect everyone to be good at everything.

To 'include' doesn't always mean to be inclusive

It is essential to check and challenge the practice of inclusion. In many situations, we might think that we are being inclusive but we are actually steering towards integration or segregation. Ensure that you know the differences and that you take a proactive approach to establish high-quality inclusive practices.

Watch your language

If you listen out, you will hear that there is a lot of negative language within SEND. It can be subtle yet powerful – for example, referring to a child as 'suffering' from autism rather than having autism. The way in which we speak about children and families often communicates how we internally view them and their experiences. Focus on areas of need rather than on delays.

Develop your own unique inclusive pedagogy

Inclusion will not look the same in every setting; for example, a nursery will differ from a childminder. Don't be afraid to get creative, push boundaries and challenge outdated mindsets.

Signposts and resources

'Every kid needs a champion'
TED Talk by Rita Pierson
Available at: www.ted.com/talks/rita_pierson_every_kid_needs_a_champion?-language=en#t-1214

'Changing education paradigms'
TED Talk by Ken Robinson
Available at: www.ted.com/talks/sir_ken_robinson_changing_education_paradigms

'Unlocking us' podcast
Brené Brown and Dr. Vivek Murthy on 'Loneliness and connection'
Available at: https://brenebrown.com/podcast/dr-vivek-murthy-and-brene-on-loneliness-and-connection

2 'We must, we should and we can': Understanding and implementing key SEND policies and procedures

Starting points

One of the key concerns of practitioners is feeling overwhelmed by the number of policies and procedures relating to SEND and inclusion. Think about the following:

- Do you actively use the SEND code of practice?
- Do you know key SEND processes and how to put these into practice?
- How confident are you with integrating key SEND concepts into your everyday EYFS practice?

Introduction

Getting it right

As a sector, we put up with a lot especially when it comes to public policy. In more recent years, the sector has become weary of the dominant agenda to standardise Early Years education. For example, the introduction of the controversial baseline test on entry to Reception seemed anything but child-centred, and four-year-olds could be seen marching to Parliament for the 'More Than A Score' campaign. We are also now implementing the EYFS reforms and there has been a mixed response from the sector. In particular concerns around how fit for purpose the reforms are for children with SEND. For many practitioners, there is a concern that we keep being subject to changes that do not clearly show how EYFS practice and SEND support become aligned. This leaves us in the position of often having to come up with something different or additional to the main documentation and guidance. So while the EYFS reforms have a very clear intent to reduce general educator workload, this is not appearing to be the case when it comes to SEND support in the Early Years. The issue that emerges is that practitioners become reluctant to engage with policy changes, because their benefits and impact are not always clearly rationalised. The following case study demonstrates this reluctance:

Case study: Supporting whole-team development

Shelley manages a nursery and has ten practitioners under her leadership. They have been discussing the consultation process of the 2021 EYFS reforms (DfE). Shelley explains to her team that the local authority has encouraged the team to review some of the consultation questions together so that everyone's voices can be heard. She is met with lots of disheartened responses from her team, who don't see the point in engaging because they are rarely actually listened to anyway. They explain that they are so fed up with the constant changes. Shelley feels frustrated by her team for not being passionate enough but can also relate to their feelings because she too feels that it is just another vicious cycle of change. She realises that there are more important things to be getting on with, so she drops the task from her team meeting agenda.

- Does this experience sound familiar?
- How do you approach public policy, reforms and reviews within your setting?
- Do you understand the role of policy changes and reforms, and in what ways do you think that Early Years settings can engage?

Discussions around inclusion, special educational needs and disability are hugely important but can also feel very emotive when we are navigating a fractured SEND system. I have often noted that practitioners can become overburdened by the amount of statutory and non-statutory guidance that they must follow and the 'human element' of inclusion often becomes lost. I remember once reeling off the requirements of the Equality Act (2010) to a practitioner who was trying to work out how he could adjust his pre-school room to meet the needs of a child. He responded, 'You take the heart right out of it when you come at me with all your technical language and rules.' He wasn't being difficult, but his focus was on the individual situation and the child; blanket statements about possible discrimination did not help him to be active and solution focused. Sometimes the 'rule books' can really hinder us when we are in the thick of it. We spend so much time trying to interpret different sets of statutory and non-statutory guidance that our common sense moves further and further away from us. Within this chapter, I want to introduce what you need to know but in a more accessible way. We must be mindful of the fact that we are subject to many policy changes, reforms and shifts within legislation. And so if we take it back to basics and focus on what we can practically do to support children and families, these changes should not always feel so heavy going. I say this because of the many changes I have observed, the underlying principles and practice largely remain the same.

The Early Years sector is political. As practitioners, we should engage with the current debates and tensions within our field. Still, there are pockets of professional snobbery where we can feel totally out of our depth and not switched on enough to have our say. But we need to keep getting louder (when we are not tired and exhausted from the daily demands of the job), because something needs to change. As Aynsley-Green says about the importance of politics in his book *The Betrayal of British Childhood*:

> 'Why is it important? Well, politics is the vehicle for change in society, politicians are the engine, policy is the fuel, and changing practice, the wheels for practice. Public opinion is often the driver.' (Aynsley-Green, 2018)

This is something we have to keep at the heart of Early Years practice, for it is those working on the ground with children every day that should influence and shape policy changes. We should be listening intently to their experience of delivering early education and by adopting participatory approaches, the sector might have more opportunities to lead practice in the right direction.

Getting to the heart and harsh reality of public policy

I recently delivered a training session on child protection and safeguarding. Most of the practitioners had explained that they had completed some form of similar training before. Still, I picked up on a real disconnect between the principles of how we protect children and how this translates into our everyday practice. I recently heard someone say that we must always be prepared to think about the 'unthinkable'; it is our duty to be alert and responsive to child protection. Most practitioners have a 'horror' story of how children face adversity or abuse. Still, these events often seem distant from our everyday experiences. One practitioner put her hand up and said, 'I have worked in the Early Years for a long time now, but I have never really understood my safeguarding responsibilities. There are so many flowcharts and procedures that I don't really get involved.' It may shock you to read about such a blasé attitude, but I think that many practitioners feel that mandatory training is just that… mandatory. It does not necessarily serve them within their roles, and in many cases, it can feel like a barrier. For example, practitioners will often tell me that policies may look great on paper, but they are often hard to implement in the real world. A critical concern from many practitioners is that the expectations to meet the ever-increasing needs of children is not backed up with adequate support and funding, and so children's rights do risk becoming compromised. When a sector feels undervalued and unheard, it leads to disempowerment, so the expectation to advocate for the rights of all children is difficult to achieve.

We also exist within a society where childhood still needs defending. It was only in 2005 that we had our first Children's Commissioner in England (Aynsley-Green, 2018). To put that in perspective, it was only deemed necessary 15 years ago to have a Parliament member to represent the needs and best interests of children, a role that only emerged after the Lord Laming enquiry into the murder of Victoria Climbié, an eight-year-old child who was tortured and abused by a family member and her partner. The inquiry found significant failures by social care and health services, and sparked debate around the quasi-acceptance of institutional racism within public policy. According to Goldstein (2006) public policy must seek to acknowledge the common and distinct contextual factors that could influence how well the system protects children who are at risk. The murder of Victoria Climbié led to major changes in child protection policies (DfES, 2003) but concerns remain about how misplaced cultural assumptions took precedence over the accurate identification of needs. Policies cannot be universally applied, and as practitioners, we have a duty to be culturally sensitive, and to challenge our cultural assumptions.

When I put it to the training group that protective and 'preventative' measures are often only implemented by the government reactively, in response to the occurrence of such horrific events, rather than proactively, the magnitude of our responsibilities becomes clearer. While changes, reviews and reforms indicate the 'knowing better, doing better' mentality, it is sobering to know that many of the procedures that we follow are underpinned by events that perhaps could have been avoided.

Activity

Visit the National Society for the Prevention of Cruelty to Children (NSPCC) website and read the timeline of key events and legislation. This will provide you with a good insight into how child protection has developed over time.

The right to be protected

According to Miller and Brown (2014), children with special educational needs and/or disabilities are at greater risk of abuse. Therefore, practitioners must be extra vigilant in response to the risks posed to children who may not disclose abuse due to their SEND. The NSPCC (2020) has identified that significant gaps remain in the development of support systems and processes for children who could be made vulnerable as a result of their SEND. Things you might consider around safeguarding include:

- The level and access to safeguarding and child protection training, including specific courses that address particular vulnerabilities including additional needs and disabilities.

- Communication barriers, child's 'voice' and the difficulty that a child may experience in understanding or explaining their experiences of abuse. It is a harrowing reality that children with disabilities can be intentionally targeted because of their inability to report abuse.

- Key adults not understanding signs or types of child abuse, or not deeming it their responsibility.

- Key adults feeling uncomfortable or awkward in case they have read a situation wrong. The advice is and will always be: 'If in doubt, talk it out'. Do not keep those worries to yourself.

- Key adults not valuing the views of children with SEND.

The Working Together to Safeguard Children (DfE, 2018a) document specifically states that educators should pay particular attention to disabled children, and those with special educational needs. A sufficient assessment of needs should be carried out to determine whether there are concerns relating to their level of care, or to the nature of their disability. Reflect upon how often discussions around safeguarding and SEND occur within your setting. Have additional steps been taken to understand some of the unique challenges and vulnerabilities children and families might face?

The impact of Covid-19

The impact of a global pandemic on child development is also undeniable, and disruption to essential services for SEND is bound to have far-reaching implications. For example, there has been a significant reduction in access to universal health services during national lockdowns, and while much support has moved to a virtual format, it has resulted in increasing pressures and variability in who to prioritise (Institute for Health Visiting, 2020). While we do not fully know the consequences of the pandemic, early indications suggest that there has been an increase in child development needs, and abuse rates have increased (Romanou & Belton, 2020). An important factor to consider is the preparedness of settings in supporting these children in the aftermath of Covid-19. The answers to this are unfortunately not fully clear but it will be crucial that training and support is distinct in addressing the key difficulties, and that public policy reflects the diverse experiences of living through a pandemic.

Understanding the foundational legislation

Table 3 shows a timeline of key policy moments for the broader EYFS and for SEND. As you explore aspects of these throughout the chapter, you will see how specific approaches and processes have come to be. You may also recognise key policy moments that, while good in theory, have been more challenging in practice. We will not examine all in detail but will focus on those that are most relevant to your practice.

Table 3: Foundational legislation

Policy	Outline
SEN code of practice (DfES, 2001)	• Strengthens rights to mainstream education • Introduction of individual education plans (IEPs) to outline additional support • Needs categorised into four broad areas • School Action and School Action Plus to monitor SEND
Children Act 2004	• Multi-agency working becomes a legal force
Childcare Act 2006	• Requirement to register as a provider • Duty for local authority to provide information, advice and training to childcare providers • Requires that local authorities in England secure sufficient childcare as far as is 'reasonably practicable' for working parents and those undertaking training with the intention of returning to work • Obliges councils to have regard for disabled children and make sure that there are enough free early education places
The Early Years Foundation Stage Framework (DCSF, 2008)	• Provision is personalised and aspects of the 2001 SEN code of practice are embedded across the framework • The provider must take necessary steps to safeguard and promote the welfare of children, including children with special educational needs • Providers must maintain records, policies and procedures required for the safe and efficient management of the settings and to meet the needs of the children, including special needs status
Achievement for All (DCSF, 2009a)	• An initiative of the National College for School Leadership that evaluates existing good practice of inclusion in mainstream schools
SEND review (Ofsted, 2010)	• Identifies the over-identification of SEND and highlights that high-quality universal teaching should be the greater focus
Equality Act 2010	• Highlights the types of discrimination an individual can face • Outlines the requirements for reasonable adjustments that should be anticipatory • Clear outline of the protected characteristics • Justifications
Children and Families Act 2014	• Provides statutory changes to the SEND framework
Integrated review at age 2: implementation study (DfE, 2014a)	• Combination of the Healthy Child Programme and development review used by health visiting teams, and the statutory EYFS progress check used by Early Years practitioners to assess children's development between 24 and 36 months • Highlighted as an early intervention tool
SEND code of practice 0–25 (DfE & DoH, 2015)	• Provides radical reforms for SEND provision, including the transition from statements of special educational needs to Education, Health and Care Plans • The removal of Action and Action Plus and replacement with SEN support • Greater focus on the views and rights of parents and children

Table 3: Foundational legislation (continued)

Policy	Outline
Disability access fund (DAF) and special educational needs (SEN) inclusion fund	• If you provide places for any three- or four-year-olds who receive disability living allowance (DLA), your setting is eligible to receive disability access funding • Every local authority must have a SEN inclusion fund to support Early Years providers in meeting the needs of individual children with SEN
Education inspection framework (DfE, 2019)	• The quality of support for any children with SEND must be assessed, including those children who may not be fully accessing their full educational entitlement • The framework also examines to what extent the curriculum and care practices that the setting provides meet the needs of the range of children who attend, particularly children with SEND • Inspectors will pay particular attention to children with SEND, and will be keen to understand how a setting ensures that progress is made
The Early Years Foundation Stage reforms (DfE, 2021d)	• Revises early learning goals • Rewrites 'Development matters' and removes age stages.

As you can see from Table 3, different acts, reviews and policy moments have informed the code of practice that we have today. The purpose of this table is to demonstrate the progression of inclusion, and where key working practices have emerged. These changes are often built on a strong evidence base of research and allow us to further expand our knowledge and skills when working with children and families. The way in which these policies are translated or communicated to the sector is important as this can influence whether the changes will be welcomed or resisted. The arrival of the 0-25 SEND code of practice (DfE & DoH, 2014) was initially welcomed as we saw the reduction in bureaucratic systems. Unfortunately, however, the implementation of this has been much harder. And this is why it is so crucial that we are given a voice when reviews occur, because without providing feedback, we have less opportunity to influence how policy will be shaped going forward. Practice should inform policy. As practitioners, we need to be the policy-shakers to the policymakers.

I will not cover all the key policy moments in great detail. Still, I have selected those that are most relevant to your everyday practice. Each policy will break down what you must do and where appropriate what you should do. The conclusion of the chapter will explore what you will do with your increased knowledge.

The building blocks of inclusion policy

Many of the documents we use are interlinked and so by using a building blocks approach, we can examine what we need to have in place, and how we practically and realistically implement the SEND code of practice: 0–25 (DfE & DoH, 2015). I will also be unpicking some myths and confusions because there are many. Here is a visual of the building blocks, and we will follow each one, understanding the basics of what we must do, what we should do, and, most importantly, what we can do.

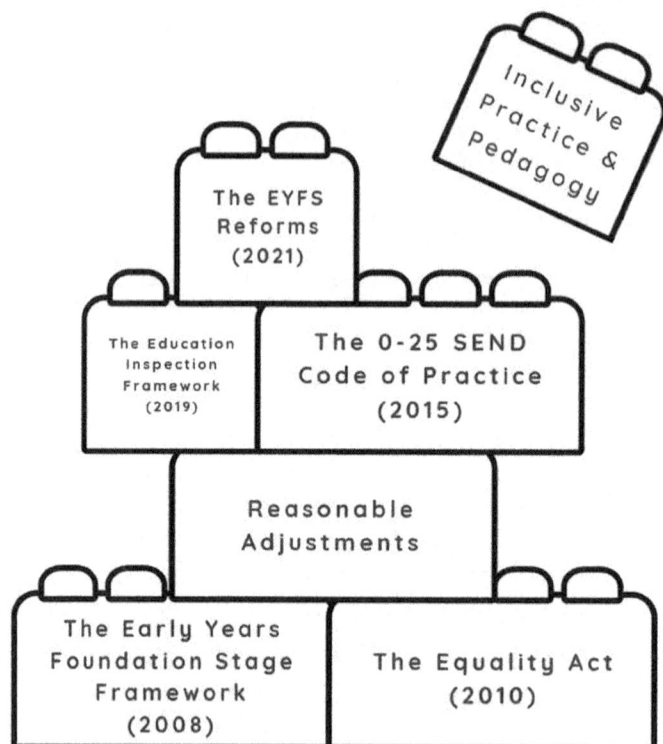

Figure 3: *The statutory framework building blocks*

The Early Years Foundation Stage (EYFS)

'All those who work with young children should be alert to emerging difficulties [early identification] and respond early [early intervention].' (DfE & DH, 2015, para 5.5)

One of the first things to understand about the EYFS is that it aims to be an inclusive framework. Practitioners have legal duties as per the statutory guidance (DfE, 2021a). However, this does not always go to plan. There have been scenarios where children have been excluded or not accepted to a setting or school based on their SEND. Practitioners will, at times, suggest that it is not 'their job' to look after children with varying needs. This is usually born out of the frustration that there is not a better infrastructure to help settings support those needs. The percentage of SEND needs is also increasing within Early Years provision (DfE, 2021b) which is likely to add increasing pressures on the Early Years sector if it is not adequately equipped. The expectation for practitioners to adapt under already pressured systems is quite unfair. It is akin to building a house on quicksand and expecting it not to sink. We cannot simply go around demanding inclusion without discussing and considering the context. The victim of the current system is often the child who ends up in a setting that is not equipped or able.

It would be unwise to simply list your statutory duties because there is without doubt challenges in doing this, but it is important to have an awareness of what is expected and to think about how to navigate these systems so that the child's needs are adequately met.

According to the Council for Disabled Children's SEND toolkit (2015a), the EYFS is based on a set of inclusive guiding principles that allow equality of opportunity. Settings can do this by:

- promoting and implementing a play-based and child-centred curriculum that is responsive to individual needs, including those of children with SEND
- meeting the requirement to have arrangements in place to identify and support children with SEND and to clearly communicate these with parents
- ensuring that practitioners review children's progress and share a summary with parents, including the statutory assessment points at age two and at the end of the Foundation Stage
- ensuring that systems are in place for the good health and care of children, including those who require medical assistance and support
- allocating a SENDCo who will fulfil the leadership duties involved with SEND and inclusion
- focusing on high-quality teaching and learning that improves the outcomes for children with special educational needs and narrows the attainment gap.

  (Adapted from the Council for Disabled Children's SEND toolkit, 2015a).

Registered Early Years providers are inspected on the implementation of the EYFS framework and this, again, includes the ways in which children with SEND are supported, assessed and monitored in terms of progress (DfE, 2019).

Assessment points

There are two statutory assessment points within the EYFS, and these consist of the progress check at age two and the Early Years Foundation Stage Profile, which is completed at the end of the Foundation Stage.

'We must, we should and we can'

The Equality Act 2010

Must

All Early Years providers have duties under the Equality Act 2010. In particular, they must not discriminate against, harass or victimise disabled children, and they must make reasonable adjustments, including the provision of auxiliary aids and services for disabled children, to prevent them being put at substantial disadvantage.

Activity

Read the following scenarios:

Scenario 1: A Reception class refuses admission to a child who has incontinence issues due to a medical condition, because it is not their job to provide childcare.

Scenario 2: A nursery has introduced 'Speaker of the Week' for children who engage in circle time. Three children in the group have speech and language differences, including a non-speaking child, selective mutism and pronunciation difficulties.

Scenario 3: A four-year-old girl has speech, language and communication needs that makes it difficult for her to pronounce her words. Two practitioners find some of the ways in which she says things funny and often do impressions of her.

Scenario 4: A parent challenges a setting's practice, which angers the practitioners, who say that they are not making any more effort to do anything else for the child. They can't wait for the family to leave.

Scenario 5: A boy with sensory processing differences can become overwhelmed in large groups. When he is experiencing sensory overload, he will bite or hit out. The nursery expels him for three days, citing zero tolerance for aggressive behaviour.

- Would you define the above scenarios as discrimination?
- Is there any way in which the scenarios differ?
- Have you observed any similar examples in practice?

If you skip to 'Unpicking discrimination' (page 41), you can see the answers to these reflections.

The Equality Act 2010 is something that you will hear about quite a lot, but we must delve a little deeper to understand it in practice:

1. The Equality Act replaced nine different acts and almost a hundred different sets of regulations and was amalgamated into one single legal framework. Imagine if we still had to get our heads around those previous acts and regulations!

2. The Equality Act recognises that 'equality is rooted in equal treatment' but, for disability, this must also be equitable.

3. Equality means treating every child the same, but equity means making sure that every child has the right support to succeed, making the education system fair and inclusive of varying needs.

4. The Equality Act outlines nine protected characteristics, and it is important to recognise that in your everyday professional work, you may be working to protect several of these at any one time, including your own.

Unpicking discrimination

The Equality Act sets out the four main forms of discrimination, defined as 'prohibited conduct', that apply to children who share protected characteristics. If you think back to the scenarios described earlier on, you can see how the types of discrimination can be broken down.

PROTECTED CHARACTERISTICS

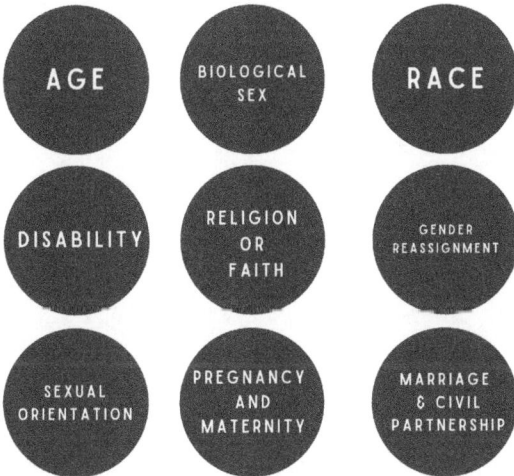

Figure 4: *The protected characteristics of the Equality Act (2010)*

Direct discrimination – to directly discriminate against a child's protected characteristic and to treat them less favourably than they would other children.

Scenario 1: A Reception class refuses admission to a child who has incontinence issues due to a medical condition, because it is not their job to provide childcare.

Indirect discrimination – to indirectly discriminate against a child in relation to a protected characteristic.

Scenario 2: A nursery has introduced 'Speaker of the Week' for children who engage in circle time. Three children in the group have speech and language differences, including a non-speaking child, selective mutism and pronunciation difficulties.

Harassment – engaging in unwanted conduct for example, by being hostile towards a child based on their protected characteristic.

Scenario 3: A four-year-old girl has speech, language and communication needs that makes it difficult for her to pronounce her words. Two practitioners find some of the ways in which she says things funny, and often do impressions of her.

Victimisation – singling out or targeting a child with unjust and cruel behaviours based on a protected characteristic.

Scenario 4: A parent challenges a setting's practice, which angers the practitioners, who say that they are not making any more effort to do anything else for the child. They can't wait for the family to leave.

Discrimination arising from a disability and a failure to make reasonable adjustments. In addition, this form of prohibited conduct applies to disabled children, and to disabled people in other contexts.

Scenario 5: A boy with sensory processing differences can become overwhelmed in large groups. When he is experiencing sensory overload, he will bite or hit out. The nursery expels him for three days, citing zero tolerance for aggressive behaviour.

Practitioners should also be aware that there can combined discrimination, and this occurs when a child is treated less favourably based on two or more of their protected characteristics. For example, discriminating against a child based on their disability and race, or race and gender.

Legitimate aim

In some cases, the decisions that we make have a legitimate aim. For example, we may need to make a decision based on the safety, wellbeing and dignity of children, and we must engage in transparent discussions when making decisions regarding equality and equity. The questions that you must ask yourself during decision-making are:

1. Is it proportionate rather than reactionary?

   There are times when a behaviour or experience is a 'flashpoint' for a practitioner and their reaction is not balanced. Take a moment, a breather and a step back before making a decision.

2. Is it appropriate?

   Actions must be appropriate and should certainly not further disadvantage a child.

3. Is it necessary?

   There have been times where the decision I have seen taken is in the best interests of everyone involved. If we take necessary action to mitigate or moderate risks and we can justify this, then we have made the right decision.

Reasonable adjustments

What is reasonable in a reasonable adjustment?

Reflection

- What do you think of when you hear the term 'reasonable adjustments'?
- Can you think of examples of reasonable adjustments?
- Can you think of examples of unreasonable adjustments?

'Reasonable adjustments' is a term that is not explored often enough in the Early Years. It usually makes practitioners think of adjustments relating to physical disability or impairment. Still, it is much broader in scope, and you are likely making adjustments more often than you would realise. As an Early Years practitioner, you must promote equality of opportunity. You must not discriminate against, harass or victimise disabled children (DfE, 2015). Failure to make reasonable adjustments where this is entirely possible is a form of discrimination. However, we do see the reluctance in this area. It would be easy to judge settings or practitioners. Still, I think that the more significant issue with this topic is understanding and recognition. So let's unpick what it means in practice and how relevant it really is.

A reasonable adjustment begins with your mindset and your willingness to consider changes and adaptations to your setting to ensure access and participation. When a child walks through the door, we should anticipate possible adaptations and adjustments. An important thing to remember is that not all disability is visible or yet diagnosed. Upon meeting a child, we have to explore what those needs are and what they 'look like' in everyday experiences. The common mistake with reasonable adjustments is that they require a physical change, but they can relate to a whole variety of things. Adjustments can occur in mindset, behaviours or physical accommodations. I use the following example to demonstrate.

Case study: Reasonable adjustments

Clare has started to attend a local pre-school and is 36 months. She is quite shy but loves cuddles and her teddy Ronald. He goes everywhere with her, and he is involved in lots of her role-play games. Clare has some social and emotional needs, and experiences quite intense separation anxiety. This is often exacerbated during the morning handover. Her key person and parent have noticed that the busy environment is a big trigger, and seeing lots of people come and go can be very unsettling. Clare's key person suggests a reasonable adjustment for the morning handover: she or the buddy key person will meet Clare outside the setting and they will all walk in together, and Clare can use this time to share what will be happening during the day. Clare is often comforted by knowing what is happening now and next. The nursery manager agrees that this adjustment can be managed effectively while Clare gains confidence.

Whenever I share this example with practitioners, they seem surprised and often respond that this is just something that they would do. In short, going above and beyond is already an embedded part of their practice. But practitioners must recognise how they adjust or adapt to meet children's needs. Once you see how often it happens, you also, by default, become more open to thinking creatively about reasonable adjustments.

Unreasonable adjustments

'The essence of reasonable adjustments is that they anticipate where disadvantage may arise and are put in place to prevent that happening.' (Council for Disabled Children, 2015b, pg. 26)

You must be thoughtful in the process of identifying and agreeing on reasonable adjustments. Another issue that arises is where the practitioner believes that they have to implement unreasonable or unrealistic changes. For instance, I once received a call from a setting saying that they needed to have a lift installed as soon as possible because a child with physical disabilities could not get up the stairs. While there is a broader discussion around why such ableist accessibility issues exist, it is unfair to suggest that settings should go beyond what is reasonable in the immediate moment. Many Early Years settings are based in non-purpose-built environments or are limited in terms of space, funding or resources. The crucial factor is the willingness and openness to ask: 'What is within your capacity?'. The conversations around reasonable adjustments should be ongoing, and if there is an identification of longer term accessibility issues, settings should always be thinking about how they may adapt in the future.

The SEND code of practice: 0–25

The right code but the wrong practice

In September 2014, the SEND code of practice: 0–25 came into effect in England. It included radical reforms to transform the SEND system. Anyone who has picked up the document, particularly the specific guide to the Early Years (DfE, 2014b), will note that the reforms provided greater autonomy in developing support systems that worked across different types of provision. A greater emphasis was placed on a successful transition to adulthood – hence the extended age from 18 to 25 – and many of the code's principles could be understood and applied from early childhood. My professional feelings about the code of practice were overall very positive, and I saw an opportunity for Early Years to develop innovative and workable practices based on the uniqueness of their setting. But before we get into the details of the code, it is important to acknowledge that the implementation of the reforms has been less than ideal, despite the radical ideas contained within. Why do you need to know this information as a practitioner? Because many of the issues that you are facing are common across different areas, local authorities and settings. And by identifying the problems, we can think of creative ways around them, because one good feature of the code of practice is flexibility within its delivery style.

Principles into practice

The SEND code of practice describes the principles that should be observed by all professionals working with children and young people who have SEND. These include:

- 'taking into account the views of children, young people and their families
- enabling children, young people and their parents to participate in decision-making
- collaborating with partners in education, health and social care to provide support
- identifying the needs of children and young people
- making high quality provision to meet the needs of children and young people
- focusing on inclusive practices and removing barriers to learning
- helping children and young people to prepare for adulthood'.

    (DfE, 2014b, pg. 5)

'We must, we should and we can'

Mind the gap

Following on from the introduction of the code of practice, Ofsted and the Care Quality Commission (CQC) devised a programme to inspect local areas for their effectiveness in delivering the code of practice. The inspections aim to examine how local areas are:

- identifying children and young people's SEND
- meeting the needs of children and young people who have SEND
- improving outcomes for children and young people who have SEND.

  (Ofsted, 2017)

In 2017, Ofsted produced a report of their main findings from their first 30 inspections, and such findings were, on the whole, quite disheartening. The full report can be found on the Ofsted website, but some of the more concerning headlines from this report included:

- 'Children and young people identified as needing SEND support had not benefited from the implementation of the Code of Practice well enough.' (pg. 5)
- 'School leaders had used unofficial exclusions too readily to cope with children and young people who have SEND.' (pg. 5)
- 'Access to therapy services was a weakness in half of the local areas inspected.' (pg. 5)
- 'In over a third of the local areas inspected, leaders across education, health and care did not involve children and young people or their parents sufficiently in planning and reviewing their provision (a process known as co-production).' (pg. 6)
- A large proportion of parents in the local areas inspected lacked confidence in the ability of mainstream schools to meet their child's needs.' (pg. 6)

  (Ofsted, 2017)

However, a positive finding was that children and young people's SEND were identified well in the Early Years, particularly for those with complex needs. Parents generally felt supported and involved in the process. This included ensuring joint working during transition and developing holistic pictures of children's needs. It is always surprising to me that the sector that is the least valued in education continually demonstrates greater skills in advocacy and rights. It is important to recognise that this is in part because we have a deeply embedded set of EYFS themes that lend themselves extremely well to the work of inclusion:

- A unique child
- Positive relationships
- Enabling environment
- Learning and development.

  (DfE, 2012)

I have recognised when working with so-called 'low-skilled' practitioners that a passion for this sector cannot be taught or gained through a qualification. You either love early childhood education or you don't.

The keys to the code of practice

Arrangements for SEND support: Early identification and intervention

---

Must

Early Years providers must have arrangements in place to support children with SEND.

One of the underpinning concepts within the code of practice is the importance of early intervention. The Early Intervention Foundation states that early intervention 'means identifying and providing effective early support to children and young people who are at risk of poor outcomes' (n.d, para 1). According to Mahoney and Wiggers (2007), it is important to respond early to any emerging concerns as the first five years of life present us with a unique opportunity to prevent the manifestation of difficulties. According to the code of practice, the arrangements that we have in place should ensure that children are not unnecessarily delayed in accessing the right support, as there is now a strong body of evidence to suggest that unsupported needs impact on long-term and future outcomes (DfE & DoH, 2015).

Case study: Emerging difficulties

According to the code of practice, 'all those who work with young children should be alert to emerging difficulties and respond early' (DfE & DoH, 2015, para. 5.5), but Nick has found that this can be quite difficult at his setting. On a number of occasions, he has highlighted emerging difficulties and been told by his SENDCo, 'Oh don't worry, he will catch up' or 'He's a boy, they take more time than girls'. This has worried Nick because it goes against the guidance, and on some occasions children's needs have become more pronounced.

What would you do in this situation? Have you ever felt reluctant to identify a child as SEND because they may simply catch up?

The case study on page 47 has been identified as a common scenario in identification. The 'Bercow: Ten years on' report (2018), which addressed the state of speech, language and communication support in England, found that early identification is still a significant issue. There is no consistent approach to accessing early intervention. It is important that, as practitioners, we develop the skills and expertise to act early but this also must be matched with responsiveness from support services. A general rule of thumb when you suspect SEND is to not rely on 'he will grow out of it' mentalities.

Top tip: Identification

Take the sameness out of observation: Record observations in a range of ways, such as random and planned note-taking and photograph sequences, which are great for examining key play and independence skills. Short videos are also great because they can be watched back later or alongside a parent or colleague.

'Look for it' observations: Sometimes we can feel unsure about whether there is a difference or a delay. While we want to focus on what children can do, we may also need to look to see whether they are demonstrating key milestones within their play and daily tasks. Setting a focus area can help you to consider development across a number of contexts, and you can share this with parents so that they can also collaborate to understand the bigger picture of development.

Explore the how and what of learning: Often practitioners can focus on the milestones and what children are learning but it is crucial to also think about how a child learns. Ensure that there are discussions and dialogue around the Characteristics of Effective Learning (Early Education, 2012), which will better help you to understand whether there is a concern. For example, you may find that a child doesn't 'bounce back after difficulties' and this may indicate that they are not feeling motivated in their learning.

What to expect when: Share a parent-friendly child development document and engage in curious conversations with parents so that you can be involved in shared decision-making about whether there is a specific need.

Utilising the EYFS

As a setting, you will follow the EYFS, which means that many of your observations, assessments and planning systems are already embedded. When it comes to SEND arrangements, you are building upon these already existing systems rather than developing additional or new ones. The benefit of the code of practice is that it is flexible in how you design and implement your SEND support arrangements. Following on from each statutory requirement is a description of the things that you should do to further strengthen your SEND support.

In addition to your formal opportunities to identify SEND – for example, the progress check at two years old – you will also have informal opportunities to build a picture of the child's strengths and needs.

Continue to use your observation, planning and assessment cycle. Still, the code of practice also recommends that you tighten up those processes with the four-stage graduated approach of assess, plan, do and review. This will be covered in greater detail in Chapter 5 but, essentially, you will use your summative EYFS processes:

- Using progress checks or summaries to summarise development at key intervals, ideally you will stage development which can become useful when needing to make referrals.

- You will need to think about how to stage development under the new EYFS reforms, and I would still recommend that ages/stages or the Birth to Five ranges (Early Education, 2021) support this well. For example, you may have a child who is 36 months but developing within 8 to 20 months across her prime areas.

- Ensure that you have shared key information with parents so that they understand how you come to make these judgements. The 'What to expect, when?' document (DfE, 2018b) is great for this.

- If you use any additional assessment tools, ensure that parents are fully aware of these and avoid ones that adopt 'red flag' approaches.

Identifying the area of need

Should

Special educational provision should be matched to the child's identified SEND using the four broad areas of need:
- communication and interaction
- cognition and learning
- social, emotional and/or mental health
- physical and/or sensory.

These areas give an overview of the range of needs for which providers should plan. However, individual children often have needs that cut across all these areas, and their needs may change over time. Providers should review how well equipped they are to provide support across the four broad areas of need.

Once a setting has identified that a child has developmental needs, they will go beyond their seven learning areas and consider the specific areas of need. It is peculiar to me that these areas are still not well known or utilised, because they can guide settings in mapping out clear support. These will be defined in more detail in Chapter 5. They also ensure that we do not become fixated on labels or diagnosis but instead on how we can develop effective provision.

It is also beneficial to frame discussions with parents around the areas of need to understand the predominant focus. Often when you identify several concerns, it can seem overwhelming, but the four broad areas of need enable you to develop a focus, as the following case study demonstrates.

Case study

Panos had been working with Ben's parents for a few weeks on identifying key areas of need. Ben is an engaged and motivated child, but he had been struggling to communicate his needs due to speech difficulties. It was not yet understood why this difficulty had emerged, but often Ben would get very frustrated when he was misunderstood. This had led to several emotional meltdowns, and Panos was keen to help. When he looked at Ben's areas of need, he could see that Ben's predominant area was communication and interaction, but that this was also impacting on his self-regulation, and so he also had social, emotional and mental health needs. However, the key was to help Ben be understood, and so Panos introduced a 'Needs and Wants' choice board so that Ben could point out and communicate and indicate what he was thinking and feeling. As Ben became confident with the board and his needs were met, the frequency of his emotional meltdowns decreased.

Parent partnership and 'voice'

Must

Where a setting identifies a child as having SEND, the setting must work in partnership with parents to establish the support that the child needs.

We will cover this in much greater detail in Chapter 6, but it is important to establish a clear understanding of the role of the parent. The Pen Green Centre team have carried out extensive research in parent partnership, and in her book *Involving Parents in their Children's Learning: A Knowledge-Sharing Approach* (2017), Margy Whalley describes parents as co-educators. We should acknowledge that 'both the home and the early child institution have important, complementary but different parts to play' (Malaguzzi, cited in Dahlberg et al., 1999, pg. 59).

In 2017, the Department for Education produced a research report, 'Study of Early Education and Development (SEED): meeting the needs of children with special educational needs and disabilities in the Early Years' (DfE, 2017a), which found that partnership and communication was generally effective with emerging SEND but those parents of children with complex needs found information exchanges more challenging. With this in mind, settings do need to consider how the systems of support are differentiated according to need, and the ways in which information exchange is handled so that it becomes empowering as opposed to overwhelming. A significant consideration for parent partnership is valuing the parents' wealth of knowledge as equal to our own. There is often a power dynamic at play, which can lead to a parent feeling 'done to' rather than as an equal and active collaborator. This can lead to information overload, and Dr Janet Goodall makes an interesting point in a blog: 'I often ask people how long their romantic partnerships would last if all they ever did was give their significant other information – if they never stopped to listen, if they never engaged in dialogue. Estimates of longevity range from a few days to a few weeks, but I've yet to find anyone who thinks that "information sharing" could be the basis of a partnership' (2021, para 4).

Local Offer

Should

Early Years providers should also have the opportunity to take part in the regular review of the Local Offer that the local authority has a duty to undertake, in order to identify gaps in provision and ensure that the Local Offer is responsive to the needs of local children, young people and their families.

When I initially saw the term 'Local Offer', I felt that settings may not understand how it could be of value. It is straightforward but, at the same time, ambiguous. It is made all the more ambiguous because the expectations for private, voluntary and independent Early Years providers differ from compulsory education.

What you need to know

Your local authority must publish a Local Offer, which you will find on their website, usually under 'Family Information Services'. The purpose of the Local Offer is to set out in one place information about the provision that families can expect to access across education, health and social care – for example, local support groups in the area for children and families with autism spectrum condition. A parent who wants to access support can go onto the Local Offer and look at available options. The SEND code of practice: 0–25 outlines its two key purposes:

- 'To provide clear, comprehensive, accessible and up-to-date information about the available provision and how to access it, and
- To make provision more responsive to local needs and aspirations by directly involving disabled children and those with SEN and their parents, and disabled young people and those with SEN, and service providers in its development and review.' (DfE, 2015, para 4.2)

Activity: CPD challenge

Find your Local Offer and have a browse.

It is vital to offer clarity here about the fact that Local Offers are variable and almost definitely a 'work in progress'. They are not the answer to effective parent partnership, but the premise behind them has some value.

Settings in the private, voluntary and independent sectors do not have to produce their own Local Offer because their local authority does this on their behalf. However, you will provide your setting details to the Family Information Service and this should include your arrangements and specific provision for SEND. Interestingly, when I worked in a local authority, most of my settings never thought to share their expertise meaning that parents had to research much more about settings. The code of practice states that it is essential for you to cooperate with your local authority to ensure that it remains up to date and is not merely a directory but also an information source.

How can we make the Local Offer meaningful?

Beyond our legal duty, we can actually use the Local Offer to strengthen our setting's practice and our communication systems. While you do not need to outline or produce your own Local Offer, it would be good to utilise it within your own provision.

When I worked in a neighbourhood nursery back in early 2000, signposting was hugely beneficial and popular with parents in terms of information sharing. Every setting that you walked into had an area or display with lots of information. To me, the term 'Local Offer' translates to that practice of signposting but actually goes further and collaborates with parents to help guide. Here are my top recommendations for bringing the Local Offer to life.

Top tip: Utilising the Local Offer

Policy and procedure: Include the link to the Local Offer in your setting's policy and procedure. Include a statement about your duty, in line with the SEND code of practice: 0–25.

Signpost it: Set up a Local Offer board in your setting or create a presentation folder with key information relating to your own SEND provision. Examples can be found at www.eyfs4me.com.

Talk to your team: Hold a team meeting and discuss what it is that you actually offer to families and what is within your expertise. If you are a childminder, network with local colleagues to discuss individual services. That way, if you have a family whose needs you can't meet, you can still engage in supportive signposting.

Capacity building: Some parents may feel nervous about how to use the Local Offer or are unsure of how it works. If you have a laptop, you can do a short screen recording with a demonstration or tutorial. An example can be found at www.eyfs4me.com.

Acronyms: Have a list of acronym translations so that parents do not get swept away by terminology.

'We must, we should and we can'

> **Have your say:** Contact your local authority and ask whether there is a feedback form for their Local Offer, and if not, email them with your feedback.
>
> **Collaborate:** Schools have a legal duty to create their own Local Offer. Contact feeder schools and ask for copies of their Local Offer so that parents know what to expect.
>
> **Use it or lose it:** Use the term 'Local Offer' so that it becomes familiar.

In 2017, Ofsted found that Local Offers were not effective in helping parents to access information and services in over half the local authority areas that they had inspected. Please keep this in mind when browsing Local Offers; they are variable in quality. However, as Early Years practitioners, we are a powerful voice. If we see the value of equipping parents with knowledge, we will utilise this new term. Even if the term 'Local Offer' is replaced or goes out of date, the practice remains a necessary inclusion.

Record keeping

> **Must**
>
> Practitioners must maintain a record of children under their care as required under the EYFS framework. Such records about children must be available to their parents, and they must include how the setting supports children with SEND.

One of the significant issues that comes up in our workforce is the burden of paperwork. In fact, some of the latest EYFS reforms were underpinned by reducing workload. We shall see about the reality of that one. The code of practice equally attempted to remove the burden of paperwork. However, the truth is that it still bombards us daily, and there is, without doubt, needless duplication and reams of forms. It is so prominent that a whole chapter within this book is dedicated to paperwork (see Chapter 6) but I thought it useful to consider what we should have as a baseline for SEND support.

To register or not to register children with SEND

This is a contested topic within the Early Years, mainly as there is no legal requirement for how you should document a child's SEND. Many schools use a SEND register, but there are enough anecdotal examples of how this has been used as a labelling system. The best advice that I can give a setting is to do what you believe to be right. Still, I believe that an inclusion schedule can be very beneficial for settings.

There are mixed feelings about the appropriateness of a SEND register because it can lead to the labelling and categorisation of children. They can, however, be useful when utilised in the right way. I usually promote the use of an Inclusion Schedule (you can access a template in the Companion resources). It is not uncommon for the setting SENDCo to have other roles, and without a process of reviewing SEND support needs, children can get overlooked. I also find that it can be a useful way to monitor what is working with a setting, and what is not, and to identify patterns and trends. For example, in one setting, there were a high number of children with social, emotional and mental health needs, and this was evident in the inclusion monitoring form. The setting was able to invest in specific training to become better at supporting these types of needs. As a setting SENDCo, I would use this form to go and check in with key people to establish what was happening for each child. Remember that key people are responsible for leading on support, and so there does need to be a way to monitor what is happening for children.

English as an additional language (EAL)

Should

Identifying and assessing SEND for young children whose first language is not English requires particular care. Early Years practitioners should look carefully at all aspects of a child's learning and development to establish whether any delay is related to learning English as an additional language or whether it arises from SEND. Difficulties related solely to learning English as an additional language are not SEND.

One of the ongoing issues within the Early Years is the continual confusion about EAL and SEND. Practitioners will often talk about these two topics as interconnected, and they absolutely are not one and the same thing. That doesn't mean to say, however, that a child who speaks more than one language can't, in addition, have special educational needs. Still, as practitioners, we need to conduct a dual assessment with parents to establish this. You can access a guide to this in the Companion resources.

Become familiar with what you must do and what you should do

You must have arrangements in place to support children with SEND, followed up by additional practices to strengthen the effectiveness of inclusion.

Know how statutory documents interlink

Just when you think you have worked out one set of statutory guidance, you find that it diverges with other documents. Make yourself familiar with key documents and how they link.

Location, location, location

No one is expecting you to know the documents inside and out. They are to be used in an ongoing way, so I always recommend having a few hard and digital copies of the 'go to' documents. It is also vital that you let parents know where they can access these documents, either within the setting or independently.

Don't let change throw you off...

It can be frustrating when reviews, amendments, reforms and changes happen. Still, it is often just part and parcel of our sector. Changes are usually minimal and require slight adaptations to practice. However significant the changes may be, the fundamental principles of your good practice remain the same.

Take it off the shelf

While you may need hard copies of written policies, there are other ways to document and record their existence. Collaborative displays, posters and team meetings or group-work to review and reshape can be beneficial. The voices of your children, practitioners and parents should be included.

Signpost your Local Offer

Think of it as a way to communicate how your setting works to be inclusive. Ensure that you signpost parents in as many ways as possible and develop your own Local Offer board, poster or booklet.

Signposts and resources

SEN and Disability in the Early Years toolkit
Council for Disabled Children
Available at: https://councilfordisabledchildren.org.uk/help-resources/resources/sen-and-disability-early-years-toolkit

Disabled Children and the Equality Act 2010 (what Early Years providers need to know and do, including responsibilities to disabled children under the Children and Families Act 2014)
Council for Disabled Children
Available at: https://councilfordisabledchildren.org.uk/help-resources/resources/disabled-children-and-equality-act-2010-early-years

3 'Oh, that's the SENDCo's job': Understanding whole-team approaches to SEND inclusion

Starting points

- When was the last time you felt like you stood up for something or someone you believed in, including yourself?
- How did it make you feel?
- Have you ever held back from speaking up when you believe something?
- How did this make you feel?

Introduction

The 'unpowerful' voice of the Early Years practitioner…

The National Association for Special Educational Needs (NASEN) produced a report in 2020, examining early identification of SEND in the Early Years from the SENDCo's perspective. This report found that 80 per cent of SENDCos felt confident in identifying SEND but recognised that whole-team staff knowledge was an important factor, which was sometimes prohibited by a lack of availability in staff training. At the time, the survey did not explore in more depth how the relationships between practitioners and the setting's SENDCo strengthened the identification of SEND, nor did they interview childminders. However, the crucial finding in this research about whole-team access to training has ignited further research efforts from NASEN about how we upskill and empower practitioners so that they can effectively carry out SEND support.

It is still concerning, however, that despite the focus on key person accountability in the 0-25 SEND code of practice (DfE, 2015), the key person remains largely absent from research and is an unpowerful voice. It brings me back to this idea that every teacher should be a teacher of SEND but how can this be measured or understood if research only ever involves the SENDCo and parents. I have recently begun providing a key person drop-in session as an opportunity for Early Years practitioners to unpick and work through their inclusive practice. What has become immediately apparent in these supervisory sessions is that key people have a wealth of untapped knowledge. They challenge, question and expand their pedagogy when they are given opportunities to engage in a professional dialogue. For example, we have recently discussed key persons discomfort with the requirement to focus on the negatives during referral, and how SMART targets feel like a tokenistic practice and continue to promote ableist approaches to learning. If we do not take time to sit alongside key people and to hear their voices, how might we see the reshaping and progress of inclusive practices. The key across this chapter is that all 'voices' count, and we need to start listening!

Top tip: Childminders

If you join a network of childminders, try to do some information-gathering via a survey so that you can feed back priority needs to your local authority. Websites such as SurveyMonkey have free versions of their software.

Amplifying voices

When I came to write this chapter, I was cautious of simply outlining roles and responsibilities without first discussing the critical concepts of advocacy, activism and courageous leadership in the Early Years. As you will have picked up in previous chapters, the sector is subject to deeply embedded tensions and so, in our inclusion work, we often find ourselves alongside parents in a 'battle' for support. It is fundamental that, as practitioners, we amplify the 'voices' of children with SEND, thus supporting the child to be an expert in their own lives. The concept of activism can seem strange to a practitioner who already feels a sense of disempowerment through continued experiences of not being heard or valued. Still, we must consider how such behaviours become part of our professional identifies, as opposed to an 'add-on' task.

Definition: Child's voice

Young children should be viewed as experts in their own lives (Langsted, 1994) and we should encourage their participation in decisions that will affect them. The concept of the 'child's voice' includes the thoughts, feelings, needs, wants, perspectives and views of the child, and in our everyday work, we need to reflect on how our decisions are informed by the 'voice' of the child. For a child with SEND, we should consider the unique ways in which they communicate and ensure that these are understood.

Advocacy, agency and activism

In 2019, The Pen Green Research Centre delivered a live webinar where they outlined the importance of developing agency, advocacy and activism as part of our everyday practice. While these terms often appear quite politically charged, they are more common than we realise.

Advocacy

Advocacy is defined as the process of supporting and enabling vulnerable people (Prowle & Hodgkins, 2020), who are often made more vulnerable by the oppressive and outdated education systems. It involves us as practitioners speaking on behalf of the child and family, but also alongside them. I often suggest to practitioners that they are the back-up system for a family. Families need to know that we are here with and for them.

Agency

Agency describes the strength of belief that we have about our ability to determine change. Developing this as a competency in the Early Years is crucial because things often appear beyond our control. But being high in agency means that we will readily become involved in challenges and seek ways forward (Whalley, 2017). Practitioners can often shy away from demonstrating their agency because they become fearful of disrupting the status quo and have fears about how they may be personally impacted. It is essential to recognise, however, that agency does not mean pointless acts of defiance. It is rooted in a genuine desire to promote positive changes. Practitioners as 'agents of change' understand the value of minor and significant changes and acknowledge those 'small wins' as steps towards greater good.

Activity

As a team or as a childminder, note down all the positive impacts or changes that have occurred over the last six months due to your sense of agency. Often, we do not reflect enough on the effectiveness of our daily work.

Activism

Activism occurs when practitioners take intentional steps to reshape their practice to support the struggle for social justice and social change (Whalley et al., 2017). A pedagogy of activism spurs a practitioner to engage in rights-based practices and affords high-quality, equitable teaching to all children rather than simply the dominant group – in this case, children who are considered 'normal' or typically developing. Dr Nathan Archer has studied the concept of activism extensively within his research, and in his interviews found that practitioners 'are activists both against and for policy developments, but overwhelmingly were motivated by the best interests of children and families' (para. 26). He also referred to the importance of valuing the powerful acts of 'quiet activism' (para. 23) that occur within our everyday actions and practices. The Early Years sector has also become more acutely aware of social justice and how this intersects with race, gender, class, disability and language, to name a few.

If we think about the above descriptions, you can likely see yourself in them and you will be able to come up with examples where you have demonstrated all three. The case studies below also highlight the many shapes and forms of advocacy, agency and activism, in particular where 'quiet activism' emerges.

Case study: Advocacy

At the end of each day, everything is tidied and put away ready for the practitioners to set up the following day. A few children have become upset because they will have to start their play all over again. The teacher sits down with the children and apologises, saying that he didn't realise that they may want to come back to it. He suggests a 'come back to it' table and says that children can place favourite items or unfinished work on the table, and if there is something that they do not want cleared away they can stick a note on it. Although the environment seems messier, he immediately notices increased engagement and a high level of recall from children.

Case study: Agency

Dalia is a nursery manager and encourages her key people to complete referrals. She notices that there is a lot of duplication of work when referrals need to be made to several services, and this takes time away from being with the children. She contacts the head of Child Development Services and suggests that a multi-referral form be devised. She raises this a few times before any change occurs, but eventually they develop a universal registration form and a multi-referral form. They make this available on the local authority website with clear guidance.

Case study: Activism

Varinder has been told that the children with SEND will need to be taken off to a separate space each morning to do a focused activity while the rest of the class has 'carpet time'. Varinder asks for the rationale behind this decision. She is told that this is because the children cannot sit still or follow Golden Rules. Varinder asks whether she can be given an opportunity to lead a group circle time involving all children, because she would like to demonstrate that sitting still is actually counterproductive to learning. She expresses that she is not comfortable with a setting that suggests that they are inclusive but then carries out exclusionary practices. Varinder provides research to her leader about movement-based experiences and films her circle time for her leader to watch back later. Her leader admits that this circle time looked much more fun, and that they were impressed with how engaged the children were.

Whole-team approaches

Imagine if we all adopted the skills of agency, advocacy and activism in our daily practice? In an ideal world, we would be able to dismantle many outdated practices and rebuild. Still, where this is not the case, it becomes the whole team's collective responsibility, and their micro-actions can begin to weaken old systems. The 'whole team' for a childminder includes their networks with other childminders and their families. Often when we think about leadership, we look to a hierarchy of professional roles, and we might immediately think of the manager or setting SENDCo. Still, leadership exists across the sector, and we can choose to take the lead to develop our own personal pedagogy. Think back to the jigsaw analogy which acknowledges that each individual should be valued as being autonomous, accountable and active with their role.

Courageous and distributed leadership

In their book *Courageous Leadership in Early Childhood Education*, Long et al. (2016) write about the importance of informed, consistent and deliberate actions. That is to say, it is not enough to think about the things you want to challenge but you also need to act upon them, especially around issues of social injustice. For many of us working within the Early Years, we do not exist in settings where equality and equity are a given. We exist within complex communities faced with 'systems, practices, and dispositions that perpetuate educational privilege and inequity' (Long et al., 2016, pg. 7). More alarmingly, the intersections of race, ethnicity, social class, disability and gender can leave children in even further educational debt. I say debt as opposed to gap because so often such narratives suggest that the onus is on the child, rather than the way in which the education system is designed.

'Written off'

Whatever our position, we can never be advocates for just one thing, and so in our work to support children with SEND, we are also supporting children who face others forms of oppression. Through several discussions with Liz Pemberton, director of The Black Nursery Manager Ltd, we connected on our shared disillusionment that black and brown children are often subject to much higher degrees of teacher bias, and are more frequently mislabelled and misdiagnosed (DfE, 2018). The implications of this are long lasting and can lead to a lack of timely and appropriate support. Liz shared a case study from her time as a nursery manager below.

Case study: Black boys and misdiagnosis

At the nursery that I manage, I had a two-year-old boy join my setting who had previously been excluded from another setting due to behaviour that they had labelled as being so poor that they wouldn't be able to have him attend the nursery any longer. They had told his parents that they believed he had some kind of behavioural problem, possibly ADHD, and advised that he go and 'be tested'. They concluded that this could have been the only possible reason for his behaviour.

When the parents came to me, they were filled with anxiety, doubt, fear and confusion. It seemed that their son had been 'written off' at two years old. It was their feeling that the nursery could not be bothered with their son and they said that they believed the reason he was being excluded and singled out was because he was Black. The parents deemed the nursery as being ineffective in their ability to manage their son's behaviour because they lacked cultural understanding; they believed that the nursery wasn't genuinely interested in the wellbeing of their son and they believed that the pre-existing stereotypes of Black boys being naughty and disobedient overshadowed the nursery practitioners' ability to look at their son as an individual.

The child started at my nursery and we all identified that his environment was what needed to be changed, and nothing else: communication, strong parent partnership and an investment in the child's wellbeing. Within a few months, the parents noted a significant change in their son's behaviour. He was happy and more engaged and his emotional responses were met not with 'behaviour management techniques' but with empathy and space for him to express himself.

This case study tells us that working with children is not merely defined by the job description or a set of tick-box role requirements. It is a process of unlearning, relearning and engaging with uncomfortable truths. It can seem unfathomable that black and brown children are subject to more negatively charged experiences and labelling. Still, research has found a disproportionate exclusion rate of black Caribbean children (DfE, 2018b) and that unconscious and conscious bias has been found to influence educators' views on behaviour and expectations. The behaviours of children from different ethnic groups are, according to Rudoe (2014), viewed more harshly than those of their white counterparts. According to research by Wright et al. (2010), such negative views lead to children feeling undervalued and disrespected, and so we begin to see children placed at a disadvantage by the very people who are supposedly best placed to protect their interests. This can seriously undermine their ability to maintain good levels of resilience and engagement with their learning. I recently spoke with a parent whose turmoil was rooted in the fact that all her child ever heard was the negative views that her key person had about her. Regardless of the biological and genetic underpinnings of any type of SEND, it is the environmental and relational experiences that embed the way in which children think about themselves. Gershensen (2015) found that non-black teachers have significantly lower educational expectations for black students than black teachers do *when evaluating the same students*. The level of expectations by black teachers did not differ dependent on how the child was racialised. These findings are concerning, as research consistently suggests that a practitioner's views of a child can contribute to the outcomes for learning.

Definition: Ableism

Favouring able-bodied and neurotypical traits and development.

As Early Years practitioners, before anything else, we must become champions for all children. I always say to practitioners that it is not enough to simply like children; you have to be actively interested in their learning and development, and to develop a working knowledge of their experiences. There are many ways in which to develop this, but these six features of courageous leadership are great places to start, whether you are at the top, working on the ground or multi-tasking in several roles (which is commonly the case in the Early Years). A courageous leader:

- challenges 'one size fits all' curriculum models, including those that are mono-cultural and ableist
- seeks to understand the whole child

- addresses the lack of equity-based professional development and regularly engages in the development of their own courageous pedagogy
- dismantles deficit views and negative profiling of children, while considering the uncomfortable truths about race, ethnicity, social class, disability and gender
- values children and families and does not allow their own dominant views to take up space
- goes beyond verbalism, which is talk without action, by insisting that the work of advocacy for children is non-negotiable in their setting space.

(Adapted from Long et al., 2016)

Whole-team SEND approaches

All practitioners should be developing their SEND-based skills and knowledge

The best way to learn about SEND is by supporting and teaching children with SEND. Learning is not a one-way process, and while the children are learning from you, you are absolutely learning from them. My first SEND experience was on the first day that I stepped foot into a nursery as a summer volunteer. I wasn't there by choice; I was there because my mother insisted that I help out now that I had broken up for the summer from university. I wasn't particularly interested in children, so I agreed to do assisting duties like cleaning. Still, anyone who works with children will know that they do like to curiously stare to the point of awkwardness. One little girl stared at me with fascination for such a long time, but I avoided interacting with her entirely. Later, she got stuck trying to climb the stairs to a slide and she reached out to me. Given no other option, I cautiously approached to help her. I hazarded a guess that she was about three years of age, and I assumed that she could talk, but when she spoke to me, she could not pronounce or speak many words. The act of her holding out her hand for help has stayed with me throughout my career. It seems like a trivial, unimportant event, but it cemented my understanding that my role was to be a helping hand as a practitioner. This is echoed in Tamar Jacobson's book *Don't Get So Upset* (2008), where she describes the importance of developing a relationship with children that tells them that we are by their side. This 'I'm by your side-ness' goes against the educator's usual power dynamic of being in charge of the child; rather, we walk alongside them to guide, cultivate and support their learning. Funnily enough, the fascination that this child had with me led to my fascination with her. I think that the differences in her development ignited my interest in SEND because I had to work harder to understand her.

There are far more complex anecdotes that I could share about children with SEND, but I think that it is unhelpful to only focus on the 'worst-case scenarios' and how we got through them; that just builds anxiety. I would instead say that supporting children with SEND helps us to understand differences, and those differences lead to innovation in our teaching. Our mainstream spaces could not progress without the diversity and uniqueness of the children that occupy them.

While I will write about the ways in which we can feel equipped, as a starting point the best way to be equipped is to be available. So much focus is on the 'to-do' list, but uninterrupted time being with children is absolutely the best teaching technique in SEND.

Staff quality

According to the European Agency for Special Needs and Inclusive Education (2017) review, the quality of practitioners is one of the most essential factors in early education. High-quality interactions and sound pedagogy are strengthened by progression through qualifications and ongoing access to training, often referred to as continuous professional development (CPD). However, with such an assortment of qualifications within the current workforce and a lack of representation, high-quality teaching is considered variable.

The review also identified that, across Europe, including the UK, more qualified staff tend to work with older children. When I first read this, I felt concerned about two things: first, that caregiving in the earliest years is overlooked as a skillset and is therefore only considered as a career by those with lower-level qualifications, when it is actually highly skilled work; and second, that those children who have emerging SEND are supported by staff who have less access to training, qualifications and resources.

Top tip: Identify training needs

Have a training matrix to identify any gaps in accessibility to training – for example, do baby room staff get out as often as pre-school staff? If ratio maintenance is an issue, consider different training modes, such as in-house training, online training or webinars.

Top tip: Childminder networks

Join a local or national network – for example, The Childcare Business Hub offers a support group and regular online training from guest speakers each month.

My utopia involves qualifications within early education becoming recognised at a higher professional standard. Anyone engaged in early education should be required to develop a specialism within five years of qualifying. As practitioners, we currently rely heavily on health specialists to provide support, but there is no reason why we cannot develop on-site specialisms as a sector. There is currently no compulsory element in the qualifications when working with children with SEND in Early Years settings, and it is worrying that the expectations are much clearer within compulsory education. If we are truly effective in early intervention, we need to see a more evenly distributed investment for the Early Years. By not equipping us with training, skills and qualifications, we are adding to the work of the school SENDCos, surely?

The role of the Early Years SENDCo

Let's get the mundane definition out the way and then delve into the reality of the role. According to the SEND code of practice: 0–25, 'those in group provision are expected to identify a SENCO. Childminders are encouraged to identify a person to act as SENCO and childminders who are registered with a childminder agency, or part of a network may wish to share that role between them.' (DfE & DoH, 2015, para 5.53) No matter who takes on the SENDCo role, they should be doing it because they have the skills, passion and knowledge for the job, not for the sake of ticking your 'named person' list.

According to the SEND code of practice: 0–25, the SENDCo is responsible for the following:

- 'ensuring all practitioners in the setting understand their responsibilities to children with SEN and the setting's approach to identifying and meeting SEN
- advising and supporting colleagues
- ensuring parents are closely involved throughout and that their insights inform action taken by the setting, and
- liaising with professionals or agencies beyond the setting.'

    (DfE & DoH, 2015, para 5.54)

'If I want something doing, I do it myself.' (Early Years SENDCo)

The SENDCo role must be viewed as a leadership role because the SENDCo oversees all SEND-related tasks. Unfortunately, we still see task burden with SENDCos, leading to a weaker support system overall. The above quote from an Early Years SENDCo highlights some of the issues we can face when there is a belief that the skills can only be demonstrated by one person. Settings should aim for shared responsibility for SEND provision, and this includes key people leading on individual SEND support.

SEND leadership

The reality is that a SENDCo or anyone engaged in SEND leadership is often involved in other roles. It is not yet the case that an Early Years SENDCo can be a role within its own right. While some settings don't necessarily need to allocate the position to a full-time role, others are in desperate need of time, capacity and resources. In fact, when I worked in an Early Years setting, I became the full-time SENDCo because the level of need was very high and we wanted to establish our provision and Local Offer to families.

While a SENDCo will often oversee SEND, the role is very much rooted in distributed leadership, which is defined as 'a deliberate organisational strategy in which aspects of behaviour and actions are shared with some, not necessarily all, staff throughout an organisation' (Lindon et al., 2016, pg. 119).

In her book *Leadership in Early Childhood*, Jillian Rodd interviews a senior lecturer who described a leader as someone who 'has a vision about their future expectations for self and others' (2012). It is one of the most apt ways to describe anybody leading on SEND, whether for a setting or for an individual child. To succeed, we have to have a vision for the child, family and for ourselves as practitioners. SEND leadership is not just a set of practical tasks, but the development of a deeply embedded approach and commitment to inclusion. Leadership should inspire others to play their part and the SENDCo must develop this network of skills to ensure that when children attend a setting, they are not viewed as solely the SENDCo's responsibility.

Practitioners come with combined knowledge, and together the following essential skills are beneficial for developing a whole-team approach:

- Sharing, discussing and inspiring ideas and thoughts, such as creating a toolkit of collective strategies or offering a fresh perspective.

- Providing feedback and recommendations to each other, such as offering an alternative perspective on a situation.

- Modelling good practice and demonstrating key skills, such as talking about what has worked well and what has not in your own practice.

- Positively influencing each other's behaviours and taking a solution-seeking approach, such as in moments of stress using active listening but offering constructive ideas rather than 'jumping on the bandwagon'. For example, avoid saying 'I agree that child just does not fit in here'.

- Helping each other out, delegating and making space for each other's priorities. For example, 'I know you are keen to do that non-participant observation today. I can cover for ten minutes if that helps?'

- Being hands-on with partnerships and using expertise and knowledge to inspire but not to intimidate. For example, offering to demonstrate a technique or to send some links to research about a particular topic.

- Embracing growth and doing things differently to how they have been done before. It is often within SEND that we have to adapt or move on from particular practices. This can be hard as it can make us feel de-skilled but keeps the child's best interests at the centre of your strategy.

How to identify the right person for the setting SENDCo

When I first took on the role of SENDCo, I was doing so because the current SENDCo absolutely detested the role. It was never her area of passion and she only agreed to do it because it was the only role that didn't have a named person. As you can imagine, when we engage in tasks or responsibilities that don't motivate us, we aren't going to perform to the best of our ability or inspire others. It is important to recognise that this particular practitioner had other skillsets. We don't write practitioners off because they don't feel passionate about every single area. The practitioner needed to find ways in which to develop her SEND knowledge and skills, but she certainly wasn't best placed to lead. Below are some key questions to consider when thinking about who would be best placed to take on the SENDCo role.

Is there a practitioner who:

1. has expressed an interest or passion in the area of SEND and inclusion?
2. has demonstrated key skills in leadership?
3. has demonstrated key skills in SEND and inclusion?
4. has effective communication skills, particularly with parents?
5. has good time management?
6. is open to feedback, and is aware of potential bias around SEND and other intersections such as race, class and gender?
7. believes in a strength's and rights-based approach to SEND and understands the harm of ableism?
8. has potential in any of the above areas, given the right support?

The key isn't to know, it's to be prepared to find out…

Something useful to remember is that you absolutely do not need to know all the answers as a SENDCo. I still continually get asked about different conditions and often think, 'I haven't heard of that' or 'I don't know what that acronym means'. I often find that potential SENDCos are afraid of losing face or feel embarrassed about not having in-depth knowledge. It is helpful to accept that you cannot know everything but you should be proactive when it is time to find out. Honesty is the best policy when navigating the SENDCo role.

Top tips: SEND leadership

Find your way around: Save the relevant SEND code of practice: 0–25 to your desktop to have on hand. You will jump in and out of this document as you go, but you will also find that everyday practice doesn't always match the script.

Check and challenge: If you are new to SEND leadership, be proactive in understanding the setting's approach and philosophy. The first place to start is with the policies and procedures relating to SEND, inclusion, equality and medical conditions. Become familiar with these documents and check that they are in line with current statutory guidance. Make notes on what you are currently doing well as a setting and where you need to develop.

Roles and responsibilities: Agree on how SEND leadership will be carried out and ensure that this is in some way reflected in all job descriptions. Consider what you can realistically do in terms of resources, time and capacity. If you are a childminder, ensure that your roles and responsibilities are childminder-specific, and consider priority tasks.

Knowledge, skills, expertise and training: You may have already completed SENDCo-specific training, but also consider how you will continue to develop your knowledge through CPD. Set up your own training plan, highlighting those areas that you know you will need to develop knowledge and skills in. Consider the different modes of learning; not everything has to be face to face.

Whole-team approaches: If you work in a nursery setting, you should also expect that all practitioners will commit to ongoing CPD for SEND-based knowledge. As a baseline, all practitioners should complete an introduction to SEND. A good signpost for this is the National Association for Special Educational Needs (NASEN), who offer a full suite of free SEND training.

Action plan: High-quality SEND provision does not happen overnight, and while you don't want to be burdened by paperwork, it can be a good idea to have a SEND-based action plan. This does not need to adhere to any particular format and should work for your own learning preferences. Some SEND leaders have bullet journals or use digital notes, while others have a full action plan. Choose what works for you and remember that slow and steady wins the race.

Set up a SEND toolkit: SEND leadership and pedagogy is a knowledge-building task. There is always something new to learn, unlearn, relearn and reapply. A way to reduce the information overload is to have a SEND toolkit. This can be either digital or a hard copy, and it is good to break it down into different sections, such as: policy and procedures; referrals; areas of need; assessment tools; and information exchange. This can then become a shared document and will help you to delegate and feel organised. *Side note: Do not keep confidential information in your toolkit.*

'Oh, that's the SENDCo's job'

Local authority procedures: Each local authority has its own systems, which can be frustrating, especially if you have to go cross-borough. Make sure that you collate these as soon as possible and have them in an accessible place. It will make life so much easier when you can signpost staff and parents to the right services.

Local Offer: Make yourself familiar with the Local Offer, and if you think it isn't good enough, your first SENDCo job is to contact the local authority to let them know.

Introduce yourself: Make sure that parents, colleagues and local services know your role. You can get creative here by developing a one-page profile or SENDCo passport.

The complexity of key people

Parent's voice

Having a key person that understood my child made the world of difference. I felt comfortable to share my vulnerabilities.

You will likely be unsurprised to know that there is very little that explicitly supports key people within the domain of SEND. While there is a wealth of resources and SEND-based training, there is an absolute need for targeted support so that an Early Years practitioner can feel equipped and confident. Let's begin with a case study to consider how valued the key person currently is in SEND support.

Case study: Key people

Sarah is the key person to Ben, who has been at the setting for a year. Ben loves the water play area and exploring how things work. He has speech, language and communication needs, and Sarah has developed a close bond with him, supporting his alternative forms of communication. Sarah has a detailed knowledge of Ben.

One day, the parents come into the nursery and invite Sarah to a Team Around the Child meeting. The SENDCo comes over to explain that she will attend instead because she is more experienced at information sharing. She turns to Sarah and asks for all information relating to Ben.

The case study is a variation on a real example where I supported an agitated key person who was holding on to a lot of anxiety about her key child's needs and access to support. The critical issue here is that the 'voice' of the key person was overlooked, and they were not actively empowered to take a lead in SEND support. This is unfortunately a common occurrence and can lead to disengagement. By Sarah not being at the meeting, important information will be missed. Key people often have intricate knowledge of their key children because they spend lots of time supporting and caring for them. To ensure that support is personalised, we must value the underpinning values of the key person approach in line with SEND & inclusion.

Hard to love?

Along with practical help, there is often another overlooked aspect of SEND support: the notion of love as pedagogy. We form attachments to our key children, and love forms an important basis with which to support children's development (Loreman, 2011). The very existence of the key person model is underpinned by the fundamental principles of attachment theory (to be covered in more detail in Chapter 8). We often lead with love and belonging, knowing that if a child does not feel safe and secure, they will find it very difficult to learn.

Professional love

Love as a concept in the Early Years can become a difficult topic to navigate, as can any work involving emotions. We have to be very clear about boundaries and we must recognise that there exists a risk that children can end up fulfilling the unmet attachment needs of practitioners. During a keynote speech in 2019, Dr Eunice Lumsden asked the audience a pertinent and telling question about whether they had ever been into the baby room to have a cuddle with the babies. She asked, 'Is that for you or for the child?' A strange discomfort entered the room as we each reflected on the complexity of *professional love*. The reality to consider here is that our actions should be driven by meeting the child's needs, and not our own emotional needs. Emotional support is undoubtedly vital for a practitioner, but the degree to which we depend on it from children should be carefully understood. The truth is that none of this is straightforward. Still, when we advocate for children, we should be aware of the experience of professional love, a term coined by Dr Jools Page (2014) to describe the ways in which a practitioner manages their feelings and emotions for a child.

When it comes to children with SEND, this can become even more complex still. We generally tend to gravitate towards those children deemed 'easy' to teach, and it can be more challenging when a child presents with needs that we do not understand. These early experiences of finding a connection can be tough, as they are often continually disrupted by 'bumps in the road'. I remember so many moments as a practitioner where I felt a multitude of complicated feelings about children with SEND, and it is within these moments that you need colleagues who have empathy for the child and the practitioner. Someone who says, 'It's his way of asking for help' or 'Think of it from the child's perspective'. Or someone who recognises that its tough and says 'Just take a moment' or 'Tell me how I can help'. Connecting with colleagues, if you are able, is vital. For a childminder, identifying a colleague as a sounding board, or even sending a voice note or text message, is key in those moments of discomfort.

Practitioner's voice

I have always believed that the Early Years is an environment of relationships. It does not matter to me what role you are, or whether you have a specific named responsibility. For anyone working with children, our main responsibility is to connect with a child, so they feel safe, secure and able to thrive. In my practice as a nursery manager, I encourage my practitioners to recognise that relationships will look and feel different between children, and that this is OK. We cannot provide a 'one size fits' all type of care because it has to be personalised and based on that unique connection. It has always been so important to me that my practitioners have time to cultivate those attachments with children.

Head over heart

Another reality that I wanted to touch upon is that professional love also means professional heartbreak. Seeing any child struggle, face adversity or suffer from their situation is painful for a practitioner. The emotional whiplash that occurs in our sector is largely ignored, and it comes back to this concept that we need to leave our 'baggage at the door'. In all my years of working with practitioners, suppressed emotions are among the most common things that I observe. We learn to swallow down worry, hurt, sadness, grief and anger as we engage in head-over-heart practices. At a recent training event, a practitioner shared how her mental health had declined in her job because of a difficult child protection situation, and that by night-time, she lay in bed wide awake, unable to switch off. Isn't it unusual that this is not talked about more often? Why is there an unspoken shame about the fact that we mentally carry our children around with us? While professional and personal boundaries must be defined, where is the room for growth through vulnerability?

During a SENDCo training session, I once decided to share my own vulnerability about my job. I am concerned that sometimes we become so committed to maintaining our professional selves that we miss opportunities to hear about how people's personal stories of practice have become shaped into a pedagogy. I often notice that people who are invested in SEND have a story to tell, and so I told mine. During my early career, I cared for a little girl in the baby room alongside my colleague Louise. Louise was the primary key person and I was the SENDCo. We both knew early on that the child's needs were complex, but we were optimistic and working hard to support those early milestones. I remember the first time that she rolled from back to belly and the screams of joy from me and Louise. Those first baby milestones never stop being utterly joyous – but then it all completely stopped. Quite rapidly, discussions went from progress to palliative care, as we were informed that her condition was life-limiting. You hear 'life-limiting' and hope for years, but we were told months. We didn't cry and we didn't break down, which we should have taken time to do; instead, we became proactive, first requesting that she remain in the nursery to still experience normality. We invested our love in providing that normality and then we did our jobs. I supported and observed Louise leading on support, including learning how to use feeding pegs and specialist equipment. We were informed that each of the little girl's functional skills, such as vision and hearing, would slowly decline and so we came up with ideas to help her to still feel safe and secure. Looking back at this time in my career is difficult because I did not acknowledge the fact that I was allowed to feel pain about the situation, and so I shut it down. I did not allow myself to grieve for a very long time. I rarely get through a sentence when I speak of this child, and in front of 30 practitioners that day I cried. Working through my mortification, I explained that the lesson about SEND is that it can be very painful, and it is OK for us to *feel*. It is likely one of the best training sessions that I experienced, as the practitioners began to share their own heart-shaped stories of pedagogy. There is so much that can be gained from leading with love.

Practitioner wellbeing as a platform for SEND support

A significant aspect of the work in Early Years revolves around our ability to support and to help children manage their feelings and behaviours. To do this, we need to be able to effectively manage our own feelings and behaviours, and this becomes a relational model for learning. According to Prowle & Hodgkins (2020), the Early Years role is emotionally and physically demanding, and there exists a risk of failing to meet our own basic needs. Garboden Murray refers to us as 'practitioners of care' (pg. 136) but if we do not demonstrate the care we have for our own wellbeing, what message could this send to children? I often explain to practitioners that wellbeing is not just cultivated through organisational practices but is a dynamic between individual ownership of prioritising basic needs and the expectation that your place of work cultivates a culture of wellbeing. Reflect on the following?

- In what ways do you communicate your basic needs?
- In what ways does your workplace meet your basic needs?
- How do you create boundaries?
- Does your place of work provide emotional safety, security and support?
- How are you made to feel valued?
- Does your workplace build your confidence?
- How do you appropriately challenge situations where your basic needs are not being met?
- Does your job provide fulfilment?

While you may not have perfect answers for these questions, it is important to consider whether your needs are met in a good enough way for you to 'bloom' at work.

Top tips: Practitioner wellbeing

It is important for practitioners to recognise that their own wellbeing may be impacted upon during SEND support. Consider the following when thinking about maintaining your wellbeing:

Normalise feelings: It is perfectly normal to experience a range of feelings and emotions when working with young children and families. Talking about how you feel, even when it doesn't feel comfortable, is essential. If you hold everything in, how can it be resolved?

Recognise feelings to be able to identify strategies: One of the issues with leaving our baggage at the door is that we then don't have the opportunity to develop strategies to resolve problems. By identifying a feeling, such as stress, and talking about it, you can then consider the strategy that might help. For example, 'I know that when I feel stressed, I need to take five minutes to do some breathing. Can I do this alongside children, or do I need to ask to be excused for a moment?'

Speak kindly to yourself: When supporting children with SEND, we can sometimes focus on all the things that are not going right. Speak aloud and recognise the positive steps that you are taking. Accepting that you are doing your best and identifying what works will help you to think more clearly about solutions for the things that don't seem to be working.

Put things to bed: We often carry a lot of thoughts around in our heads. Write your to-do list, worries or anxieties down before bed and put the list away. By emptying our minds of these things, we can hopefully rest better ready for the next day. Similarly, when you come back to that to-do list, consider halving it; it is better to get three jobs done right than six jobs half-done to the point of exhaustion.

Don't ever feel ashamed to ask for help: Often, key people can work themselves to exhaustion and get to a point where they think they cannot make mistakes. Part of the learning process within SEND is understanding our own capacity for providing support. Ask for help when you need it. Do not suffer in silence. SEND support is hard work.

Activity: Joint observation

Whether you are a SENDCo or a practitioner, try to get into the habit of observing together or sharing observation notes and discussing perspectives. It is usually through our curious conversations that a real picture of the child's development emerges. This will also provide an opportunity to consider whether the concerns are about the child or about the quality of practice. Joint observations also serve as a support system. Trying to work everything out by yourself is difficult, and sometimes that shared dialogue leads to new ways of thinking about things.

But I am a childminder…

Case study: The team around the child

Rosie is a childminder and has been developing her SEND support over the past year. She is becoming more confident in her SEND leadership and has actively been completing referrals and liaising with specialists. One of her children attends both Rosie's childminding setting and a local nursery. Rosie has reached out several times to ask whether she can attend a Team Around the Child meeting so that she is consistent with her support. When she finally gets to go along, she overhears a specialist ask why a childminder would need to come to the meeting when the nursery does all the work.

As a childminder, it can feel like such an isolating experience, and despite attempts to devise supportive systems, I still see massive frustration because they often feel forgotten. I delivered SEND training to childminders in the evenings. They were the most passionate and feisty group, and when I asked why, they responded that they work alone a lot so any opportunity to collaborate and learn is reviving.

Ideas for developing the SENDCo role as a childminder

Make connections

You are likely geographically close to other childminders, and I would suggest contacting your local authority and asking them to facilitate networking. In my local authority, the childminders allocated a SENDCo out of a cluster, and it allowed them to discuss and share good practice. Having a confidential WhatsApp or Facebook group can facilitate discussion.

Use social media support

I still see this considerable fear from people around the use of social media for SEND, but lots of research tells us that it is actually a significant source of support. If you intend to access social media, put together a short policy to establish your professional parameters. I don't want to be responsible for lots of practitioners sharing names and dates of birth of their children with SEND.

Local Offer

It will be crucial for you to have your signposting systems in place because you may need to call on these spaces.

Connect with a local setting or school

This is something that I often recommend to childminders, and there can be some nervousness around this. I cannot guarantee that you will always be met with a friendly response, but most nurseries will appreciate the importance of collaboration.

Continuous professional development

SENDCo training is just the start…

Consultant: What forms of continuous professional development have you undertaken recently?

Practitioner: Nothing, I never get the opportunity to go to courses.

This exchange is quite common. For a long time, I saw continuous professional development (CPD) as the face-to-face, usually day-long courses offered by a local authority or another training provider. Early Years practitioners are often so busy with the day-to-day aspects of their job that CPD has been an additional burden of guilt because they just never find the time to get around to it. It is similar to the situation with books: I see so many practitioners investing in books, but actually having the time to sit and read them? Not really.

I realised that CPD is another misunderstood process that can rarely empower a practitioner if they do it as a means to an end. I see so many practitioners attend training or refreshers and often get the distinct feeling that it becomes another thing to tick off the list. I think that this is why we see such an obsession with certificates. The evidence that practitioners have been accountable often overrides whether they have actually taken something worthwhile from the course. I have myself sat in training courses disengaged, all the while thinking, 'Well, at least I can still add it to my CPD file.' The very purpose of CPD is to enable us to impact our field of expertise by either strengthening our current knowledge or developing new knowledge and skills. It is essential to recognise that this can be done in a multitude of ways. Training courses are not the start and end of CPD; they are simply one aspect.

The continuous part of professional development…

Professional development in the Early Years is defined as the 'teaching and learning experiences designed to enhance practitioners' knowledge, skills and dispositions, as well as their capacity to provide high-quality early learning experiences for young children' (Snyder et al., 2012, pg. 188). It is likely, as a practitioner, that beyond your formal qualifications, you have engaged in additional training or attended courses to enhance your knowledge. According to Bubb and Earley (2013), engaging in professional development can motivate and refresh your thinking while making you better at the job that you do. This will, of course, be dependent on how open the practitioner is to the opportunities to develop and on the quality of the professional development on offer.

The continuous aspect of professional development consists of all the things that we do regularly, many of which most practitioners entirely overlook. When practitioners tell me that they have done 'nothing', it only ever takes a slight prod to find out that they are actually carrying out a high volume of micro-actions that strengthen their pedagogy. I asked lots of practitioners to name all the continuous ways in which they undertake CPD and generated this list, which is not exhaustive:

- books
- magazines
- conversation and debate with colleagues
- podcasts
- online courses
- webinars
- blogs
- TED Talks
- YouTube videos
- social media messaging, threads, groups, pages, live broadcasts, reflective posts, chats, hashtags, stories and story features
- following well-known Early Years specialists and accessing their websites and channels
- membership to Early Years organisations
- journals or portfolio work
- transferring knowledge from other interests
- team meetings.

So, as we can see right away, it is a continuous process, but many of these modes of professional development do not get the credit that they deserve. They must, however, be recognised as valuable *if* they enhance our knowledge. Naturally, many of the above examples can also hamper our knowledge or reinforce our 'weaker' practice. This is usually down to social media and how we can have a tendency to curate our 'feeds' to nurture our personal beliefs about education and teaching. Opposing opinions are not always welcomed in these 'safe spaces' and so we must consider how we are expanding rather than reducing our professional development when interacting online. More on that shortly.

Putting the joy into CPD

Like children, we have to be engaged to take something from our learning. So often, social media or e-learning becomes a preference for practitioners because they can choose what they wish to learn or have more options. There is a harsh reality that access to face-to-face

CPD is now considered a luxury for many practitioners, as so many local authorities have become financially limited in terms of what they can offer.

Social media

Practitioner's voice

There have honestly been times when I have gotten more from an Instagram live than a full day's training on the subject.

I recently had a discussion with a practitioner who was keen to learn more about autism and parent partnership. The practitioner had been to a training course but found that it was very dry. She explained that she wanted to understand the parent's and child's perspectives and stumbled across an Instagram account collaboratively run by some parents of autistic children. Each week they did a live broadcast focusing on different topics, and the practitioner watched along, hooked. She explained that she had learned more from watching those live sessions than from any of the courses that she had been on.

Activity: CPD challenge

Choose a SEND-based topic to research – for example, autism – and over the space of a week, complete a bitesize piece of CPD each day. Some ideas:

Monday: Listen to a podcast on the commute to work.
Tuesday: Read a blog post.
Wednesday: Read a short chapter in a book.
Thursday: Watch a TED Talk.
Friday: Read some hashtag posts.

At the end of the week, note down what you have learned and how you will apply it in practice.

In policy but not in practice

When working as an Early Years practitioner, exploring policies and procedures is usually the last thing on your mind, because you are often far too busy with the practical aspects of work. When I was a SEND consultant, I often had to review SEND and inclusion policies.

I found that they were out of date, referenced the wrong legislation or were written using a general template in many cases. Policies have a place and a purpose, but they are somewhat mundane to deal with. Getting your team – or yourself as a childminder – excited about reviewing policy is hard work.

I often get groups to invest in policy to give them a voice in devising said policy. For example, during my 'Rights of the Child' module, rather than simply reel off the United Nations articles (rights), I got students to think about what they defined as a 'right'. We did mind-mapping, and together we created a document that was real and relevant. I am against this system of policies all being in neatly typed Word documents. A policy should be a glorious representation of reality – a cover sheet to get the basics down, sure, and a procedure, yes, but beyond that, we should be asking, 'What we are going to be doing to bring the policy to life?' If policies are devised by the people who implement them and are informed by good practice and pedagogy, they are more likely to be sustainable in practice.

Get off the shelf

When I was a nursery manager, my first task was to buy loads of large ring binders, a laminator and a printer, and carefully print out (in Comic Sans) my beautiful labels. It was the psychologically comforting process of 'I am an organised and efficient manager'. I then printed 60 templates of policies that I had purchased from an educational website, making a few amendments with the logo and some word changes, and voilà, my operational organisation was done. I created a checklist and said that all staff must be familiar with the policies in preparation for inspection. I made the mistake that many of us make when trying to manage a nursery: I used stale systems to feel in control, and I was doing this for the wrong reasons – for inspectors. The Early Years is a variety-filled sector with lots of lumps and bumps, and sometimes we try to be too system-driven and almost too professional. How many times have you taken a file off a shelf and thought, 'This is filled with paperwork that is essentially not very useful'? One of my most distinct images of a nursery manager is them flicking through folders for that one piece of evidence that has been asked for. I blame Ofsted for this bureaucracy. We need policies and procedures to come off the shelf.

Once policies are in place, it is important that these are made accessible to parents and carers by putting them on the setting's website or making them available in an induction pack for new parents. Settings should also ensure that all staff are aware of their inclusion policies.

Advocacy, agency and activism

Our everyday practice should be underpinned by our ability to advocate for all children's rights. Despite the challenges, we know that our voice makes a difference in children's lives.

The SENDCo is a leadership role but not a 'know it all' role

A good SENDCo feels secure enough to say if they do not know something and has the initiative to seek more information. It is a role that requires leadership skills, not expert knowledge in every matter relating to SEND.

The key person should lead on SEND support

The best person to support a child is the key person, who has a bond with and knowledge of the child. They should lean on the SENDCo for help when needed but should be accountable for the main tasks in SEND support.

Ensure that roles and responsibilities are outlined, communicated and understood

We can still fall into the trap of thinking that the SENDCo is responsible for all SEND-related things. All practitioners' roles and responsibilities must be clearly outlined and communicated – for example, via job descriptions.

Observe together, learn together

The collaborative relationship between a SENDCo and a practitioner can be powerful. Taking time to observe and discuss children's development can lead to more meaningful plans for support.

Work within your setting's expertise but embrace beyond the comfort zone

It is essential to discuss what you are skilled at and be open-minded to supporting children with different needs. However, clarifying what is beyond your setting's expertise is vital in establishing the quality of support that you can offer.

SENDCo training is just the start...

All practitioners should be engaging in SEND-based training, whether it is online, face to face, through additional reading or via new qualifications. Have a training matrix to ensure that professional development is ongoing.

There is no 'I' in the whole team

Supporting children with SEND can be a stressful experience, and no practitioner wants to feel alone in that situation. Taking into account each other's needs is crucial because good wellbeing in practitioners leads to good wellbeing in children.

Signposts and resources

The role of the Early Years SENCO

Available at: www.foundationyears.org.uk/wp-content/uploads/2018/05/The-role-of-the-Early-Years-SENCO.pdf

4 'I should only have to voice it once': Understanding helpful and harmful approaches in parent partnership

Starting points reflection

Are we helpful or harmful?

'It's such a shame, she is so beautiful!'

'You must be so worried!'

'Your child is still the same, even with the diagnosis.'

'Boys are slower to talk, don't worry.'

'Oh my God, how do you cope? It must be so hard!'

'It's such a shame because it's not just his life but all of you.'

'It's so sad that his sister won't have a normal life!'

'Don't worry, in my opinion everyone's a bit autistic.'

'It must be like grieving the loss of the child you thought you would have.'

- How did these statements make you feel?

- Have you ever been subject to a statement like this or said something similar?

Introduction

The term 'parent' means any adult with a significant caring responsibility and is not limited to a mother or father or blood relative.

The above statements are real examples from parents of children with SEND, and they demonstrate some of the well-intentioned but harmful thinking that we may have about disabilities. When I ran my SEND leadership training, I became very reluctant to do a 'parent partnership' session because there isn't a fool-proof way to work in partnership with parents. We all talk about parent partnership a lot but it can be a rather complicated experience for both practitioners and parents. Although most of what we do as practitioners is well-meaning, our thoughts about SEND can sometimes become apparent in our words and actions.

If we take one of the above examples, 'It's such a shame, she is so beautiful', we can likely understand that it is quite hurtful for a parent to hear this. If you listen carefully, you will hear these statements echoed in lots of discussions. A strange series of projections can occur between parent and practitioner as they navigate their personal thoughts about the existence of a child's SEND. For example, if you were caring for a child with complex needs and continually thinking, 'What a shame', 'He is going to have a tough life', 'He won't cope' and so on, do you think that some of those beliefs would be mirrored in your practice? How proactive can we be if we place the onus on the child and his disability, rather than considering how the mainstream societal structures are actually disadvantaging differences within children? Rather than 'It is so sad, he won't have a normal life', we should surely be asking what we can do externally to expand our perceptions – for example, by thinking about what normality looks like for that child and adapting our provision as best we can to meet their needs.

When I work with practitioners who hold onto these harmful thoughts, I also tend to hear lots of discontent about how difficult it is to meet a child's needs. It is challenging to practise inclusion if we lean towards deficit thinking and the very perceptions that we hold about SEND become the barriers to inclusion. When I discussed the statements with the parent advocate who shared them, something that stood out to me was that these types of statements can exacerbate deep anxiety. For example, parents often get told 'not to worry' when they share concerns and are told that their child will 'catch up'. To avoid being seen as fussy or neurotic, a parent will often push that worry to one side, but this unheard experience is anxiety-provoking. It can be incredibly tricky when a professional insinuates that they know best because it creates a power dynamic within the partnership. Yes, we *may* know more about child development theory, but a parent knows the child intimately as a person. Often when a parent shares concerns we should first recognise the courage that it takes to do this, because it is the first step in asking for help, and we should also believe what they have to say and offer in terms of parent expertise. Whatever perceptions we may have about how parents parent, we should trust that their concerns are valid because they are often attuned to their child's met and unmet needs.

Intriguingly, when I completed my dissertation on parental self-efficacy, I interviewed six mothers about their early intervention experiences and all six said that they knew within the first year that 'something wasn't right'. The culture of ascribing hysterical or neurotic labels to mothers, in particular, is concerning, especially since most of the early intervention research suggests that the outcomes of the child are predominately shaped by a warm, responsive and proactive carer. However, if parents' voices are unheard from those earliest moments, what are we communicating about the value that we place on that partnership?

'If a community values its children, it must cherish its parents.' (Bowlby, 1951, pg. 84)

'I'm by your side-ness'

In the previous chapter, I spoke about the concept of 'I'm by your side-ness' in relation to children, but it absolutely relates to parents too. The term 'partnership' is problematic in education because there is a general tendency to attribute more power to the practitioner – the usual discussions that we hear about parents feeling 'done to', rather than 'done with'. By reframing our position as being alongside parents during SEND support, we offer some crucial opportunities for the relationship.

Shared learning

During early intervention, we, as practitioners, are often engaged in new experiences and systems. We, too, are navigating through unknown territory and we also have things to learn. By acknowledging this, practitioners can be more open about their own vulnerabilities, leading to greater connections with parents – for example, explaining to a parent that while you have an in-depth understanding of child development, you have never completed a referral before. So while you are absolutely willing, there is also learning going on for you. I often find that when practitioners try to act as though they know what they are doing when they don't, parents can figure this out quickly.

Intentions

We often see parent partnership as having to be on the same page, but the reality is that the intentions of a parent and practitioner diverge, and while they might be singing from the same song book, it's rarely always from the same page. Parents might feel obliged to focus their intentions on 'learning' so that they match the practitioner, but in truth, this might actually be the last thing that they want to do. They might be thinking about how they can achieve a full night's sleep, how to find moments for quality time with their child or how their child might make friends. Taking a moment to ask about intentions beyond typical 'milestones' may help you to hear something new. Sometimes we also need to remind parents that the experiences that we plan for children span beyond reading, writing and numeracy. The 'What to expect, when?' guide (DfE, 2018b) is an excellent induction document for parents to know precisely the development areas that you are supporting.

Interconnected expertise

To confront the unequal distribution of power, practitioners must also seek to value parents' expertise as interconnected with their own. While you may take the time to teach a parent a specific strategy for learning, they will also be equipping you with ideas. Key interests or experiences from the home provide examples of how they support their child. This is one of the most crucial steps in forming a meaningful partnership with a parent because we begin to learn from the main expert in the child's life.

Emotional scripts

In our SEND support, we are often working from different emotional scripts, and to be aware of this is essential because tension can fill the air between a parent and a practitioner. From my discussions and interviews with parents, they will often ruminate over whether the SEND results from something that they have done within their parenting; we see so many mass media headlines that attribute blame to parents. It can be challenging to develop trust when you are processing the different scenarios that could play out – for example, 'Will this lead to diagnosis?'. I often speak with practitioners who are frustrated by parents' perceived lack of engagement. I find it curious that they believe that a lack of engagement with them as the practitioner means a lack of engagement full stop. There is often a lot of processing and work going on in private. Research is increasingly demonstrating that parents turn to social media and other parents as a support network. For all its faults, social media allows some level of protection. Parents can ask questions, engage with others going through the same process and feel a certain degree of safety by feeling less confronted by others.

Equally, as a practitioner, you will be emotionally processing the situation and developing coping mechanisms. I recently submitted an ethics application and left blank the section that asked, 'How will you look after your own psychological wellbeing when interviewing parents?' – the worrying aspect of this being that, as a professional, I believed that I was above feeling feelings. For the record, it was a privilege to hear parents' stories but very emotionally painful. The lesson? Do not overlook your own wellbeing.

> ### Case study: 'I'm by your side-ness'
>
> Kila had always been confident working with parents but she had recently started supporting a parent whose child had quite significant SEN. Kila felt really anxious and found that she was avoiding having conversations with the parent in case the parent asked her a question to which she did not know the answer. The manager informed Kila that she would need to complete some referral paperwork and potentially begin the request for a statutory assessment. This made her feel totally overwhelmed, as she didn't entirely understand the child's needs. Kila shared with a more experienced colleague, Muna, that she didn't know what to do or how to connect with the parent. Muna suggested that she be honest with the parent about her own vulnerabilities because often this helps to build trust in parent partnership.

> The following week, Kila met with the parent and explained that she had the best interests of the child at heart but she had never completed some of the tasks, such as a referral, and she was new to navigating some of the systems. The parent breathed a sigh of relief and explained that she also felt clueless and was nervous to share her own confusion about what to do. Together, they worked out a plan and agreed to catch up on a weekly basis to check in with each other.

The parent trap

Another reason why I resist delivering training on parent partnership is that I feel that parents cannot be summed up or understood by bullet points or blanket statements. Parents are not a homogenous group. If we fall into the trap of thinking that one approach suits all, we will find ourselves stuck when faced with more emotionally complicated situations. Generally, practitioners have to successfully navigate multiple relationship dynamics. I often envisage them as a human pinball, springing off lots of complicated relationships, interactions, handovers, meetings and awkward moments, just trying not to fall down a hole somewhere. Obviously, some settings establish really close connections with parents, but we each find ourselves initiated into the 'Awkward Relationship with Parents Club' (at some stage). For the Early Years, a 20-second handover, a day sheet and a nappy bag of soiled pants is not really the best time for those sensitive and supportive interactions. After a hundred or so of those short exchanges, we tend to get more comfortable with parents, and the relationship is built on those micro-moments of connection. When it comes to SEND, a lot does need to be considered to retain and protect parent partnership.

The essential conversation

> 'Children's relationships with adults are the centre of our key concern, but don't forget that there is also a complex relationship between a child's teacher and a parent. Sometimes navigating this bond can seem more like walking through a minefield than having a mutually supportive dialogue.' (Christakis, 2017, pg. 258)

In her book *The Importance of Being Little* (2017), Erika Christakis talks about how parents' expectations and anxieties can loom over a practitioner like a threat. She refers to the work of Sara Lawrence-Lightfoot, who focused on the dynamic of parents and teachers during progress meetings, describing them as 'natural enemies' (Stelmach, 2004). It sounds controversial but what is refreshing about this perspective is that Lawrence-Lightfoot speaks about the thing that we are all too afraid to speak about. That is, parent partnership is not automatically 'smooth running' just because two people have a vested interest in a child. Coming back to the earlier point about intentions, it is crucial to recognise that priorities differ. A parent's 'view of their child is highly subjective, intimate, protective, and very loving, whereas a teacher's view of the same child is more distant and dispassionate, balancing the needs of individual students with the development of the classroom community' (FAN, 2014). It is an essential conversation to have with a parent about what you hope to achieve out of that partnership. How often do you as a practitioner ask a parent:

- What do you hope to get out of our partnership?
- What are your goals or ideas for your child?
- What can I tell you about myself that will help you to understand my intentions?
- If we disagree on the direction of things at times, what ways or approaches do you find helpful?

I recently asked this to a practitioner, who stared wide-eyed at me and simply said, 'I'd be too scared.' To be fair, I would be too scared too, but only when we open that book, can we finally begin to read each other's pages.

Parent types

I had been working alongside a parent whose child had SEND and she kept referring to the fact that she was pushy – 'I know they will just see me as pushy.' I found it interesting that this was considered bad. It got me thinking of all the labels that I have heard over time, and I thought it useful to consider how helpful or harmful those labels can be.

'Hard to reach' parent

Harmful: This is a term often used to describe a parent who does not engage in the way in which we would like them to, and we therefore attribute the blame to them. These parents often get accused of not engaging with the advice and support that we offer, and so we are left to do all the 'work'.

Helpful: This is a parent with whom we have not yet found a way to connect, but with whom we continue to engage and offer support and advice. We take into account the possibility that their engagement may be occurring elsewhere, or that they are still building trust with us. As a setting, we continue to expand our repertoire of strategies for engagement.

Pushy parent

Harmful: These parents never stop asking for things and always pick holes in everything we do. They become invasive and overly involved and have too many requests. They need to pipe down.

Helpful: This is a parent who is doing their upmost to ensure that their child gets everything they need, and is right to be assertive. To effectively engage with this parent, I need to be clear with them about my own capacity and level of expertise in meeting the needs of their child. I know that it can sometimes feel personal when the parent pushes, but within those words could be ideas and ways forward. Before my defences go up, I need to remember that we may have the best intentions but our intentions may be different.

Passive/avoidant parent

Harmful: This parent just doesn't seem to care. I keep asking them for information, and they conveniently forget. They won't carry out the strategies that I give them.

Helpful: This is a parent who is still processing what is happening and is unsure of the systems and procedures. I recognise the fact that I or others may be overwhelming the parent, and so we need to take smaller steps in supporting the parent's confidence. I will reassure the parent when I can and focus on developing trust before we take any bigger steps. I will continue to support the child within the setting, knowing that this can still make a significant difference.

The 'in denial' parent

Harmful: This is a safeguarding issue because they refuse to let me refer the child and they just won't listen. They say that the child does not have SEND and that the child does all the stuff we say they can't at home. They are obviously grieving.

Helpful: This parent needs space and patience from me. They need me to be sensitive to their situation and offer gentle guidance. Suggestions will be carefully considered and information will be shared in manageable amounts. I can clearly state my concerns for transparency but work at a pace that will suit the child and family.

Most of the above examples share one common feature: to support a parent, we have to first identify their pace and mirror it. This can go against early intervention principles, particularly for those parents who need much more time. However, it is better to adjust the pace of support than to negatively disrupt the trust that you are building with a family. When I was a consultant, I made an error in judgment early on in the job. I rushed a family who was not yet ready. I was taking strides as they were taking steps. My actions looking back were utterly wrong. Not only did I damage the trust that the parents had in me as a professional, but they also became fearful of engaging with the setting that I was supporting. They removed their child from the setting and completely disengaged. This situation was complicated because there were also safeguarding concerns, but it serves as a reminder that being too assertive or aggressive in intervention can actually create a more significant issue for long-term engagement. Once that trust with the 'system' is broken, it can be tough to repair. We live in a tick-it-off, to-do list world, and sometimes early intervention falls victim to this too. We focus on getting a referral done quickly rather than strengthening the relationship, or we 'chase up' parents rather than giving them the benefit of the doubt. The best advice is to meet the parent where they are and know that the connections you are building are part of a more sustainable outcome.

Good grief

'I can clearly see that the child is delayed, but the parents are in denial.'

I wanted to labour on this point briefly because it is often cherry-picked from the grief stages that are now commonly discussed in relation to SEND. There is tension around the appropriateness of this, and for transparency, I do not prescribe to the grief model as a practitioner. Still, I can understand how parents use it as a framework for processing their own experiences. However, the original use of the stages was to describe the experiences of terminally ill patients and their coming to terms with their own death. It is problematic to automatically associate the experience of finding out your child has SEND with grief and death. It offers little hope and does not reflect a balanced perspective of SEND. We see this example when using the 'in denial' narrative, which is often used to describe any parent who isn't engaging at the pace that we would like.

'When all educators recognise parents' transformative experiences as potential family strengths, empower parents by accepting their current level of understanding regarding disability, and honor each family's unique experiences, they will help create an atmosphere of trust and respect.' (Allred & Hancock, 2012, pg. 16)

Capacity building

'A little at a time, of each new thing, is best. Too much too sudden is too frightening.' (Hughes, 1995, pg. 1)

While we must not ignore parents' emotional experiences, including the recognition that there may be feelings of loss, it is not the loss of a child, but the loss of what they might have envisaged for that child.

There are transformative events that occur throughout the SEND pathway. Adopting a capacity-building approach helps you to address the challenges and shift focus to a strengths-based approach.

Research has found that our perceptions of the child and family are instrumental in empowering parents (Dunst & Trivette, 2009). Our own attitudes about SEND can help to shape the parents' outlook. For example, if we choose to talk positively about the child, the parent will be spurred on to do this as well. I was speaking with a parent who said that he rarely shared his positive interpretations of his child's development because he thought they would be considered as insignificant to more experienced practitioners. With this in mind, we must consider how we break down this barrier to welcome and embrace all types of development.

Partnership in practice

Do we welcome what parents bring to our settings?

In *The Essential Conversation* (2004), Sara Lawrence-Lightfoot shares an anecdote about two parents who join a setting. In their eagerness to participate, they bring along a big sugary cake and several litres of fizzy drink to celebrate their child starting at the nursery. Lawrence-Lightfoot explains that it became quite apparent that this act of celebration was met with hostility and displeasure from the teachers. Instead of focusing on the act of human kindness, they used the opportunity to make judgments. As practitioners, I am not going to proclaim that we should simply be non-judgemental because it is a deeply rooted aspect of our human behaviour, and judgments often spring up from both our conscious and unconscious bias. We do not flick a judgemental switch and, voilà, judgments have gone. Instead, we exercise our way into anti-bias or non-judgemental practices. The reality is that we are skilled at making judgments, we make them all day long in our practice and they form a crucial part of understanding children. I spoke with a childminder recently who was being overly judgemental about a parent's competence, before we swiftly moved on to her talking about the pain of being judged as 'just a childminder' – if only she had applied the same empathy that she affords to herself to the parent. As the saying goes, it is easier to hold up a magnifying glass than a mirror. It is important that we check in with ourselves when making judgements and tune into what parents can bring to our settings. Sure, cakes and sugar aren't always best practice, but deeper connections can emerge when we adopt a welcoming approach.

Don't believe everything you think…

> 'I know my life is better when I work from the assumption that everyone is doing the best they can.' (Brown, 2019)

I had the privilege of recently hearing Jane Lane speak; she is an Early Years advocate for racial equality and wrote the book *Young Children and Racial Justice* (2008). She said something that I think would do anyone well to remember when thinking about how judgemental we can be. She noted that we don't have to go with our first thoughts about something; we can stop, think and reframe those thoughts. This concept of 'catching yourself' will definitely expand your anti-bias practice because it allows you to relinquish some of your deeply held beliefs. For example, we may view a parent with limited English as unintelligent or a family living in poverty as incapable. I often speak to practitioners about their own experiences of being judged. The Early Years practitioner is so often viewed as insignificant due to caregiving being viewed as low-skilled. There has been a longstanding tension about the relationship between care and education, and it is not uncommon to hear Early Years practitioners refer to themselves as 'just a practitioner'. There is undoubtedly an impact on our professional identity based on the judgements of others. When practitioners talk to me about how this feels, I use this as an opportunity to translate that experience to parents and the judgements we might make. For example, we often hear SEND being linked to social deprivation and poverty, and this can lead to us placing blame on families due to their circumstances, which often are the result of wider systemic issues. I have moved away from describing families as living in poverty, and instead use the term 'living in an under resourced area'. Acknowledging this inequity and poor distribution of funds helps me to understand the barriers a family might face in seeking and accessing the right support.

Compassionate spaces

'Liking a child is a such a priceless currency, that it should be offered unreservedly and often.' (Christakis, 2017, pg. 261)

If a child comes to your setting, it is crucial that the parent also feels that sense of belonging. To achieve this is not necessarily an easy task, but we should consider fostering compassionate spaces. According to Dobson and Melrose (2020, pg. 14), you can have 'impeccable credentials, excellent qualifications and a commitment to hard work but that which doesn't appear on an application form is disposition and attitude'. Being good on paper is not a guarantee for being good in practice. Being present with someone through challenging 'human moments' is an ongoing action. I heard someone recently say that the way in which we develop emotionally can be viewed from the perspective of a lump of clay: we continue to mould and reshape continuously over time. Our task is to ensure that we do not harden in the face of complicated relationships; we grow and mould into them.

From partners to co-educators

The work by Whalley (2017) at Pen Green Research Centre has focused on parents' roles within their child's education. Viewing the parent as a co-educator gives us the potential to develop meaningful collaborations. Co-education can be defined as 'parents being involved in supporting their own child's learning and development 24/7 – this needs to be recognised, and home learning and nursery learning needs to be shared' (Whalley, 2015). Often when I speak with practitioners, I find a real misunderstanding of 'home learning'. For some reason, the mind wanders to activities or explicit acts of teaching. In reality, home learning, as Whalley states, is quite literally never-ending. It comes in the form of getting dressed independently, spotting things on the walk to nursery, nestling in for big snuggles and a book, rummaging through purses and wallets and pressing buttons, pointing to items in the supermarket aisles, playing rough 'n' tumble, eating and trying new food, singing together to songs on the radio, and all the uninterrupted play that often occurs in the home. Home learning is not the worksheets, phonics packs or 'homework' that we send home.

Equal and active

Whalley (2015) recommends that practitioners take an 'equal and active' approach. By recognising that learning looks different across different contexts, we can become curious about the many 'looks' of learning. It happens so often that a parent says, 'but he always does that at home'. So often, a practitioner will think, 'Yeah, right.' Still, children very much adjust their behaviours according to the environment, including those children with SEND. It is well known that children with sensory processing differences learn to contain themselves in a school environment because they are expected to conform. They will then get home and have a sensory 'blowout' to relieve all that excess energy. Alternatively, a child may feel more comfortable speaking at home because it is not commanded of them in the same way that it can be in a classroom environment. We, as practitioners, have to be prepared to explore those differences.

> 'Nothing gets under a parent's skin more quickly and more permanently than the illumination of his or her own children's behaviour. The effects of participation can be profound.' (Athey, 1991, pg. 66)

Feedback

> '"Do you actually like my child?"
>
> Parents can tolerate a lot of unsettling feedback if they know the answer to that first question is a resounding yes.' (Christakis, 2017, pg. 261)

Earlier on in this chapter, I mentioned the ways in which we build relationships during the daily handover. When I worked as a room practitioner and SENDCo, I noticed how quickly the handover could become dangerous territory. Trying to share concerns via a 'quick word', especially after a long day, can be challenging. I fully acknowledge that we are often backed into a corner with this, particularly as we do not always have the luxury of time and space. Still, we do need to figure out how those sensitive discussions can take place without creating conflict.

I often role play handovers during SENDCo training because it always helps practitioners to think about how their sharing of concerns is received. One of the most common opening phrases I hear during parent–practitioner exchanges is the dreaded words: 'I have concerns.' I have said it countless times myself, and I suppose on those occasions I still saw these concerns as something to be fixed rather than understood. The varying rates at which children develop can disrupt the environment and learning that we had hoped for, so we can fall into the habit of reporting children to their parents in a confronting way. But we should be viewing the parent as an ally, exploring collaboratively to understand what these concerns might mean.

> 'We know that young children achieve more and are happier when Early Years educators work together with parents and share ideas about how to support and extend children's learning.'
> (Athey, 1990, pg. 1)

Open-ended questions can be helpful in these situations, along with observational language – for example, 'I have noticed…' or 'What are your thoughts?' This then becomes a reciprocal conversation rather than an accusation. We also have to listen to parents and give them space to talk. Through active listening, we may pick up on important information.

The reason why concerns can feel so frustrating is that, deep down, we want happy, healthy and thriving children. The reality that this is not always the case can be complicated for all involved. So how do we approach those initial discussions? These are my top tips.

Top tips: The handover

Wearing our hearts on our faces: I have lots of discussions with parents about the exchange of information, and one thing that consistently comes up is the dread of seeing a key person's face on pick-up – the dull thud of hearing 'he's bitten again' or 'she's had another bad day'. Parents fear that we will grow to dislike their children, and so when we wear our hearts on our faces and begin with this information, we are essentially and unfortunately fracturing aspects of our relationship with that family. It sounds like such an incredibly harsh thing to say, but I have seen enough parent mortification to last me a lifetime. Yes, we may have some unsavoury news to deliver, but we always eagerly await the parent and we begin with the positives. There are no positives? There are always positives… If we truly tune in to a child, we find the positives. And if you still can't find them, acknowledge the bits where they tried, even if they didn't get it quite right.

Avoid hallway overshares: Far too often, because we don't have the safe spaces in which to have sensitive conversations, we do the hallway overshare – that is, giving out lots of sensitive information in an open space, where other practitioners, parents and children lurk.

Silence is not so golden: The other thing that I fell into when I felt that there was no genuine time or space to have a sensitive discussion was to stop telling the parent entirely. I was more focused on just getting them out of the door. Why? Because I had grown tired of trying to manage a tricky conversation but not getting anywhere. Develop practices that allow practitioners to follow up with sensitive discussions.

The sensitive sandwich: We have all heard of this method and some may find it a cliché but it genuinely works if it is matched with good intentions and empathy. So how does it work?

Start with good news...

'Hi Peter, how has your day been? Charlie did so brilliantly today when he was in the water tray. He got totally stuck in and created our first nursery tsunami. He was in his element!'

Pause and let the parent enjoy this good news moment, the fact that their child feels safe and secure enough to fully revel in play.

Address the area of need... and reflect

'He was having so much fun that he did forget to take turns, but as you know, we are working on that. How are you finding that at home?'

The positive pathway...

Always end on a proactive note so that the parent can see that this isn't a permanent situation; it is something that you are open to supporting. It can also be good to talk about the ideas in relation to all children so that the parent doesn't feel that their child is the 'problem child':

'We have introduced a few turn-taking ideas for the children, so we are going to use the timer if there are lots of children wanting to be around the water tray, and we are going to play some general turn-taking games.'

Mind your manners: I felt some reluctance to include this one, because I know that in almost all cases, we do our very best to maintain positive relationships with our parents. However, I think in all honesty that sometimes our frustration with a child or a situation can be projected onto the parent. That is something that I believe practitioners need better support in – acknowledging that it is OK to feel frustration with parents.

Keeping each other in the loop

The Pen Green Loop effectively demonstrates the ongoing flow of partnership in SEND support. Coming back to the earlier point about parents' and practitioners' interconnected expertise, Pen Green (Whalley, 2017) outline that:

- Professionals lead with a 'public' knowledge of the child, understanding broader child development theories and pedagogical expertise.

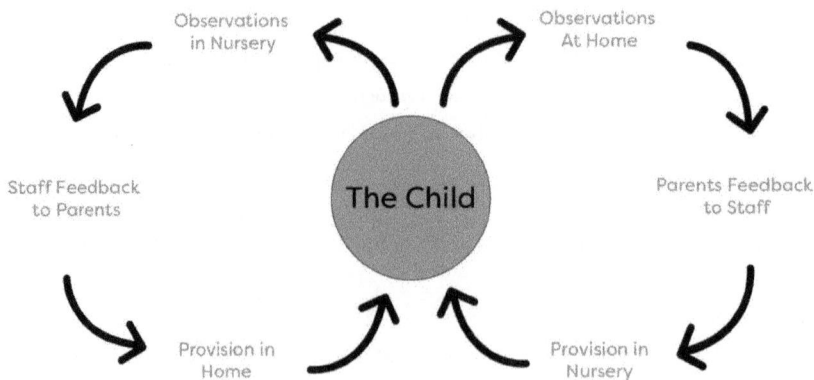

Figure 5: *Pen Green Loop, adapted from Pen Green (2018)*

- Parents lead with a 'personal' knowledge of the child, understanding the inner working world of their own child and connecting that to the wider social world.

These knowledge sources have equal value. Through meaningful interactions, the important adults in that child's life demonstrate a shared knowledge and a more in-depth understanding of the child's needs.

Closing the information gap

A significant aspect of parent partnership is ensuring that parents are equipped and knowledgeable about their child's SEND. In many cases, parents will conduct research about their child's developmental differences and delays. One of the most important steps we can take is to acknowledge that the expertise between a practitioner and a parent will differ but merged can narrow the information gap. For example, it is not uncommon to hear that a setting is implementing a set of strategies but has not adapted them so they can also be adopted within the home setting. Similarly, if parents are accessing therapy or specialist support for their child outside of the setting, those strategies do not always make their way into the setting. This creates a degree of inconsistency and by creating a co-interventionist approach, we can ensure that knowledge is more consistently shared.

Parent and family workshops

Timing, capacity and resourcing are often cited by practitioners as a barrier to developing a parent workshop approach, but there are creative ways around this. In the first instance, you may signpost to digital content, webinars or video clips. The charity SENSE, for example, has a full range of play skill videos on YouTube.

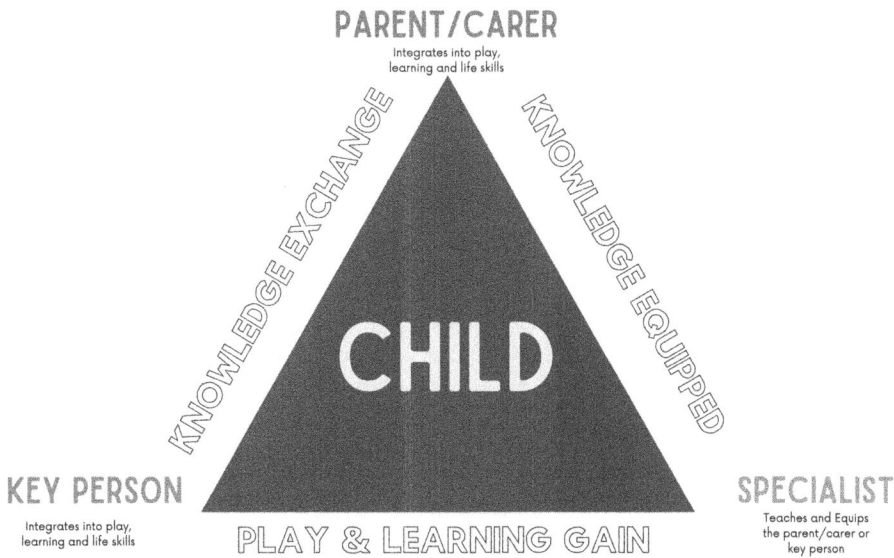

Figure 6: *Developing a co-interventionist approach*

Let's suppose the setting wishes to carry out these workshops themselves. In that case, I frequently recommend that a wall calendar and mapping out a schedule for workshops is essential. The workshops can be delivered by yourself or by an external visitor, so it is crucial to consider what will work. I usually recommend that you combine workshops based on what parents ask for and what you wish parents knew more about. How often they are and how long they will be will depend on the type of setting in which you work. If you are a childminder, you may run more intimate workshops or arrange a Saturday coffee morning or early evening meet-up. Ideally, workshops would combine 'stay and play' and child-free elements to allow for both theory and play practice. Where a workshop is child-free, it can also be a good idea to film it on a recording device so that parents can watch it again afterwards or those who missed it can watch it.

If you do not feel that workshops can work for your setting face to face, you may perhaps deliver an online workshop. You can also contact local services to see whether they have drop-in workshops or schedules. Where Children's Centres remain, they often have really high-quality options.

You should also consider how inclusive your workshops are and whether targeted workshops could be of benefit – for example, targeted fathers, trans, gay or lesbian families. It is essential to also be mindful of cultural variations for families and how perceptions of SEND may differ.

Virtual support

The global pandemic has expanded everyone's capacity to access the virtual world, and partnerships between the home and the setting are no different. We have seen the innovative ways in which technology can keep us all connected, and this is no different even in more ordinary times.

Suppose that you don't necessarily have private spaces in which to have sensitive conversations. In that case, it might be that you offer a virtual meeting, ensuring that you take into account some of the lost emotional connections that this format can result in. However, it is better to have as many open communication channels as possible so that you don't always feel like you are chasing the parent for that quick chat.

You may also want to set up an email list, sending out useful articles or resources, or upload YouTube videos with ideas and strategies.

SEND toolkit

Parents will often need guidance on particular strategies or techniques. Developing a SEND toolkit that parents can also access will be useful when you need to talk through a specific strategy. It is also helpful to think about those parents who may want to independently access information. One of the settings that I supported had a toolkit file, and over time they filmed a short YouTube video of each strategy.

This can be particularly beneficial for those parents who might not feel confident in discussions about SEND. Sometimes people like to process things privately. Being multi-modal with your toolkit can increase engagement.

Top tip: Consider language

When sourcing resources from websites, check whether they have translated versions. This will increase accessibility. For example, the National Literacy Trust provides several translations of their 'Talk to Your Baby' documents.

Parent observations and 'stay and play'

Earlier on in this chapter, I mentioned the different ways in which children can behave across different settings. It can be useful to invite a parent to observe alongside the key person. Often practitioners say that this can be too difficult, as they cannot take a step back, but it can still work if managed effectively. First, it is important not to place an emphasis on the child not being able to interact with the observers. Second, it is useful for a child to observe the interactions between the parent and practitioner. These observations do not need to be long or formal. Still, they can support parents and practitioners to develop a shared knowledge of the child.

Parent planning sessions

Inviting parents in for planning sessions can be done on an individual or group basis. These can support the practitioner in developing a good understanding of the child. The use of floor books or mind-mapping generates conversations around play, teaching and support. This can also be an opportunity for a parent to develop confidence in speaking with professionals. Imagine how intimidating it might be for a parent to have to continually engage with professionals. In those cases, this can go some way to being a mediating factor in reducing barriers.

Collaborative planning

While doing my daily scroll through social media a few weeks back, I noticed a post about empowering parents during transition or SEND support meetings. The post asked basic questions: Do you offer the parent a cup of tea and encourage them to make themselves comfortable? Is there a place to hang a coat or to put a bag down? Can they get a drink of water or access signposts and resources? Small environmental adaptations can make the setting feel welcoming and homely. We can go beyond this when we begin planning for children, whether it be a Team Around the Child meeting or a general discussion. The post suggested that giving parents a pad and pen when they arrive along with the agenda helps them to feel equal.

I also avoid at all costs filling in sections of forms designed for parents – for example, 'parent's voice'. By encouraging parents to annotate the work that we are doing, we are adding to its quality and relevance.

Safe spaces

We often do not work in spaces that allow for separate discussions. Still, on so many occasions, I have walked around a setting that has said 'we don't have the room' only to find a nook, a cranny or a wasted space that could become that safe space. Sometimes it just takes a little bit of creativity. One setting I worked with actually asked the parents themselves to help create a space for meetings, which is the perfect way forward. Sometimes fresh eyes can offer new perspectives so that wasted corners can become the cosy corners.

Resource lending

This is obviously dependent on your own access to resources. Still, a parent often needs us to lend some items to support a particular activity or experience. Having a lending library, particularly for SEND-based items, can be really helpful. For example, parents might not always have laminators or a printer at home. They may struggle to maintain a visual routine because they do not have the resources to make one. Offering parents use of resources helps them to feel competent in being able to be proactive.

Local Offer support

Something that has been wrongly assumed with the Local Offer is that all parents have readily available access to the internet. In fact, when I was in local authority, many parents did not have access to a computer at home. I recommended to settings that they ensure that parents knew that they could book in to use one of the setting's computers to browse the Local Offer. This came with the additional benefit of a parent asking questions to a key person or practitioner.

Setting up a guest account on your computer or laptop can lead to opportunities for parents to engage in some of the research that they cannot do from home, or they may feel more comfortable having you on hand. If you are going to operate a system like this, do consider the capacity. A booking system means that you can allocate certain hours to be on hand.

Play dates and hashtags

When I supported a nursery, they explained that they had quite a lot of children with SEND, and some parents felt quite isolated. The setting devised a play dates approach. When completing the registration form, parents could opt in to be informed of any potential 'link-ups'. For example, two parents both had children on the pathway for a social communication diagnosis. By introducing the parents, they were able to arrange play dates outside the setting. This proved invaluable for the setting, families and children, as they developed support networks. They also went on to host Saturday Socials, where all parents and children met at local places for days out.

Another setting had a large display in reception, which included popular hashtags for parent support, including children with SEND, along with social media support groups.

Parent does not only mean mum

Top tips: Engaging ALL significant people

What matters to children should matter to us: When we think about who mattered to us growing up, whether that be a mother and father, one or the other, two of the same or another significant other, we would have wanted them to be included in the decisions that affected us. When working with young children, we need to be aware of that child's important people and need to make opportunities to build trust. 'Getting to know you' questionnaires can give you an opportunity to find out about parents, common interests and conversation pointers.

Eagerly await and seek to know parents: When parents who are less familiar come to the setting, it can be a daunting experience. Clear signposting and name badges can be a small but powerful way to help guide a parent. For example, fathers may still hold the view that childcare is a woman's space and they may feel out of sorts or awkward. We too may feel uncomfortable as we may be used to speaking with mothers. Try a simple 'Hi, you must be one of our dads, do remind me of your name so that I can remember for next time.' Often, learning parents' names is a big step in actually getting to connect with them beyond their parenting roles.

Don't say what you think parents want to hear: If we want all parents to engage, we need to find authentic ways of connecting through conversation. Sometimes when we feel nervous of a parent, particularly fathers, we may talk about gender-reinforced stereotypes – 'Oh, he loves messy play' – in the hope that we are giving the male parent something to relate to. During feedback, try to share what the child has been interested in and ask questions – for example, 'Have you noticed at home that she is fascinated with how things work?'

Be mindful of gender-heavy environmental layout: Male and female spaces are often reinforced by how we 'decorate' those spaces. This can have an impact on both children and parents. Fathers, for example, may feel that they are invading spaces that are predominantly made up of women. It isn't about putting more 'manly' things into your spaces but developing a more neutral space that invites fathers into that space. Alistair Bryce Clegg suggests in his 2016 blog 'Gender schema, your space and you' that we should ask ourselves 'what gender would this be?' in order to challenge some of our predispositions to dominate space.

Get specific: According to the Fatherhood Institute (2007), the use of the word 'parent' can make fathers feel excluded. Their advice is to be specific and to ask how parents like to be individually addressed.

Don't assume the motherload: Despite research suggesting that mothers carry out the main tasks associated with early intervention, we should not just automatically assume this, and we should again consider whether we are making our SEND support gender-specific. Have parent-specific practices. In our quest to be inclusive, we may need to carry out some targeted work – for example, hosting 'Dads Day' or providing specific guidance on the benefits of fathers' involvement in early intervention.

Some final points

Sharing is caring: Parents are a powerful source of knowledge and expertise and this should be valued, but they have not studied child development in the same way that a practitioner has. It is important not to provide ambiguous advice or to assume that when you recommend a strategy, a parent should automatically know how to carry this out in a home-based setting. Providing 'how to' leaflets or guidance should be matched where possible with demonstrations or further signposting, so that the parent can learn more. Taking the time to do this early on means that the child is receiving holistic support and will save time later on.

Take a capacity-building approach: Practitioners will at times need to share when progress is not as expected, but parents also need to know what is going well. If parents receive lots of negative feedback, it can be difficult for them to apply ideas or strategies at home because the task may just appear too overwhelming or out of reach.

Time to share: Research has found that it is crucial that a parent receives feedback in order to feel confident and able in providing SEND support. If you are going to recommend an idea for home learning, make time to discuss how it is going, provide feedback and use these opportunities to build on support. Equally, ask for feedback from parents on how they think you are doing. This makes the relationship collaborative.

Patience and understanding: Some parents may not have the time, understanding or resilience to apply strategies at home. This doesn't mean that practitioners should halt their work, but they should continue to be consistent in the setting and to gradually develop the use of these strategies at home. If a parent struggles to apply a strategy, it may be too overwhelming; therefore, the practitioner may need to break it down further so that it is more manageable.

Parent's voice

The things I need you to know:

- Recognise my child's potential, and the unique ways in which he develops.
- Become an expert in my child, and not simply through working from blanket assumptions of his needs.

- Gain an understanding and a love for his different ways of learning and experiencing the world. I am not just looking for your acceptance of him but your love for him.
- Be an advocate for him and for us as a family, because we are an advocate for you. We are so often in a 'battle'; be with us, not against us.
- Always presume competency and be driven to help him flourish.
- Be honest but positive.
- Be as proud of him as we are.

Parent's voice

The things I need you to know:

- Communicate with me honestly and be in touch. Updates help.
- Challenge your views of her SEND and see beyond the usual narrative that it's a bad thing.
- Surround her with comfort and care.
- Respect her personal needs and be protective of her dignity.
- Bring her happiness and joy.

Parent's voice

The things I need you to know:

- To me, my child is a person, not an assessment score or outcome. Please know him through his strengths, and not the way he performs on a test.
- Actively listen to me and let me know that my input is valuable. I am the expert on my child (regardless of my educational background).
- Believe what I tell you. Do not make me scream inside when I feel disregarded.
- Please take the time to know me; don't rush me through meetings, words or feelings.
- Do not underestimate my child's efforts; they might not always look the same as another child's, but they are efforts, nevertheless.
- Think outside the box when it comes to your approaches. My child is unique, so your adaptations should be too.

'I should only have to voice it once'

Approach parent partnership with compassion

We need to work effectively with parents, but we need to approach this with compassion for both ourselves and the parent. We seek to form a connection, so we must take time to listen, be available and reflect.

Be patient but proactive

Early intervention can make us feel that if we don't act now, then all is lost and we have failed. Take time and be patient. It is better to be responsive than reactionary.

Not everything you think is true

We can fall into the trap of making assumptions about parents based on what we see in the small windows of drop-offs, pick-ups and setting engagement. Challenge these assumptions and choose to see parents as doing their best.

Co-educators and co-interventionists

The parent is our equal partner so we have to treat them as such, recognising their unique expertise and knowledge. They are a source of information and so we should work alongside them and not against them.

Open-ended and curious questions

If you see the parent as an equal, you will work together during discussions. Asking open-ended questions or making observation comments leaves space for them to also ponder.

Capacity-building relationships

Remember that there will be times when you possess knowledge that the parent does not, and vice versa. Capacity is built through collaborative partnerships.

Be all-inclusive to parents

Try to recognise your tendency to think of 'parents' as the mother. Expand beyond this to include all types and dynamics of families. Be flexible with your expectations around engagement and reflect on how inclusive your setting is for all kinds of parents.

Signposts and resources

Independent Provider of Special Education Advice

Available at: www.ipsea.org.uk

5 'He will grow out of it':
Understanding SEND support and the graduated approach

Starting points

- Have you ever experienced a gut instinct or a sixth sense that a child may have specific needs or said 'I just have a feeling'?
- What do you think that this tells you about your skillset and knowledge of children?
- How often have those concerns turned out to be accurate?
- When they haven't been accurate, have you reflected back on your knowledge or practice?

Introduction

I have had countless conversations with practitioners and parents who told me that they instinctively knew there was a concern. I was recently speaking to a childminder who said that she sensed that something more was going on for a baby she was caring for. This gave us an opportunity to explore this 'knowing' feeling. The first thing to note is that we spend a lot of time around young children as practitioners. An essential aspect of our role is the ability to tune into those intricate developmental steps that tell us that the child is progressing. If you speak to a parent or practitioner about a child they know well, you will find that they can provide a great amount of detail about that child's unique development. Yet so often, they overlook how much knowledge they possess about children. Therefore, the first thing to recognise is that it is not just instinct that tells us there is a concern. It is also our child development knowledge, which becomes significantly more valuable when we engage in professional development. The second thing to consider is empathy. According to Wong (2004) and as cited in Prowle and Hodgkins (2020), the intuition or gut instinct that we feel is actually linked to our skills of empathy. By tuning into young children, we come to develop an insightful awareness of the child. We mentally read children's desires, intentions, wants, needs and unspoken concerns. As practitioners, we are primed to act when these concerns emerge, as we want to be as responsive to the child's needs as we possibly can. This does, however, throw up quite a few challenges.

'They will grow out of it'

Definition: Early intervention

Early intervention is a loosely defined term that refers to trying to resolve issues, before they become more difficult to support. In an Early Years context, widely but not exclusively considered to be from conception until a child reaches the age of five, there is a strong body of evidence to suggest that early interventions can be used to identify children who may be delayed within their development. Such interventions are said to help to develop their skills and competencies in a range of areas, including in relation to health, cognitive development, and social and emotional skills. It is important to be mindful, however, that for children with developmental differences, early intervention should seek to support and enhance individual learning, rather than try to cure, fix or stop atypical behaviours.

Our initial reactions to concern are often to seek help, and as per the guidance, we follow early intervention procedures. The issue that often arises is that you may be met with obstacles, barriers and reluctance when you raise those concerns. I have lost count of the times I have been told by a practitioner that they have been told by specialists to wait or to give the child time to grow out of 'it'. When speaking to a childminder, she shared that she knew that she and the parent had to 'go it alone'.

This is a horribly isolating experience, which is why practitioners develop reluctance in supporting children with SEND. They can feel so alone. If you know early intervention will result in some form of 'battle', how quickly might you become disheartened? How many times can we keep showing up, particularly when these systems appear to be getting harder to navigate? Eventually, this does lead to caregiving fatigue, as demonstrated by the following practitioner's voice.

Practitioner's voice

As a nursery manager, creating an environment that encourages a supportive and inclusive climate for SEND children and families to thrive and flourish is imperative.

What is important to recognise is that the emotional reserves this draws on can take their toll on an already undervalued and underpaid workforce who are viewed as low-skilled workers by wider society and who have been directly influenced by the narrative that, in particular, this most recent Tory government has built around the Early Years.

> Without the additional support of area SENDCos, speech and language therapists and Early Years consultants to offer guidance, support and CPD, the ability to provide the best SEND support is limited for many practitioners on the ground.
>
> In my experience of supporting countless SEND children at my nursery setting, the relief that has been felt when we have been able to lean into additional support has been invaluable. The children and families have felt seen and supported, and been guided through what would otherwise have been a very emotionally turbulent time.

We also need to focus on re-framing early intervention not as simply a way of fixing problems, but rather see it is a way for us to be accountable, responsive and prepared for children who need different types of support. Some practitioners reject or have moved away from using the term early intervention, but I think it is an important concept that holds us all to account when ensuring children get what they need at the right time and in the right way.

Scapegoats and purse strings

I need to clarify here where my finger is pointed. It is not generally at specialists, who are also victim to budget cuts and constraints. They are also often stuck between a rock and a hard place. I have worked with many specialists who face the same challenges and emotional drain that we, as practitioners, face throughout our careers. In fact, as a local authority consultant, I, too, became one for spinning tales to cover the gaps within our service. The eradication of teams and services is an everyday threat for local authorities, who continually find themselves having their purse strings tightened. Any team or service working beyond capacity will become weakened in quality as a result. It may seem defeatist, but a significant investment in the Early Years or SEND is unlikely under the current government structure. So we have to engage in activism from the ground up. One such way to do this is to reflect on what we are currently able to offer in terms of early intervention and to place value on that which is working well.

Case study: Finding solutions

I have a really strong relationship with my local authority. I have observed redundancy, the loss of services, the redesign of services and the coming and going of different professionals. However, they have always been a phone call away, and though I do not get the intensity of support that I previously received, I get the encouragement and reminder that there are things within my knowledge and control. We have been supporting a child with high needs for around a year, and the journey for this family has been slow, at times stressful and frustrating. I was working alongside a highly stressed parent and I picked up early on that I could either add to her chaos or be her calm. I was truthful about the limitations and barriers, but also optimistic that we had enough knowledge and skills to make a difference. The best advice that I was given by the local authority is that smalls steps forward are better than big stomps standing still. We focused on key goals, we planned for transitions and we kept talking about the breakthroughs. Over time, the parent's stress levels eased, and when we found ourselves less stressed, we actually had capacity to do more.

When I spoke to the nursery manager about the things that helped them to focus their mindset in this way, they suggested the following:

- feedback that they were at least on the right track, along with additional ideas

- reinforcing progress by focusing on what was working well and breaking down the barriers into smaller achievable actions

- removing the burden that it was the nursery alone that was responsible for the early intervention, thus doing what was within their expertise and focusing on doing this well, rather than taking disjointed steps in all different directions

- reminding practitioners as much as they could that they were striving for 'good enough' and not perfect.

This case study demonstrates something that I regularly speak to practitioners about, which is this tendency to focus on what others are not doing rather than focusing on what we as practitioners can do, and so across this chapter, we will consider what is within our control...

Can-do approaches

Milestones and inchstones

Parent's voice

It took time for Zac to teach me how to see the joy and beauty in his own development. Once I had freed myself from the tick boxes and restraints of 'developmental norms' perpetuated by the narrowness and ableism of the Early Years curriculum and 'milestones', it was a huge relief.

The arrival of 'Development matters' (Early Education) in 2012 saw a shift in how we assessed and planned for children's development. As a document, there is no denying that it is good, particularly because of the inclusion of the Characteristics of Effective Learning, which focus on *how* children learn, and not just *what* they learn. 'Development matters' has, however, always been problematic for children with SEND. This was followed up by Pen Green Research Centre. During their DfE-funded project 'Building on Being 2', they found it difficult to demonstrate progress using the 'Development matters' statements (Pen Green, 2018). I do not think that this issue lies purely with 'Development matters' because most child development milestone documents do not account for the diversity within SEND development. Pen Green Centre identified some key challenges (2018) which remain concerns with the EYFS reforms:

Normative statements of development

Despite 'Development matters' previously being 'ages and stages', allowing for the time that it took for children to meet key development milestones, they follow a typical development pattern. The early learning goals as a measure of attainment essentially mean that children with SEND just do not fit into a normative set of descriptions.

Deficit model

'Development matters' encourages a deficit approach because when children do not fit in, we begin to view them as being on the periphery of the EYFS development statements.

Spiky profile

The focus on prime and specific areas suggests that children need to demonstrate key skills before progressing. Still, some children may have strengths in one area and needs in another. These needs, however, may be ongoing and met in alternative ways. 'Development matters' does not always allow for that progress to be truly celebrated. The child is essentially still defined as not being good enough in their development level by the time they reach compulsory school age.

Practitioner's voice

I became so fed up with reading development statements that did not describe or celebrate the child I was seeing every day. So, I decided not to be dictated by it, and started to write more personally about the child. When you trust your own knowledge, you start to see with new eyes. Sure, I do the 'tick box' stuff but it never dominates my time like it used to.

Celebrating the whole child

The implementation of revised early learning goals and 'Development matters' have further exacerbated the worry that the whole child is being lost to the continual push for standardised education. This is often referred to as the 'schoolification' of the Early Years.

Using different developmental documents

The issue that can arise with some SEND-based development documents is that they focus on the 'red flags', and so the document becomes focused on what the child cannot do as opposed to what they can. Developmental milestone documents that account for differences should take a celebratory approach and recognise those aspects of development that are still hugely significant. We often hear these referred to as small steps documents, but it is important to recognise that these steps are no less important, rather they are broken down so that we can more clearly see the different ways in which children learn.

Defining development

When considering development, we should be thinking about whether a child can do something consistently and across different contexts. You are also assessing whether a child is independently demonstrating learning skills and behaviours, bearing in mind that independence is relative to the need. For example, a child may only be able to do something independently with reasonable adjustments. The terminology that we most commonly hear when describing development is outlined below:

- **Emerging** refers to those developmental behaviours that you are beginning to see for the first time. Remember that a child with SEND may present differently and make note of the differences or alternative way of doing things – for example, a child with speech and language differences may use a Makaton sign for the first time to indicate a need, and so has successfully expressed a need.

- **Developing** refers to those behaviours that a child is actively working towards and is beginning to demonstrate skill development. The child may demonstrate these skills differently depending on the context – for example, a child with SEND may be developing a milestone with more ease at home rather than in the setting, because that environment might present with more opportunities to engage in a particular skill or type of learning. Try not to 'write off' milestones just because you haven't seen them for yourself. For example, a child may be following the sequence of handwashing at home but has not quite developed the same skill within the setting because the set-up is different. The child is still demonstrating a capacity for self-care.

- **Accomplished** is when we are seeing milestones often and they become embedded across different contexts independently. For example, a child may follow a routine with the aid of his visuals and be able to anticipate what happens next.

- **Accomplished+** is when we see development that is unique to the child and which potentially looks different to the 'normative goals' we might follow but which is still significant for that individual – for example, an autistic child may form a connection with a peer while retaining his individual social skills. 'A+'s should be celebrated, acknowledged and discussed because they will often provide a platform for further learning or a 'way in' to development. For example, a disabled child may not engage in running and jumping but may be physically active in lots of other ways.

As you can imagine, the design of many child development documents actually hinders our opportunities to celebrate individual children and their unique and alternative ways of learning. We have thankfully seen the publication of documents that break development down further and think about specific skills and needs. Still, we are yet to see a tool or guidance that becomes universally applied across the Early Years. Some of the most significant non-statutory documents that exist at the moment include:

- Pen Green's 'Celebratory approach to SEND' (2018), an assessment tool for identifying and supporting children with SEND.

- The 'Early Years developmental journal' (Council for Disabled children, 2013), designed for families, practitioners and others to use to record, celebrate and support children's progress.

In addition to this, many local authorities have devised their own versions of assessments for SEND, and on many of their websites SEND toolkits provide a wealth of resources. It is essential to be selective with these so as not to become overwhelmed. Still, the lack of support means that many services have become creative in developing tools that can really make a difference in setting practices.

Activity

Explore alternative development documents that account for SEND and consider how these can be used alongside your non-statutory guidance. Add these to your own SEND toolkit so that they can be accessed with ease when supporting children with SEND. A link to examples can be found in the Companion resources section of this book (page 213).

'He will grow out of it'

SEND support and play-rich foundations

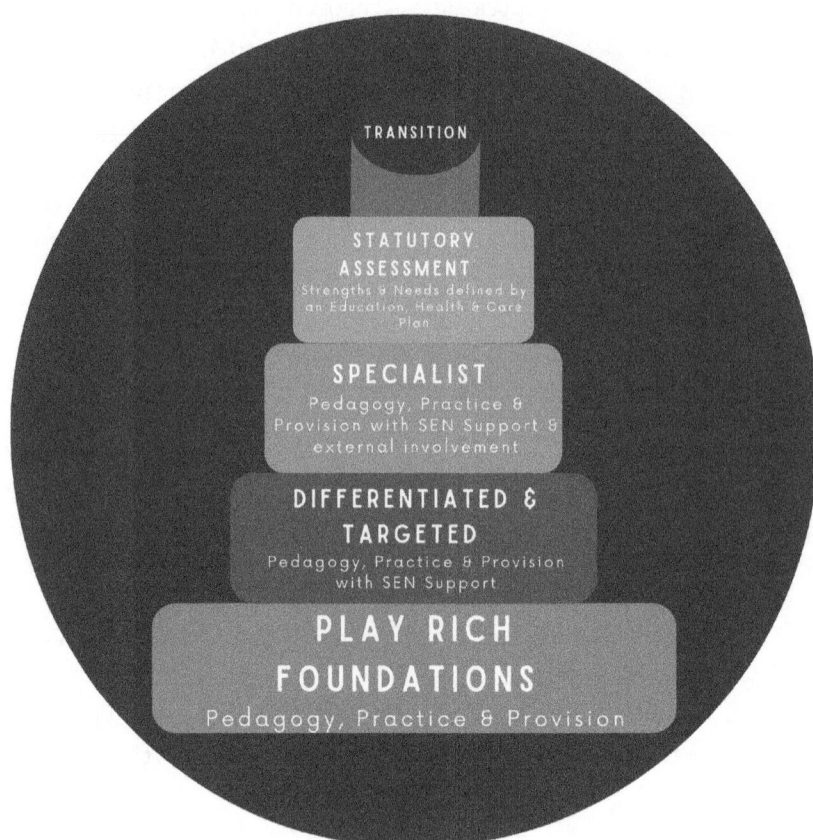

Figure 7: *Play-rich foundations*

Play-rich foundations

Much of the terminology we hear in SEND relates to primary education, and beyond. High-quality universal teaching is just one of the terms we hear which describes what we offer to all children. I call this 'play-rich foundations' because in the Early Years that is our main vehicle for supporting learning, and we need to ensure this remains central to our support for children with SEND. I first became interested in the concept of high-quality universal teaching when I became aware of a review by Ofsted in 2010, which stated that:

> 'As many as half of all pupils identified for School Action would not be identified as having special educational needs if schools focused on improving teaching and learning for all, with individual goals for improvement.' (pg. 5)

My first concern was the many parents who had been told inaccurately that their child was a problem. This felt uncomfortable and disconcerting. For so long, I had felt frustrated that practitioners and teachers focused so much on intervention, 'SEND strategies' and the role of specialists, but rarely on their own individual impact. SEND support begins within our everyday practice and provision.

There is a lot of tension and debate around the concept and definition of teaching in the Early Years. At times, it seems that we have to grapple with professional bodies to recognise that, as practitioners, we actually teach. The current Ofsted Early Years inspection handbook (updated in 2021) defines teaching, as broken down here:

> 'Teaching should not be taken to imply a "top down" or formal way of working. It is a broad term that covers the many different ways in which adults help young children to learn.' (Ofsted, 2021, para. 173)

In the Early Years, we start with and follow the child's lead, using different skills involving differentiation, which enables us to support every child's uniqueness.

> 'It includes their interactions with children during planned and child-initiated play and activities, communicating and modelling language, showing, explaining, demonstrating, exploring ideas; encouraging, questioning, recalling; providing a narrative for what they are doing; facilitating and setting challenges. It takes account of the equipment adults provide and the attention given to the physical environment, as well as the structure of the routines of the day that establish expectations. Integral to teaching is how practitioners assess what children know, understand and can do, as well as taking account of their interests and dispositions to learn (Characteristics of Effective Learning), and how practitioners use this information to plan children's next steps in learning and monitor their progress.' (Ofsted, 2021, para. 173)

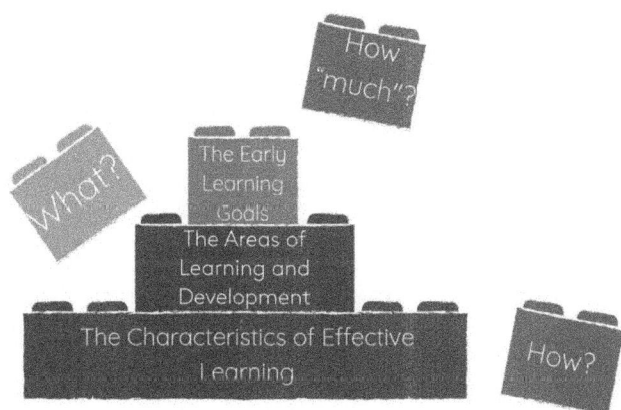

Figure 8: *Focusing on* how *children learn, before* what *they learn*

One of the key aspects of our teaching is that we seek to understand not just what children are learning, but how they learn. This has been integral to my work with children with SEND because the Characteristics of Effective Learning often afford us much greater opportunities to embrace children's individual learning blueprints.

Play-rich foundations for inclusion

An analysis of examples of inclusive early childhood education across Europe conducted by the European Agency for Special Needs and Inclusive Education (2017) highlighted similar features, including each child's 'belongingness' and active participation in learning and social activities. A 'self-reflection tool' was developed to help settings review the quality of their provision through the lens of inclusion. It consists of eight sets of questions that address:

1. overall welcoming atmosphere

2. inclusive social environment

3. child-centred approach

4. child-friendly physical environment

5. materials for all children

6. opportunities for communication for all

7. inclusive teaching and learning environment

8. family-friendly environment.

The full self-reflection tool is linked in the Companion Resources at the end of this book.

It is important that we regularly address questions around inclusion and think about the foundations on which children learn. Without this foundation, it becomes very hard to see effective differentiation and targeted support. One of the most important things you can do when developing inclusive spaces is to ensure that you take a participatory approach that gathers the views and perspectives of others. When I worked in a nursery, we had a disabled parent, and we asked whether she could feedback her experience of the setting based on the above considerations. Some might feel uncomfortable about this, but it is important that we challenge the idea that it is offensive to acknowledge a person's disability. The parent was keen to provide feedback and to have the opportunity to talk constructively about the ways in which the setting was ableist. Similar feedback can also be gained from children through different activities and experiences, such as asking a child to select their most liked and disliked spaces or routines.

Differentiation & targeted support

There may be children within your setting who, despite your play-rich foundations, need greater differentiation and targeted support. There is space for creativity here, and it may exist in the form of scaffolding, differentiation, targeted strategies or techniques. As a setting, you may also have some targeted intervention approaches that you build into everyday practice. For example, you may have training in adult-child interaction approaches and utilise particular skills to support the development of communication. You may also draw on your SEND toolkit or prior knowledge about children with similar differences or needs.

Differentiated and targeted support should involve collaborative approaches between the home and the setting, and there may be the process of involvement from beyond the setting, but you as a practitioner in partnership with the parent can plan support that can exist between both settings. Examples of targeted support include:

- making a reasonable adjustment so that a child is not denied access and participation in learning
- differentiation – for example, using objects of reference or visuals to support with routines
- using Makaton or consistent non-verbal actions to support understanding
- breaking instructions down into more manageable chunks
- using backward chaining to help a child complete a task
- adapting rather than lowering expectations to promote engagement – for example, shorter time spent sat down during circle time.

A crucial point for targeted support is that it builds upon those play-rich foundations. The targeted support should be embedded where possible into the child's everyday routines and naturalistic environments are best for children's engagement and wellbeing. So often, targeted teaching is viewed as 'in addition to and separate from', but it should be 'in addition to and within' everyday experiences.

Specialist

As a setting, there will be times where you identify a child who needs support beyond your expertise. In some cases, it might be that you can gain expertise through training or support from specialists but essentially, you need the advice and guidance with specific knowledge and qualifications. This is often the trickiest teaching stage because there is usually a lot to coordinate and navigate, including discussions with the parents to identify the best pathway for support. It is also likely that initiating specialist support doesn't mean getting access right away. There are timelines and waiting times throughout.

In some cases, children will come in with specialist support already in place, but this often looks different from child to child, area to area and authority to authority.

Examples of specialist support include:

- specific strategies as advised by specialist reports or programmes of support
- continuation and embedding of intervention programmes
- introduction of specific strategies that require training – for example, Makaton
- higher adult-to-child ratio
- environmental adaptations and reasonable adjustments
- out-of-environment interventions and parent-led interventions
- specialist equipment
- specific therapy.

Knowledge is power during specialist support, but we cannot always access the training that equips us with the knowledge. This is often frustrating and can make practitioners feel de-skilled.

Another complexity within specialist support is that the child may access therapy or interventions that actually draw on universal approaches. This can be incredibly challenging when you are asked to carry out techniques that exist within your universal practice. It is important to keep in mind that the parent is often learning different skills and techniques, and so we need to acknowledge that sometimes the therapy is for home-based environments rather than setting-based.

Where possible, access to specialist reports or programmes of support can be beneficial because you can identify the main strategies or techniques, and then agree on how they might be differentiated or adapted within the setting.

Once specialist involvement occurs, practitioners will need to work closely with children and families to agree which is most suited to the child's needs. It is important to be aware of the pro-neurodiversity stance that not all interventions are beneficial for children with developmental differences. For example, many practitioners, parents and neurodivergent people find the practices of Applied Behaviour Analysis (ABA) harmful. It is important to speak with specialists and to establish the purpose of choosing such interventions, and to check whether they are strength- and rights-based for the child.

Top tip: Neurodiversity organisations

Follow pro-Neurodiversity organisations and individuals who provide a wealth of information about specialist support – for example, Emily Lees (www.autisticslt.com).

Meaningful personalisation

When working with families during specialist support, it is crucial that they understand their entitlements of choice and control about the interventions or approaches that are being chosen. Personalisation is an important aspect of this and is defined as an 'approach to health, social care, education and support services that sees children, young people, or adults as individuals with unique skills, talents, aspirations, preferences and support needs. It also sees the young person and their family as part of, and firmly rooted in, their local community' (Sibthorp & Nichol, 2014, pg. 9). With this in mind, we must think about the interactions between education, family and specialists and ensure that there is shared decision-making and transparency about how support is organised. Duffy (2011) describes two models of specialist delivery, as described below:

- **The Gift Model** views children 'in need' and so professionals assess and allocate resources based on their perspective of what is best for the child. The gift model adopts a 'professional knows best' mentality and so professionals become 'gate-keepers' of how support should be delivered.
- **The Citizenship Model** challenges the gift model and recognises that individual children and families should have autonomy and control in making decisions that affect them. This model focuses on personalisation and makes it clear that everyone's contributions are valuable to a broader understanding of needs.

Play-rich foundations

Below are some examples of how we can build upon play-rich foundations across the four broad areas of need:

Communication and interaction

Table 4: Stages of intervention (communication and interaction)

Play-rich foundations	Targeted	Specialist
The setting uses a photo routine so that children know what to expect across the day. The key person refers regularly to the routine and prepares children for unexpected changes by using Velcro® so that photos can be swapped around.	The setting also uses visual routines for children with SEND, utilises 'Now & Next' boards and choices boards, and uses a range of symbol and line drawings.	The setting is trained in using Widgit for structured visual routines for non-speaking children.

Social, emotional and/or mental health

Table 5: Stages of intervention (social, emotional and/or mental health)

Play-rich foundations	Targeted	Specialist
The childminder has set up a space so that children can retreat when they need space and time to relax. There are a number of self-regulation items so that the child can engage in self- or supported soothing.	The childminder also has a calm-down box for a child who has specific difficulties in calming down. This includes fidget items and a choice board so that they can point to a specific self-regulation strategy.	The childminder has been advised to use a weighted blanket for a child who can become very anxious and dysregulated. This is accessible to the child so that they can use it independently when stressed.

Cognition and learning

Table 6: Stages of intervention (cognition and learning)

Play-rich foundations	Targeted	Specialist
Practitioners model ways of doing activities or tasks before expecting a child to be able to do this independently. They will use visuals, objects of reference and demonstrations and then support children in their attempts.	A practitioner breaks tasks down further to ensure that a child is able to follow along with instructions. The practitioner usually waits for about five seconds between each instruction so that the child has time to process the information.	A practitioner has been advised to use backwards chaining so that the child learns the steps within a sequence backwards but still has the sense of achievement. For example, the practitioner will provide hand-under hand support for the first four steps in hand-washing, and the child will complete the last step independently. As time progresses, the child will attempt more steps independently.

Physical and/or sensory

Table 7: Stages of intervention (physical and/or sensory)

Play-rich foundations	Targeted	Specialist
The setting has a balance of colours, ensuring that areas are not cluttered or busy as this can distract children, often referred to as visual noise. Bursts of colour are used to emphasise spaces, but natural tones help children to focus on key information.	Different paper textures on walls and furnishings are used to demarcate changes so that children with visual impairments can use the subtle changes in acoustics to navigate around the space.	The setting has been advised to use yellow tape around the room as a child with visual impairment can identify the colour and is able to identify obstructions.

Communication and interaction

- Children with speech, language and communication needs (SLCN) may have differences and difficulties in their interactions with others, including peers and adults.

- They may have difficulties in being understood (speaking) or understanding (thinking and processing).

- They may have differences or inconsistencies in attention and listening and may be easily distracted or overwhelmed in busy environments.

- They may take time to understand social rules, reciprocal conversation or order of language – for example, following instructions or understanding sequences of routines.

- They may use a range of behaviours to communicate their wants, needs, interests and emotional states.

- They may have a specific or broad profile of differences – for example, speech sound difficulties (specific) or social communication difficulties (broad).

- Their speech and communication abilities or difficulties may present differently across different contexts and spaces – for example, selective mutism may only be present within the setting.

- Children who speak more than one language may have speech, language and communication needs but their ability to learn and speak two languages is NOT a special educational need.

- Speech, language and communication needs may be indicative of neurodivergence, and so the practitioner must be mindful that different styles and ways of communicating are not necessarily signs of a delay. It is the setting's responsibility to understand the unique communication profiles of children.

Social, emotional and/or mental health

- Social, emotional and/or mental health is an overarching term for children who may have difficulties with emotional regulation, self-esteem or social interaction.

- Mental health was introduced in the SEND code of practice: 0–25 (DfE & DoH, 2015) in recognition of the importance of good mental health in development. Where children have challenges in their mental health, this too can impact on development, both in the short and long term.

- The code of practice also recognises that social, emotional and mental health needs are often a vulnerability in other areas of need. It is important to point out, though, that a) 'mental health needs' in itself is not a diagnosis, and b) mental health can be maintained even with other areas of need.

- Children with other developmental conditions can be at risk of poor mental health if their difficulties and differences are not understood or if they are required to mask aspects of their condition, for example, being expected to sit still for long periods when experiencing hyperactivity as part of ADHD.

- Good mental health is not the absence of a mental illness and we must recognise the difference between mental health and diagnosable mental health conditions.

- Children may demonstrate social, emotional and mental health needs through withdrawn or isolating behaviours or challenging behaviours.

- Practitioners should be mindful of developmentally expected and appropriate behaviours versus behaviours that could adversely disrupt learning and development.

- Children may have difficulties in forming friendships and may engage in conflict or inappropriate social skills.

- Social, emotional and mental health needs should not be overlooked in the Early Years as they can have a significant and ongoing impact across development, but practitioners should be mindful of the way in which terminology around mental health may be perceived by parents.

Cognition and learning

- Often practitioners become anxious at the use of the term 'cognition', but it is essentially what is occurring in the brain and refers to the mental processes of thinking, memory, attention and emotions. These brain activities are largely invisible to us, as we can't see inside the brain, but the executive function of these processes enables us to learn.

- In most cases, we rely on these processes to help us to function and to engage with everyday activities – for example, your memory enables you to follow routines in the correct order, such as making a cup of tea.

- Self-regulation is our ability to manage stress and emotional states (Shanker, 2016) and provides the foundation for these mental processes to occur successfully, hence why social, emotional and/or mental health was covered first. It is absolutely crucial that Early Years settings understand that self-regulation cannot exist without an adult who first co-regulates with the child and helps them to work through emotional states, feelings and experiences.

- This area of need encompasses both general and specific difficulties in our cognition and learning. You may support children who have general differences and difficulties with cognition across their learning and everyday experiences, particularly with their independence skills, and these children can have a mild, moderate or severe learning difficulty. There are also children who have profound and multiple learning difficulties

(PMLD), and these would be considered complex needs due to the range of health and social needs.

- Children may also have specific learning difficulties, and this usually impacts one main domain of learning, such as dyslexia, which impacts on reading and writing, or dyspraxia, which affects motor coordination. Of course, we know that these conditions a) are rarely diagnosed in the Early Years, and b) can extend beyond one domain, but they are generally labelled as specific due to the clearest area of impact.

- Cognition and learning does refer to neurodevelopmental conditions such as global developmental delay, autism and attention deficit/hyperactivity condition. As we well know, these types of conditions overlap with the other areas of need but fall under this area due to the growing understanding of the structure of the brain in relation to developmental differences.

Physical and/or sensory

- This area of need includes visual impairment (VI), D/deaf and multi-sensory impairments (MSI) and differences, which affects both vision and sight.

- Physical needs can include disability and specific conditions that affect mobility, such as dyspraxia (although this is also found under 'cognition and learning').

- This area is also associated with sensory processing differences, which commonly occur among neurodevelopmental conditions such as autism.

- Sensory processing refers to how people use sensory information (sight, sound, texture, taste and movement) to integrate into the environment and to understand that environment.

- Impairments in sensory integration can impact on learning and development and are categorised into three sub-types: (1) sensory modulation disorder, (2) sensory-based motor disorder and (3) sensory discrimination disorder.

- Sensory modulation disorder refers to how the central nervous system responds to external stimuli. Children can be over-responsive, under-responsive or engage in sensory-seeking behaviours.

- Sensory-based motor disorder involves a child's control of movement, and difficulties may be experienced with posture, balance, strength and control.

- Sensory discrimination disorder involves differences in managing sensory input, and the child may perceive sensory information differently – for example, using excessive strength when only a light touch is needed.

The graduated approach

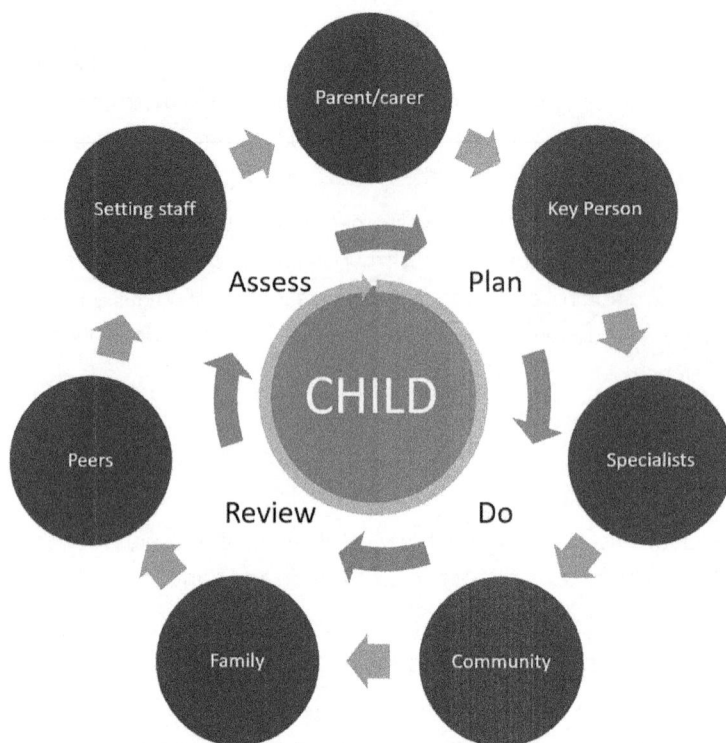

Figure 9: *The EYFS Observation, Assessment & Planning Cycle & Graduated Approach (DfE, 2015)*

The spiral approach

When the revised code of practice came into effect, I spoke with many practitioners who complained about the changes, namely that there were always new systems to be learning. The graduated approach (formerly the graduated response) is in place to ensure that we, as practitioners, remain attentive in our monitoring of a child's SEND. Still, as Figure 9 shows, it is not a new system; it is an extension of the systems in which you are already engaged. The best way that I have heard this described is by NASEN, who explain the graduated approach as a spiral. It is about tightening up our already existing systems with increasing frequency and detail. Once I took this on board, I took a much more pragmatic approach to SEND support.

The use of a cycle of assessment in SEND (DfES, 2001) has been in place since the original code of practice. It remains aligned to the Early Years Foundation Stage (DfES, 2008). Practitioners are expected to work through several actions to establish and embed support. With the introduction of the revised SEND code of practice: 0–25 (DfE & DoH,

2015), it was identified that educational settings should be developing a holistic approach rather than responding only when issues emerged. The use of the term 'approach' suggests that settings can prepare for support in a timely and measured way.

One of the difficulties with the existence of a code of practice is that it often comes with systems and procedures that feel separate from the everyday practice of Early Years. During training sessions, I always aim to show how the graduated approach fits around and complements the cycle of observation, assessment and planning.

While we are engaged in this experience, we may identify that children have specific needs. It is crucial at this stage that we revisit our OAP (observation, assessment and planning) cycle with increasing frequency and detail. This is where the spiral comes in with its graduated approach, which is described as 'Assess, Plan, Do, Review'.

Assess (linked to EYFS observation and assessment)

During the 'Assess' phase, consider:

- formal and informal observations
- dialogue with professionals
- noteworthy documentation
- staged development or data
- using a celebratory profile
- inclusive play-rich foundations
- home learning experiences
- what is currently working and not working.

Plan (linked to EYFS planning)

During the 'Plan' phase, you should:

- consult with colleagues, parents, child and professionals
- consider how your plan will be embedded into the EYFS and home learning
- decide on the appropriate format and whether the current planning system supports children with SEND
- consider what child development documents will be used and whether they appropriately describe the child
- consider how outcomes are devised and how progress will be celebrated
- consider the timeframes and dates for review
- consider whether any training will be required and how this will be accessed (e.g. online, face-to-face, CPD).

Do (linked to EYFS OAP)

During the 'Do' phase, you should consider:

- informal observation, assessment and planning is happening at all times and there are many 'in the moment' opportunities to support development
- whether all practitioners are aware and carrying out the teaching and support
- whether there is consistency in the delivery of teaching and support
- whether home learning is continuing
- whether the SEND support is being embedded into everyday experience
- whether the SEND support is leading to positive outcomes.

Review

During the 'Review' phase, you should:

- ensure there is time to check in and review what has been happening
- engage in professional dialogue
- consider this a key decision-making opportunity to decide on what is next
- consider any changes or adjustments to the SEND support.

Co-intervention

When a child has identified needs, it is likely that you will be using all your skills and knowledge to support progress and development. You are equipped with knowledge about child development and have likely completed a qualification so, when faced with developmental differences, you can put something into place. It can often happen that we judge parents for not possessing the same skills and we wonder why the home learning experiences do not appear to be consistent with the setting practice. There are a broad set of reasons why intervention differs between environments, and we should not assume that a parent should know. One of our key skills is equipping parents with the knowledge that we already possess. Below are some ideas for supporting parents as co-interventionists:

1. film the interventions, strategies or aspects of teaching
2. lend resources
3. invite the parent into the setting to observe
4. design strategy sheets or create top tips for different skills
5. email ideas
6. provide signposts via displays, newsletters or during handovers
7. collaboration on ideas

8. provide pens and writing pads to empower parents

9. agree an agenda ahead of any meeting

10. explore options for joint parent and practitioner training (it is good for parents to see that you are a learner too).

It is likely that there are many children who come into your provision who may have minor developmental differences and the pace of progress is supported by your universal provision. High-quality provision can minimise the escalation of SEND. It is likely that you are reducing the risks of delay through your everyday practice.

Top tips: Inclusive teaching

Lead with empathy and you lead the way: Be open-minded and welcoming and seek to understand rather than to make a judgement. Try not make assumptions about what a child can and cannot do based on first impressions, such as an obvious disability or delay – for example, don't assume that a child cannot communicate just because he or she is non-verbal. The communication will just be different.

Have high yet realistic expectations: Try not to view SEND as a deficit but instead focus on what the child can do rather than what they cannot. The purpose of education is to find out what you are good at, and so our role is to meet the child where they are and to provide the learning conditions to thrive. For example, if a child has particular fascinations, use these as a foundation for teaching and build this into planned experiences rather than trying to redirect the child.

Be adaptable, differentiate and get creative: One size does not fit all so be flexible and creative with your teaching. Consult with the children directly or tune into their preferred styles of learning. For example, if a child has inconsistent attention and finds it difficult to sit still during circle times, adapt your expectations and consider other creative ways of engagement, such as movement-based songs or acting out stories. As Sally Neaum says, 'Children do not learn to sit still by sitting still' (2017, pg. 74).

Make reasonable adjustments: A child's SEND should be considered thoughtfully to ensure that the setting's practice or mindset does not put a child at a disadvantage or limit their participation in everyday setting life. For example, if a child has a physical disability, consider the ways in which you could adjust the environment so that the child can have similar experiences to other children, such as additional equipment or extra adult support.

Model and inspire: Children are curious about similarities and differences, and therefore practitioners should support children's understanding when they ask questions about other children's SEND. For example, 'You are right, Clare uses a walking frame. What could we do so that Clare can join in with your activity?' These are key 'teachable moments'.

Consult and gain feedback: If you are stuck for ideas on how to develop inclusion, speak to those people who experience such barriers every day, such as the children, parents and specialists. Be mindful, however, that is not the sole responsibility of the SEN or disabled person to provide all the answers, and it requires us as adult to address the existence of ableism.

Broaden your mind: If we don't understand something, it can be difficult to plan for. Inclusion is about developing understanding, knowledge and skills. Ask for advice, guidance and training or complete your own research, which will make you feel better equipped.

Promote independence and the 'more than one way' approach: Developing independence is an important part of inclusion, and therefore the setting should have different opportunities for children to develop skills such as self-care, communication and movement. Does the setting have visual prompts/cues so that children understand the steps within an action? Are resources at children's level? Do practitioners model the different ways in which a task can be achieved?

Don't be tokenistic: Often settings will buy 'inclusive resources' to demonstrate their acceptance of difference and diversity, but this doesn't always translate into practice. Positive images of disabled people hold little value if the setting isn't accessible, clutter-free and safe for people with a range of disabilities. Be mindful of viewing SEN and disability through the inspirational or superpower lens also. The SEND community often find this patronising and it sustains ableism.

Develop a repertoire of inclusive practices and communicate these to your community: Inclusion is about progression, and settings should continually strive to meet a broad range of needs. It is important to promote the ways in which you are inclusive – for example, if you have staff who are trained in the use of a certain piece of equipment, such as EpiPens®, or who have specific skillsets, communicate these to your community so that families who fear exclusion or isolation know that there are many options out there.

Chapter summary

Milestones and inchstones
When thinking about children's development, try to think beyond the traditional statements, and engage instead with different development documents that celebrate the uniqueness and variation of development.

Strong universal high-quality teaching (play-rich provision)
No matter what needs a child has, our universal teaching, such as the EYFS, must form any support foundations. You can still ensure that high-quality teaching is happening even if you need to access additional or specialist support.

The stages of intervention
As a setting, begin to develop approaches that you can use once concerns emerge, and embed these into your everyday experiences. Practitioners need to recognise what is within their own expertise and develop a toolkit approach to inclusion. Develop a repertoire of targeted and specialist strategies.

The graduated approach and EYFS cycle spiral together
Sometimes it can feel that there are just too many systems. Sometimes there really are, but in this case, they are essentially one. Every day, you will be engaged in the EYFS cycle of observation, assessment and planning, and when concerns emerge, you spiral into the graduated approach (Assess, Plan, Do, Review).

Plan for the four broad areas of need
If you anticipate that children will have areas of need, you can plan suitable provision and match these needs. Understanding these is crucial for effective SEND support.

Signposts and resources

'See differently' guidance for the Early Years
Royal National Institute for the Blind
Available at: www.rnib.org.uk/information-everyday-living-education-and-learning-young-childrens-education/early-years

'Early Years education' resources
National Deaf Children's Society
Available at: www.ndcs.org.uk/information-and-support/being-deaf-friendly/information-for-professionals/early-years-education

'Support for children with special educational needs and disabilities'
Sense
Available at: www.sense.org.uk/get-support/support-for-children/send

6 'There's just too much paperwork': Developing a celebratory framework for SEND children

Starting points

On a piece of paper, write down as many examples of paperwork associated with SEND as you can think of. How many do you believe actually enhance the quality of SEND support?

Introduction

Too much reliance on paperwork is the absolute enemy of effective SEND support. I have engaged in endless debate about how it can lead to paperwork fatigue for both practitioners and parents. Curiously, some of those debates happen with practitioners who will often complain about the intensity of paperwork yet struggle to break away from it. Freeing yourself from formats, templates and checklists can be quite scary, especially when practitioners perceive them to be the only tangible proof that they are doing their best to support the child.

When I meet with practitioners, they often assume that my first intention is to see written evidence. What follows is a flurry of SEND files, plastic wallets, support plans, specialist reports and observations. The volume of paperwork often means that you are dealing with a jigsaw of documentation, and rarely do the pieces fit together because SEND support is messy and a bit chaotic. While I know that some people may judge a practitioner harshly for not having all their paperwork in order, the real evidence comes from the professional dialogue and knowledge of the child.

For clarity, I am not saying that we need no paperwork; we just need less of it. When completing the background reading for this chapter, I was saddened but unsurprised to see that children with SEND have way more paperwork in their files. Unfortunately, too little of this relates to their strengths, dispositions and characteristics of effective learning. In so many ways, SEND support is an accountability measure rather than a process to help us deeply understand a child. We need to go back to the roots of why we observe, assess and plan.

We also need to think of the ways in which we engage with referral processes and statutory assessments. The biggest obstacle that we face here is that no local area aligns their processes. Therefore, across the country, we likely have many variations of the same form and many variations of the same support pathways. Research tells us that this is actually to the child's detriment and accessing timely support has become a 'postcode lottery' (Longfield, 2019). This became apparent when I spoke with practitioners from different areas who reported entirely different experiences for similar needs. The fact that one setting can make a phone call and gain support and another has to fill in a six-page referral form is not good enough. There is nothing equitable here. While the guidance that I provide throughout this chapter should help you to reflect on what works and what does not in paperwork, it cannot necessarily solve some of those wider issues. It can feel futile but developing the confidence to provide constructive feedback to local services is helpful. As an inclusion consultant, I often got the best ideas from practitioners because they had the practical accounts and experiences that we no longer had.

Observation

The sticky note has become symbolic in the Early Years because it represents what we spend a lot of our time doing. The practice of observation, or look, listen and note, is the key task for us to develop a deep understanding of children. But as we will know, the work of understanding children spans way beyond a sticky note that won't stick. When exploring observation and documentation in SEND, there is a tendency to think immediately of concern forms or individual education plans (IEPs). The paperwork often overrides more in-depth discussions about how we can meaningfully support children. When I visited settings to support children with SEND, I would view observations that were often kept away from the child's main learning journey. This was because they captured the delays or difficulties rather than actual learning. The learning journeys would also have far fewer observations. I would often hear the same narrative that the child didn't really do enough to be observed. Granted, observing children with SEND can be more challenging, but this is rarely because they aren't learning. They are just learning in a way that might not feel known or understood to us. It is important to point out here that the moment I entered into a dialogue with practitioners, they could list endless learning examples. Still, they struggled to articulate this when discussing milestones that described typically developing children.

According to Heiskanan et al. (2018), the extensive documentation of a child's SEND is rarely questioned. Therefore, we begin to see descriptors that outline how a child does not fit into our normative expectations, rather than examples of our differentiation. By repositioning the child from problem to learner, our approach to observation can be much more dynamic. An example of this is captured well in a TEDx Talk by Bettina Love

(2014). She explains that a child banging endlessly on a table is not just a child defiantly banging on a table. He is actually playing the drums or seeking a rhythm based on the hip hop music he has heard. Play and learning are often mistaken for bad or trivial behaviour because they take place out of the context in which we would expect to see them. But if we believe that play is a natural-born urge, then it does not need to be limited to one thing or one place. My point: to be a good observer is to see learning with 'wide eyes and open minds', regardless of the needs of the child (Nutbrown, 1996, pg. 15).

> ' "If only you had seen all I had to do." The child wants this observation. We all want this. This means that when you learn to observe the child, when you have assimilated all that it means to observe the child, you learn many things that are not in books – educational or psychological. And when you have done this you will learn to have more diffidence and more distrust of rapid assessments, tests, judgments. The child wants to be observed, but she doesn't want to be judged.' (Malaguzzi, 1994, pg. 54)

It is common for these points to be counteracted with 'so we just never talk about the child's difficulties, then?' and I recognise that shifting long-held beliefs and systems for SEND can be difficult. Still, I think it is good to remember that the practice of observation often leads to new knowledge. The first time that a practitioner observes an autistic child will be the beginning of new understandings and new learnings. The practitioner can choose to interpret the autism as a problem or they can view it as a different way of learning. If we go with the latter, I can guarantee that the practitioner and child's relational and planning experiences will be infinitely better.

Tuning in & zooming in

Developing the skill of 'tuning in' is one of my most favourite aspects of observation. It is the process of focusing so intently that you come to understand a child's uniqueness, intricacies and ways of learning. If you speak to most practitioners, they are way better at tuning in than they realise. This becomes even more apparent in the minute detail that they know about children in discussions but haven't necessarily written down. Spending lots of time with children means that you come to know all their 'tells', including all those verbal and non-verbal behaviours. This gives the practitioner an insight into the inner workings of their mind. It all sounds very new age, but it is an underexplored aspect of our sector because we place such a heavy emphasis on paperwork and progress measures. When we think about professional dialogue, we frame it under 'moderation', which becomes another accountability pressure. I implore anyone to go and have a conversation with a baby room practitioner. The amount of knowledge that they possess will blow your mind. Granted, I don't think that practitioners always have the best ways of demonstrating the interlinking theoretical knowledge in these discussions. As a sector, we need more support to do this, but practitioners know their stuff at the roots. We aren't as bound by routines or timetables, so we tend to spend more uninterrupted time with children, although still not nearly enough. There is something very synchronous between the child and the Early Years practitioner. This comes from the observational practice of tuning in.

Observing not only for concerns

When I was running SEND training, I set a gap task for practitioners to document observations that intrigued them but that did not link directly to typical learning. We used these observations to try to work out motivations, interests and needs, and these examples highlight the importance of seeking to understand the child beyond a concern.

Observation 1

Child A had been jumping up and down near the main door and becoming distressed. It was assumed that he wanted to get out of the room or was indicating wanting to go home, but actually, following further observations, he knew the light switches were near the door and he wanted to reach them. He used problem-solving skills and took different pieces of furniture to climb up, such as turning a crate upside down, which was still too low, and a chair, which worked well. This became a daily occurrence and it took all my might not to stop him or to ask him to get back down.

I was trying to decide whether the lighting was actually agitating for him, but I noticed that he would switch it off and on, and directly look up, noticing the difference from light to dark. Another practitioner mentioned that he would always head straight for the resources that lit up in the sensory room. I took a few items, including a multi-light torch and a small lava lamp, and placed them into the main environment. He discovered them quite quickly and the torch was reflected off every surface he could find, and again, he seemed to be motivated by the changes in light.

Before tuning in, I honestly would have just seen the light-switch behaviour as entirely problematic and stopped him from doing it.

Observation 2

Child B climbed on furniture and was fascinated with opening cupboards and doors. She would climb up onto tables and counter tops, and enjoyed being picked up so that she was at height. I completed a risk assessment because she was highly skilled at getting into high places.

I looked around the room and the outdoor space, and I noticed that there was not much opportunity for children to be at different levels. I researched why this might be beneficial and discovered that different modes of movement support sensory integration, balance and physical strength. The child, I figured, was communicating to me that she needed more physical challenge. My perception of her SEND just made me think that she didn't have anything better to do, which is terrible of me I know.

I made some changes to both the indoors and outdoors, and even simple things such as adding a few steps to different areas has actually led to her doing some things for the first time, such as using the paint easel, where she painted right to the top of the paper.

Understanding the child

As you can see from the above examples, time is needed to observe and interpret learning when a child has SEND. Capacity and time to tune in are rarely available across a busy day, so practitioners need to consider realistically how they can take time to observe learning. According to Cowan and Flewitt (2020), we should steer away from observing children simply to quantify their learning. Instead, we should take more time to understand how they learn. Having a file full of random observations or a highlighted 'Development matters' document (DfE, 2021) ends up being much less useful than a real high-quality observation and understanding of learning. It is not uncommon for practitioners to say to me, 'Once the child has demonstrated a milestone three times, I can tick it off.' This tells us almost immediately that children with SEND are likely to be viewed as an 'incomplete' checklist. It can be harrowing to scroll through teacher-sharing websites where you see numerous variations of the same checklists. While I understand that they do this because they will face accountability pressures, this is a problem for all children, and not just children with SEND.

When I was trained in consultancy, I did a shadow visit with a phenomenal consultant named Samira. Together we completed a joint observation of practice, and I immediately asked, 'Do we have an observation format?' I was told, 'No, use a piece of plain paper and your eyes and ears.' This felt very scary in truth, but the lesson that became embedded that day was that sometimes the best observations are the ones that are organic and unprescribed. Later on, when we compared notes, the picture of children's experiences became so much richer in detail. We found that referring to development guidance afterwards, rather than before helped us to have a more personalised view of children's learning.

The same approach can apply to practitioners when observing children with SEND. You should just get comfortable with watching and learning. Prompts and formats have a time and place, but only when they strengthen your knowledge or provide a gateway for further understanding.

Searching for signs of learning

In 2019, Cowan and Flewitt carried out a research project funded by the Froebel Trust (Cowan & Flewitt, 2020). They wanted to examine contemporary practices of observation and assessment and how practitioners perceive children's learning. One of their findings was that practitioners tended to produce more observations for particular types of children, including those who were:

- highly verbal

- outgoing

- fluent in English

- indoors

- quiet and still

- involved in group activities

- more likely to produce 'work'

- less absent.

Despite this study only focusing on three settings, it is still concerning that non-speaking or quieter children do not receive the same observation attention as more verbal children. Bradbury (2013) suggests that this is, in fact, influenced by the EYFS requirements, which 'implicitly defines desirable behavioural characteristics in an "ideal learner"' (As cited in Cameron & Moss, 2020, pg. 123). The research sought to examine opportunities for transformative change, including the following suggestions.

Filmed observations

Cowan & Flewitt (2019) found that rewatching an observation enabled practitioners to go beyond the 'snapshot' of a sticky note. They were able to tune into fleeting and subtle types of learning. Practitioners reported that the most exciting aspects of children's learning actually went beyond the former EYFS 'Development matters' (Early Education, 2012). Digital documentation and observation revealed different traces of learning.

I have always found filmed observations to be the most effective way of tuning into children with SEND. Where possible, ask children whether it is OK to record or share the fact that you intend to record short videos to learn about their learning. If this still feels uncomfortable, you could ask the parents whether they would be willing to share or let you watch some observations. Again, all this needs to be sensitively handled. Still, with the ever-expanding world of technology, it is common for parents to eagerly share videos or photos.

Depending on your intention, filming short bursts of play and learning or strategically placing a recording device so that you can still interact is useful. Try not to record endless amounts; this reduces your chance of going back and watching it because it can quickly become time-consuming. It works best when you don't have to handle the digital technology, so a strategically placed tablet or recording device enables you to still engage.

It is also important to think about the amount of agency that a child has in that form of documentation. Allowing children to watch themselves back or be part of the recording process so that you can see the world through the child's perspectives is useful for building that bigger picture of learning.

Voice recorder

This suggestion always gets a raised eyebrow and reluctance, but so often writing an observation down feels way more cumbersome. Narrating what you see and listening back will provide a new richness. Dictation apps or specific audio recording devices are relatively cheap and can be easily uploaded or translated to text. You can also capture a child's 'voice' this way and have specific examples of verbal communication or your descriptions of how they communicate. One of the most useful things that I found when using dictation was that I could ask for practitioner perspectives, and thus you can quite quickly form a 'web of perspectives' (Canning, 2019, pg. 88).

Curious conversations

A key question that I always ask is how often practitioners observe together and engage in a dialogue about what they are seeing and hearing. Perspectives of play differ and engaging in what I like to call 'curious conversations' helps us to make sense of the child. These conversations can take place during or after observation but can help to interpret what we have seen. The key thing with curious conversations is that you then only need to write down what is actually noteworthy. Conversations about observations are always guaranteed to take you somewhere.

Assessment

'Development Matters became an assessment tool rather than the child development guidance it was originally intended to be. As it reduced in form it also reduced in its wider perspective of children's development and by default it became a narrow view of children's potential.' (Chilvers, 2020, para. 7)

Understanding the child

Observation and assessment are very closely linked, and actually, in most cases, they entirely overlap in practice. As practitioners, we often begin to analyse or make sense of what we see as we see it. The EYFS framework tells us that assessment is a way to decide what observations tell us about the child. Through our reflections, we should come to understand a child's interests, ways of learning, emotional responses and level of development. We do this in the moment and then document our reflections more formally in progress summaries or through a learning journey, for example. These informed judgments contribute eventually to the Early Years Foundation Stage profile, the point at which it is decided whether or not a child has reached a 'Good Level of Development' (GLD) (DfE, 2021c).

'Development matters' (Early Education, 2012, and DfE, 2021d) has been subject to some criticism for creating a heavy workload. Still, as the original writers point out, there has been a growing practice of practitioners using the statements as a tick list for assessment purposes (Chivers, 2019), so we have actually seen the document present a narrowed view of child development. The original intent was to guide us using a 'best fit' model that recognises that children develop in different ways. It is not about quantifying children based on statements but about engaging in a meaningful exploration of development.

Moving away from the term 'assessment' for a moment might be helpful because it can make us think of measuring children's attainment. Our neighbours in Scotland released their own guidance, and the terminology and approach seem much less skewed. In the 'Realising the ambition: Being me' document (Education Scotland, 2020), the authors refer to the importance of making interpretations of development but being flexible with these, as they acknowledge that the sense-making process can change. Our interpretations of development should give us an insight into the child and help us to think about our next steps in the adult's role. It is important that we hold onto our knowledge lightly when making our interpretations. Children grow and learn at very different rhythms and paces. By removing the restrictions of checklists and assessment formats, we have a space for genuine exploration and responsiveness.

Communicating progress

With the arrival of the EYFS reforms, the key question is how we will present progress, particularly when it comes to securing support from local authority services. The answer to this question is not straightforward because what is expected in terms of 'evidence' is really local area dependent. However, there are three ways that we can approach this using the different versions of the Development Matters (2012/2021) and the Birth to Five Matters (2021).

Table 8: Presenting progress based on the available non-statutory guidance

Non-statutory guidance	Progress description
Development Matters (2012)	• Ages and stages approach is used with the encouragement of practitioners defining which age band is relevant to the child's current stage of development.
Development Matters (2021)	• The removal of age/stage makes it harder to demonstrate development expectations and current progress, but the observation check points can be used to indicate specific types of concern.
Birth to Five Matters (2021)	• Birth to Five Matters has used ranges to demonstrate expected development and current progress.

It is vitally important for local authorities to communicate their own expectations, and in some cases, they will use their own development tracking specifically for SEND.

Pedagogical documentation

'Educators should focus on process… because it is how we learned not what we learned.'
(Rinaldi, cited in Dodd-Nufrio, 2011, pg. 237)

A key route to understanding children's thinking and learning is through the process of pedagogical documentation. This form of documentation aims to develop a shared understanding of learning rather than evidence a practitioner's workload. It should not be confused with administrative documentation and is much less subject to a format. The concept originates from and is inspired by the practices of Reggio Emilia (www. reggiochildren.it/en/reggio-emilia-approach), and the common issue with this approach is that it can often be applied rather superficially in settings. Examples of pedagogical documentation include:

- children's work
- photographs
- plans and drafts of learning in progress
- audio and video recordings
- transcriptions
- comments
- interviews
- illustrations
- mind-maps
- child observations
- parent observations
- specialist observations
- collages.

If we extend this to be inclusive of children with SEND, we might also consider:

- one-page profiles
- communication passports
- play passports
- celebratory profiles (see Companion Resources).

You may well have read the poem 'The Hundred Languages of Children' (Malaguzzi, n.d.), which aims to describe the many different ways in which children demonstrate their learning, and through pedagogical documentation, the extensiveness of this learning can be captured in meaningful ways.

Planning

Moment to moment

When I was a SENDCo, if there was a child who required quite a bit of extra support, I tended to carry around a little notebook in which to add ideas on the go. Yes, at times, that information had to be brought together into a plan or as evidence towards referrals, but don't immerse yourself in paperwork; immerse yourself in the actions of carrying out SEND support. Your mantra should always be: SEND SUPPORT IS NOT JUST PAPERWORK. These systems and processes exist within our actions. A pretty individual education plan means nothing if it sits in a file on the shelf, only to reveal itself at Team Around the Child meetings.

Web of perspectives

The systems that you have in place for all children should inform how you observe, assess and plan for children with SEND. It is fairly common for settings to think that they need to develop entirely new systems or approaches separate from the main EYFS framework. Still, the starting point for any setting is to evaluate what currently works for documentation. Paperwork should not dominate SEND support. It should not be driven by tick-box tasks, especially those that aren't then utilised or translated into practice. As a consultant, I would often review the quality of the current documentation. If it was good, we would look at small adaptations to make it inclusion friendly and if it was not so good, we would prioritise some key documents to ensure SEND support could occur. If we want to do inclusion well, we need to adapt the systems that we have to suit all children rather than create new ones.

Your documentation systems should account for all voices, including key person, SENDCo, parent, specialists and child. Within the Early Years, you aren't just getting to know the child, you are getting to know the family. They are also getting to know you, which creates a microcosm or community of support and collaboration. When we begin to learn about a family, we may have 'All About Me' formats or templates that can give us key information. In truth, these can all be a little jaded and a bit 'rinse and repeat'. If they work, great, but there are more creative ways of getting to know each other. Developing one-page and partnership profiles is a great way to get to know each other, and it can often serve as a prompt for developing a collaborative relationship with parents.

Celebratory profiles

One-page profile

The 'Celebratory approach to SEND' (Pen Green Centre, 2018) suggests the use of one-page profiles, which give you key and unique information about the child. The questions usually capture key traits and needs and do not contain too much overwhelming information. Including key questions is helpful – for example, interests and needs. You can also extend this with a list of more light-hearted questions so that you can get a 'feel' for the child and family – for example, 'Describe your perfect day out together' or 'What food do you love to eat as a family?' These things can feel quite gimmicky at times but often give us an insight that we can use or transfer into the setting.

Practitioner passports

I always recommend that parents and practitioners also share a profile that is relatively light-hearted and fun. This can be really beneficial for engaging parents, as you also begin to share little insights about yourself. Where there is SEND support needed, it can go a long way for a parent to read about some of your key skills and your personality traits or interests. Equally, it can give you an 'in' for generating discussions with parents. Some settings even go as far as to record short video introductions or send a short recording of them storytelling. Remember that parents don't always get to see you fully in practice, and this can be a good way for them to see your style and personality.

Individual education plans

The right plans must be put into place during SEND support, but this should not be a tick-box exercise or lead to prolonged breaks from children. I spent a lot of time working with nursery settings to break the cycle of excessive reliance on individual education plans (IEPs). This may seem quite controversial to those working in inclusion. Still, I have always found them to be barriers to high-quality support. My own early experiences of writing the dreaded things left me feeling depleted and disconnected from child-centred pedagogy. During my time as a practitioner, I supported a child who had fine motor difficulties, which impacted her self-care and independence. The occupational therapist's suggestion was to do repetitive activities where the child used and practised manipulations with her hands. I was given an IEP that was designed using the SMART target framework. One of the recommendations was that 'Child A should thread three single beads twice a day over six weeks to build hand strength'.

At no stage did anyone check whether the child was actually interested in beads, nor was I advised of other ways in which hand strength could be developed. As a new SENDCo and relatively new Early Years practitioner, I diligently followed the target. It was ticked off at the six-week mark, replaced with another abstract activity. Once I started writing my own IEPs, I found myself writing SMART targets that in no way related to the children's everyday experiences.

They mostly remained in a file on the shelf, used only to 'prove' that I was intervening during Team Around the Child meetings. I could have presumed that my experience was unique, but then I became that consultant and was subject to the same IEP file time and time again. Whenever we put the IEP back into the file and had a discussion about what was actually going on, we found that more useful information was collated about children and their learning.

The SEND code of practice: 0–25 (DfE & DoH, 2015) removed the requirement for educational settings to have an IEP in place. Instead, it enabled autonomy for settings to decide upon their own systems of support. This was a huge hurrah moment for me, and I have since seen so many more meaningful SEND support examples beyond the paperwork. Alas, some settings have been reluctant to let go, and many replaced the IEP with a funky new name but it was essentially the same thing. In my own local authority, the inclusion team introduced the 'individual support plan', taking us from IEP to ISP. Great… more acronyms. It is essential to say here that I am absolutely not against individual planning. It is a must for SEND support, but I am against planning becoming fragmented because a child has SEND. Let me explain…

You likely already have a planning system, and you will almost definitely be planning for children on an individual level. If you have a firmly embedded system, there is absolutely no reason why you cannot use what you currently have to plan for SEND needs. The most important thing about SEND support is that it happens. All too often, I see neatly typed-up plans or resource folders, but they aren't being used in practice. Planning is meant to be a messy, imperfect, annotated, crumpled paper and scribbly notes process. Neat planning, to me, suggests that the system isn't that well embedded. Embrace the mess and only write that which is noteworthy. If you're tired of SMART targets, try the SHARE framework instead, an alternative way of looking at SMART targets that can often focus on compliance (see Companion resources). The SHARE framework takes a neurodiversity affirming approach and provides more meaningful ways to develop targets for children with SEND.

Support plan and possible lines of development

One of the most effective methods of planning has always been mapping because it can be used in an ongoing way. The example in Figure 10 demonstrates that planning formats need to be interacted with to be useful. They can have different elements, such as activity planning, reflection, evaluations, links to learning and the next steps. This plan is adapted from Pen Green Centre's 'possible lines of development' (n.d), and further examples can be found on their website. This type of format, aside from others, can be really visually helpful and can provide a holistic view of what is happening for the child. Despite the example being typed up for this book, the usual format would be handwritten because planning absolutely does not need to be neat and tidy. Practitioners can sometimes worry about their own messy thinking and planning processes being visible. Still, it demonstrates how they are responsive to a child's interests, strengths, differences and needs. If the plan needs to be shared with others, simply take a picture or scan it into a document. I have previously done this and typed around it with key points. Practitioners can also highlight

Possible lines of direction (PLOD) for SL (2 years/33months)

Sent instructions home for bubble painting activity for parents to try at home.

During attempts at language, add one word and do this across routines, for example 'water' = 'drink water'. (01/09/2019)

Use simple and clear language and make sure to be at child's height level

Instead of 'use your words', say 'Help me to understand' or 'Can you point to' or 'Take me to'. (02/09/19)

Use props for Miss Polly had a dolly to encourage actions and vocabulary. Set up dolly play station. (04/09/19 – SL loved this. Including props in other nursery rhymes. Lots of attempts to sing.)

During daily routines, model how to do tasks, such as noise wiping, pouring own drink and ask 'can you do it' (01/09/2019)

SL said 'tissue' and stretched out hands. 'We encouraged SL to self-select. Next steps: To complete a sequence of actions independently, model noise wiping and placing tissue in the bin. (30/09/19)

For oral motor:
- Use the mirror to pull funny faces
- Read Mr Tongue
- Do Mouth-Monster
- Singing nursery rhymes rather than using tablet. (16/09/19 – Working brilliantly for whole-group experiences and SL enjoying shared experience.)

SL has loved the bubbles being used, so we will continue to encourage different mouth actions; blow hard, soft, fast, slow. (22/09/2019)

SL enjoys sensory and painting experiences; set up a blowing paint bubbles activity. Place small marbles for her to blow along. (27/09/19)

Whole group:
Hand and feet floor printing using lots of descriptive words, e.g. splatter, stamp, stomp, swish, swirl. (30/09/2019 – SL slightly reluctant to point feet but, with some modelling, enjoyed the experience and enjoyed saying and acting out swish swish.)

Home learning
Parents report they have decreased use of tablet and are singing more action rhymes with SL which she loves.

Taught parents four Makaton signs for consistency at home. They have noted she is saying and acting out drink ('drink')

To support with language, introduce some whole class Makaton signs such as sit, drink, eat and toilet. (30/09/2019 – Increased confidence in indicating need.)

Will become frustrated when trying to indicate more snack/drink. Introduce 'more' Makaton sign next.

When asking questions, ensure there is an adequate waiting period for SL to respond. She becomes overwhelmed if asked too many questions.

Using whole-body communication to express instruction. Break instructions down into manageable chunks for SL. Use positive reinforcement when she is able to follow parts of an instruction. (27/09/2019 – Identified that SL can follow two sequence instruction if matched with non-verbal gesture.)

SL can get frustrated if not understood. Ms.k has kept a note of common behavioural cues for her personal communication dictionary. 'Bock' means drink. (28/09/2019 – Identified several babble words to have meaning. Focus on clearly modelling the accurate pronunciation. Reminded teachers to never correct.)

Inner diagram

Parent and child voice

Thinking, learning and executive function

Communication and interaction

Observation of interests
Painting
Dolls
Bubbles
Sensory play

Social, emotional or self-regulation

Encouraging independence

Physical, sensory or processing

Reflection and clear date for review

Met with ICO on 01/10/2019.
1. SL's vocabulary is increasing.
2. Speech sounds significantly clearer but will continue to develop
3. Makaton is effective for indicating needs
4. The use of props and whole body is having a positive impact
5. Next focus – continued speech and language clarity, and two single words together.
6. DATE FOR REVIEW: 31/10/2019 – AGREE ON NECESSITY FOR REFERRAL AT THIS TIME.

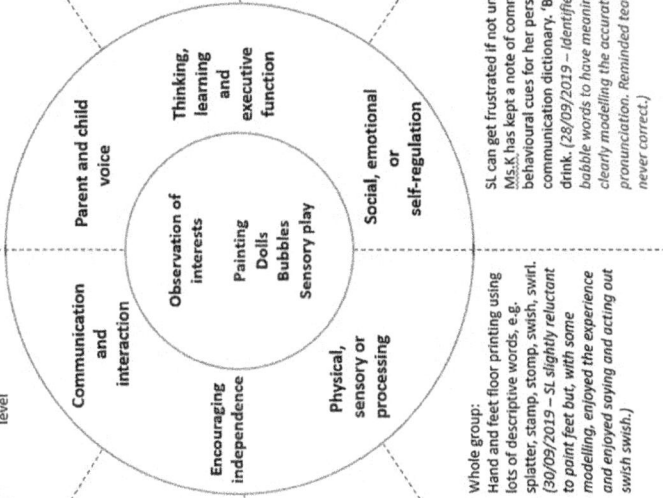

Resources:
Bubbles
Mirrors
Makaton poster

Figure 10: *Possible lines of development; a full-size version is available in the Companion resources*

important information for ease of reading. The other benefit of the mind-map is that it is not time-bound; it can continue until room runs out on the page or the practitioner wishes to summarise development – for example, through a progress check.

Equally, as a setting, practitioners may have formats that work for children. They may simply need additional considerations about how the format can be made more inclusive for SEND.

> ## Practitioner's voice
>
> Support plans are important in identifying areas of need and tracking progress, but it's also important to not be afraid of veering off them. If a child is totally engaged in making an elaborate pattern out of bricks at the only time you can take them for one-to-one activities, consider what is actually best for the child at that moment. Is it worth causing distress in order to have something to write on your focus observation sheet? Sometimes you might reach the end of a support plan and realise that one target isn't something that child is ready for. It's important not to be scared to set a target that seems like a step back or to scrap that target entirely until it seems more plausible. The child's current abilities and interests have to be central to the support plan, even if that means steering away from widely used speech and language therapy strategies to plan your own individualised activities. Progress is made when children are engaged and motivated – support plans that aren't adapted for the individual aren't functional, whereas a support plan designed to make learning exciting for that child is an incredibly valuable tool.

Coming back to those curious conversations

Earlier on, I referred to the value of curious conversations around development, which also applies to the planning stage. On the Pen Green website, there is a particularly valuable video showing a two-minute planning session, which highlights the saying that 'two heads are better than one' (Pen Green, n.d.). It is also essential to think about how these conversations happen with parents and specialists who contribute to the bigger picture of development.

Missed opportunities and 'rinse and repeat'

When working as a SEND consultant, I would receive a call from an Early Years provider who would usually outline their concerns and ask for a visit and observation. I would go along, carry out an independent observation, provide my findings and give strategies and techniques. In most cases, children's observations had lots of interconnectedness and similar patterns – for example, behaviour indicating a speech and language difference or delay. This 'rinse and repeat' support over a long period of time is not a sustainable or impactful way of raising quality. The thing that really surprised me is that I would get calls from the same settings for the same types of concern. I found myself getting so frustrated – 'Have they not learned from last time?'. I would literally be going back into the same setting and giving the exact same advice. There is something peculiar in SEND where practitioners are reluctant to transfer their learning about one child to another. The quality of SEND support is down to the person or people carrying it out and their ability to differentiate, transfer and reapply knowledge.

After a year of doing this, I went to my manager and explained calmly (translation: erratically and passionately) that we were doing a disservice to our settings. We were essentially failing to upskill and equip them because we were doing the work over and over again. The autonomy of the setting, I believe, has never really been a priority. When jobs become redundant, as mine did, there is uproar and panic until the next round of funding comes along, which funds the same broken system. The way we fix that system is to recognise that practitioners come with a wealth of skills. Instead of funding 'middle people', we should be funding our settings and our practitioners.

Waiting lists

'Your setting is the intervention.' (Ephgrave, 2020, pg. 30)

In an ideal world, when we seek support for a child with SEND, we would transition through some seamless steps and find ourselves upskilled, equipped and raring to go. Unfortunately, the harsh reality of SEND support is that there are often waiting lists, which can be such a frustrating experience for everyone involved. In my many discussions with specialists, they always remind me that they are essentially an assessment service. While they offer therapy, this is always with the aim of the parent and practitioner being able to transfer those intervention skills to a more naturalistic setting. This was quite a liberating thing to discover as a practitioner because I began to see specialist services as running parallel to what I was doing, rather than chasing them. In 2017, the Department for Education released a research report entitled 'SEN support: A rapid evidence assessment' (DfE, 2017b). Many of the findings suggested that the most effective intervention was carried out by people familiar to children and within safe spaces. The advice given was to focus on building up a repertoire of strategies and techniques across the four broad areas of need so that when SEND emerges, you are not left waiting to act.

While this may be easier said than done, there is no time to start like the present. It is highly likely that much of this repertoire of skills already exists within many of our settings.

The magic bag of strategies

I frequently receive urgent phone calls or emails from practitioners asking for SEND strategies. I honestly think that they sometimes believe I have a magic bag of strategies that I am withholding from them. There is, however, no magic bag. Most of what we provide is actually just really good teaching practice rather than a specific SEND strategy. I often encourage practitioners to view their knowledge as a toolkit of teaching practices. They may need to expand or learn new ways of using their tools, but everything that you need begins with you, the person carrying the toolkit.

Velcro® Veras

Another thing that I hear is 'She needs one-to-one' and I understand this as a response to stress, helplessness and frustration. Yes, some children need higher adult-to-child ratios. Still, we must be very mindful that children thrive best in safe, secure and familiar environments. In most cases in the Early Years, you as the key person are actually best placed to carry out the intervention, techniques and strategies because you are their secure base. While there may be times for a more skilled adult to become involved, I still firmly believe that the key person is the thread that runs between all other setting-based relationships.

The term 'one-to-one' is used a lot because often supporting children with SEND has come with this misplaced belief that attaching one adult to a child solves the 'problem'. But suppose that one adult is doing nothing more than policing and controlling a child? In that case, we are not effectively preparing that child for lifelong learning and participation. The focus of any person supporting a child with SEND is a) supporting the child to thrive and b) ensuring that the child develops independence and life skills. If a child becomes entirely dependent on us, we are not supporting a healthy pattern of attachment. One of the key pieces of advice that I give to practitioners is that if they insist on referring to one-to-one, they must also clearly outline what that person will do to support learning and development.

Specialist advice

Many children on SEND support also have specialist reports or programmes of support. Unfortunately, I have found that these often end up in the children's SEND file never to be looked at. But those reports provide planning ideas and should be embedded in everyday experiences.

The specialists essentially do the hard work for us with planning. Our task is to differentiate what is outlined in specialist paperwork. During a visit to one setting, they proudly showed me their SEND toolkit, which had lots of strategy sheets and laminated resources. We then discussed an individual child's needs and the fact that they had been advised to introduce a visual routine. The routine was in the folder and had not been used. You may be reading this and thinking 'of course I use the specialist information in planning', but you would be amazed by the amount of times the suggestions are left out. Consider in what ways you incorporate specialist advice into planning. The following is an example:

Case study: Communication and language

As per the specialist report (01/05/2020), we will use Observe, Wait and Listen (OWL) during daily interactions. Hattie can take more time to process information, and the extra waiting time gives her an opportunity to answer. This has also been demonstrated to parents.

The above is a relatively generic example but highlights how the strategy has been understood in relation to Hattie's needs. If everyone has access to the plan and the strategies are well communicated, Hattie will likely receive more consistent support.

Top tip: Building a repertoire of strategies

Specialist services often develop strategy guides and booklets. For example, if a child has a speech and language delay, it is likely that a targeted set of strategies will be shared with the setting. The next time a child has similar needs, go back to the booklet and use those same strategies. Not all reports are personalised and so we can build a resource bank.

Referrals

Practitioner's voice

The referral process is challenging and doesn't make it easy for settings, and therefore disadvantages the child. We have to allow the child to settle first and spend time getting to know them and their needs so that we can prove what we've already put in place for them. This is difficult in an already busy setting – other children may have needs requiring additional support but not significant enough to refer. It's a balancing act between doing the best for the child and being mindful of the other children attending. We're not in a position to increase staff hours to enable children with SEND to have additional support while settling in.

'There's just too much paperwork'

The referral process requires the SENDCo to attend a panel meeting – again, this disadvantages the setting, as cover is required. Settings have to contribute financially towards children with SEND, in addition to what we receive from the local authority. This is a big problem for us.

Case study: Quality over quantity

Sarah had noticed that quite a lot of referrals were being sent back to the setting due to a number of issues. She decided to call up and ask for some advice. A panel member explained that lots of referrals contained far too much information without concise explanations or descriptions. This made it very difficult for the panel to make an informed decision because they had to work through so much information. When Sarah looked back through the referrals with this pointer, she noticed that practitioners clearly thought that the more information the better, but the volume of observations, evidence and appendices made it much less clear. She decided to deliver a workshop so that the setting could decide what would be most important in completing a referral. This group exercise enabled them to develop a fairly consistent approach, and the quality did improve.

Referrals are another tricky aspect of SEND support, and the processes from service to service can be wildly different. However, there are key considerations that can support the development of high-quality and consistent referrals. When I cover referrals in training, the best way of making sense of them is to review examples. The following activity is beneficial in looking at two of the most common issues: too much information and not enough information.

Activity: Pretend panel

Imagine that you are asked to sit in on a panel for speech and language therapy. The therapists have suggested that the quality of referrals is quite varied and they are hoping for you to complete a quality check.

Referral one

Sally is two years old. We are concerned for her speech.

Personal, social and emotional development

Sally is a happy child and always comes into nursery smiling. She loves her key person and spends a lot of time with her. Sally is most happy playing on her own and enjoys playing with the cars. Sally plays alongside friends and is excited to play with all the toys.

Physical development

Sally loves physical play and enjoys spending time outdoors.

Communication and language

Sally is not using much language and can become frustrated. She babbles a lot and points at things when she wants them. She has bitten quite a few times and is at times disruptive.

Setting's next steps: To keep supporting Sally in her play.

Parent's voice

We are concerned with Sally's progress, but her key person has assured us she is doing well and will catch up with the other children.

- What would you do if you received this referral?

Referral two

Ben is two years old (30 months) and has been attending my childminder setting for 12 months. He is interested in building blocks, water play and sand. He is settled and has built a close bond with me, but he is displaying some differences and difficulties within his communication and interaction.

Personal, social and emotional development

Ben's transition into the setting goes well, and he is usually eager to see me. Ben likes predictability and responds well to the routines of the day particularly when visuals are included. Ben will demonstrate his moods by pointing at the emotions cards and likes to select items from the calm box when he is feeling upset. He does this independently. Ben is still building up confidence to play with peers but will engage in parallel play and observe others. Ben loves to spin when he is excited and will pull me by the hand when he wants me to join in with his play. Ben has a comfort bear called Bob, and he will independently access this from his bag when he wants to rest. Ben has recently spotted his picture on the coat peg he has been allocated and he excitedly points at it, and then at himself.

Possible line of development: To develop Ben's confidence in play entry with peers. Himself and a peer play alongside each other often, so I will scaffold some shared learning experiences between the two children.

Current stage of development: 8–20 months/Range 2/Checkpoint Birth to Three

Physical development

Ben is a very active child, and he will run, jump, climb and spin throughout the day. He is beginning to recognise that exercise makes him thirsty so he will run to the sink to let me know that he needs a drink. He can sit for a few seconds during story time, but much prefers movement-driven experiences and loves to dance. He also enjoys the sensory experiences of playdough and gloop. On occasion, Ben will take items to his mouth, and we are working on knowing what is safe and unsafe using visuals. Ben will let you know if he isn't enjoying something by kicking his feet or arching his back. He likes to head to the cosy corner when this happens and will stretch out on the cushions. Ben will join in with mealtimes and is particularly engaged when he gets to use the blue plate.

Ben does not currently indicate his need to go to the toilet but will spend time in the bathroom getting used to the items and is now confident with the steps in handwashing. He loves the smell of the handwash. Ben enjoys trying to do up buttons and zips. He can now fasten up the top button on his coat when I use backwards chaining.

Possible lines of development: Ben is responsive to backwards chaining, and he indicates a sense of pride when he completes a task. I will continue to utilise this strategy in physical self-care and aim to build his confidence in completing a few more steps within a sequence. Parents have also asked to be supported in developing backwards chaining as a home-based strategy.

Current stage of development: 8–20 months/Range 2/Check Point Birth to Three

Communication and language

Ben will turn when his name is called and is alert to environmental sounds. He is curious about the environment and will move between different experiences and activities, spending a short time at each. He will engage in some adult-led experiences with support but is still very much at the exploration stage. Ben can understand one-word instructions, especially when used with an object of reference – for example, showing him his blue cup indicates that it's snack time. Ben enjoys hand-under-hand support when playing with new toys. Ben makes lots of attempts to communicate, including pointing, spinning, pulling and babbling. He can become frustrated if he is not understood but I refer to his personal communication dictionary when working out his different actions. On occasion, if he is not understood, he will bite to let the person know that it's frustrating. The use of visuals and a sensory ball are supporting the reduction of this.

Possible lines of development: We have introduced a 'helping hand' visual for Ben when he is frustrated. We are encouraging him to indicate to an adult when he has a need or is becoming frustrated. He is gradually using this, and we will continue to develop his confidence by acknowledging his unmet needs. The practitioners are also using a lot of mirroring in his communicating and continuing to identify what key non-verbal actions might mean so we can build up the use of more visuals.

Current stage of development: 8–20 months/Range 2/Check Point birth to Three

- What would you do if you received this referral?

Consider the two referrals in this section and ask yourself the following questions:

- Are there emerging concerns in these case studies? Are they clear?
- Is there a necessary level of detail, including for referral if relevant?
- Is there enough information about the child's strengths and areas for development or difficulties in the three prime areas of learning and in the Characteristics of Effective Learning (Early Education, 2012)? Is there enough/accurate information on age stage of development? Will this information help you to plan effectively?
- Are the possible lines of development clear and accurate? Will the support planned make a difference?
- Would this check effectively support a referral panel? Would it tell them all that they need to know?

Hopefully from the examples in the previous activity, you can identify why referrals may be difficult to work through when they do not contain the right amount of information. Panel members often need to be able to make decisions quite quickly and so there are a number of things that we can do to make this process more efficient.

Top tips: Organising a referral

- **Photocopy referrals:** One of the most common experiences is the case of the lost paperwork. Duplicate anything that you intend to send off, because it is an inevitability that at some stage you too will hear the words 'We haven't received the referral', even though you 100 per cent know that you sent it.
- **If posting, send via recorded delivery, or request a receipt of delivery if hand-delivered:** If I am sending confidential information, I handle that information very sensitively, and if I am to hand it over anywhere, I want a record that I have followed certain procedures and protocol. If I hand-deliver a referral, I will always ask reception for a receipt due to the aforementioned issue of lost referrals.
- **Get highlighter-happy:** Specialist services receive many referrals and some of the forms require lots of information. In order to ensure that the key points are understood, I use a highlighter system, which consists of:

- ○ green (areas of need)
- ○ orange (what the setting is currently doing to support)
- ○ pink (what is beyond the expertise of the setting).
- **Always include a cover letter:** This is your opportunity to share your concerns and your contact details and to lay out the professional expectations. I very clearly and in bold put the name, number and email of the key contact and share availability.
- **Check expectations:** When I worked in a local authority, I saw first-hand how they like to create duplications of paperwork. In fact, I battled for seven years to reduce the pressures of paperwork on settings and left as a result of them continuing to make more work than necessary. One such issue is their tendency to create lots of referral forms, so you essentially end up writing out the same things time and time again or answering largely arbitrary questions. In my SEND toolkit, I had a clear procedure for each service, including the conditions in which they would accept a referral and what their statutory obligation was. In some cases, we are made to complete forms when in fact we don't need to. This is another reason why you should duplicate referrals, because if you are completing multiple, you can copy and paste the information, which is often overlapping anyway.
- **Always send a staged development check:** Panels will be examining the referral to check the significance of a delay or difference. The easiest way to highlight this is through a progress check or summary that clearly shows the stage of development. Always ask your local services how they would like the stage of development to be presented.

Education, Health and Care Plans and Assessment Requests

For this section of the book, SEND and Education, Health and Care Plans (EHCP) specialist Sarah Doyle guided me through the process of making statutory requests.

Before we begin our adventure into Education, Health and Care Plans (EHCPs), it is crucial to be transparent about their current effectiveness, particularly for the Early Years. The purpose of such a plan is to provide a single document that should describe the child's strengths and needs in a multi-disciplinary and holistic way (Palikara et al., 2019). According to Dr Susana Castro-Kemp (2020, para. 2), research has found that overall the plans are weak, badly put together and vague and have 'unworkable descriptions of needs'. Describing the current process as fragmented, Castro-Kemp argues that poor-quality plans will essentially lead to poor-quality provision. The additional disappointment for the Early Years sector is that obtaining an EHCP is still incredibly difficult, especially if it is not in a school-based setting. Therefore, it is important to forewarn you that this statutory process has many bumps in the road. With that context in mind, it's also important to view the request for an EHC needs assessment and plan as an opportunity to strive for the best support and provision for our children. One of the key messages here is not to feel dissuaded or 'stuck' due to what can be a complex process.

Outcomes and aspirations for ALL

'If a child attends a special setting in an affluent local authority, it is likely they will have a higher quality EHC plan than another child attending a mainstream educational setting in a deprived local authority.' (Castro-Kemp et al., 2019, pg. 8)

The above quote comes from a study which focused on the inequalities of the EHCP. Those children in more affluent areas were found to have higher-quality outcomes and descriptions of need. The very root of the reforms was in transforming equality of opportunity. Still, these findings suggest that we are currently moving 'further away from the inclusion and diversity agenda' (Castro-Kemp et al., 2019, pg. 10).

The big question is, no matter what the context, what do we want for our children? And what do we need to do to help them to get there? It brings us back to an old, familiar issue within the Early Years sector: the lack of training and support. This guidance, therefore, aims to help you navigate the current system.

What is an EHCP?

- The Education, Health and Care Plan replaces the statement of educational needs (DfES, 2001). It is a legal document which describes a child's strengths and interests, their special educational needs, the outcomes that can be focused on and the provision and support they need.
- The local authority must provide the special educational provision stated in an EHCP. In practice, this *should* help secure extra SEN support, rather than a child or young person being subjected to the long waiting lists we are all familiar with.
- According to the SEND code of practice: 0–25 (DfE & DoH, 2015), the majority of young people will have their needs met within local mainstream Early Years settings or schools. However, some children may require an EHC needs assessment so that the local authority can decide whether it is necessary to make provision in accordance with an EHCP.

- The EHCP must be a collaborative process between professionals and specialists across the educational, health and social care sectors, the parents and the child.

- The purpose of the plan is to ensure that special educational provision is made to meet the special educational needs of the child, which will secure them the best possible outcomes.

- The EHCP should be available across the 0–25 life span.

- As an Early Years provider, you are probably more likely to be involved in preparing a request for a child transitioning to school than requesting one for your own setting. However, it is crucial to note here that an EHC needs assessment can be requested at any age 0–25, and there are many young children in Early Years settings receiving SEND support and provision through an EHCP.

- You will likely be subject to lots of complicated systems and processes as per your local authority, and you can expect miscommunication and misinformation. You will absolutely want to become familiar with the Independent Provider of Special Education Advice (known as IPSEA), who are an independent charity in England who offer free and independent legally based information, advice and support to help get the right education for children and young people with all kinds of special educational needs and disabilities. If you are initiating a request on behalf of or alongside a parent, you should signpost IPSEA as a starting point.

EHC needs assessment requests

It seems straightforward but this is often confused. A child can only receive an EHCP following an EHC needs assessment. I often hear practitioners and parents saying they are requesting or applying for an EHCP. The first step is to make a request to the local authority for an assessment, and it's important to be clear that this request does not guarantee an assessment or a resulting EHCP. (The request is not the assessment. You are requesting the assessment.) It is important to be very clear that a request does not guarantee the assessment. (You make a request, and the local authority has six weeks to decide whether to carry out the assessment.)

When making a request for assessment, keep in mind what the local authority *must* consider by law (section 36 (8) of the Children and Families Act 2014):

- whether the child or young person has or may have special educational needs
- whether they may need special educational provision to be made through an EHC plan.

Although there is further detail on what local authorities *should* consider in the SEND code of practice 2015, essentially, if the above two statements are applicable then the local authority *must* carry out an EHC needs assessment. According to Sarah Doyle, 'Knowing this has helped me to develop my own confidence in making requests, as well as the parents and practitioners I support.'

Also worth noting is that an EHCP is not diagnosis dependant. Waiting lists for diagnostic assessment can be years so starting the process to obtain special educational provision should not be delayed.

Who can request an EHCP?

Legally, the parent or anyone with consent who is acting on behalf of the parent – for example, a nursery setting – can make the request. You will see grey areas with this, particularly if a local authority is trying to moderate the volume of requests and thus may have their own systems, but legally – and that is the key word – anyone acting in the interests of the child is able to do this.

EHCP timelines

Table 9: Education, Health and Care Plan timelines

A request for statutory assessment is received (to issue a plan).	
By week 6	Inform parent/young person of decision on whether an assessment is needed.
Local authority (LA) decides whether an Education, Health and Care Plan is needed.	
By week 16	A draft plan should be completed and sent to parent, carer or young person.
By week 18	The LA should be informed of any requested amendments by parent, carer or young person.
By week 20	The final EHCP should be issued unless there are exceptional circumstances not to do so.

It's useful to have an overview of the timeline and activities of the EHC needs assessment and plan process from your local authority. Above is a simplified overview and your area should have a more detailed version to refer to. Many local authorities are now using online processes which makes it much easier to track the progress and to know what comes next. Although you are likely to encounter some delays within this timeline, knowledge of this can help you to advocate for the child and family:

- follow up with the local authority EHC case worker if the process has 'gone quiet'
- know when to expect contact from the specialists involved in assessment
- hold space for the parent and child if delays occur.

Rejected requests for assessment

I often receive angry emails or distressed phone calls that the request has been turned down. This can be a hideous experience because we are often acutely aware of the early intervention window becoming smaller and the significant transitions creeping nearer. When I unpick the content of the requests, it can become clear that the burden of paperwork and a lack of clarity about what is needed leads to a rejected request.

I always viewed the decision-making process of statutory requests as very cloak and dagger. I asked whether I could sit in on one of their panels and I realised that, actually, it is a transparent, efficient and crucial process. I had spent a lot of time judging local authorities for rejecting requests. Still, I realised pretty quickly that they see these requests regularly and are skilled in making decisions. Similar to the discussion around rejected referrals, the panel is essentially asking two things:

1) What has already been done?
2) Despite what has been done, is progress still not as expected?

What you are essentially demonstrating in a statutory request is that 'having taken relevant and purposeful action to identify, assess and meet the special educational needs of the child… the child has not made expected progress' (DfE, 2015, pg. 103).

This was an 'a-ha' moment when I was a consultant, because I recognised that referrals and requests often consist of 'children on their worst days' with very little information about what works and what does not. My grievance with this is failure to support practitioners to understand how to effectively complete a request. The questions laid out in EHCP requests are often very arbitrary, and it can feel very overwhelming.

If you receive a refusal to assess, take it as an opportunity to learn from this, and always keep in mind the reason you made your request. Ask if there is anything else you can provide or make clearer. In my experience, an initial refusal is nowhere near a flat 'no'. The local authority must provide the reason for refusal to assess, so the first task is to check these reasons against the two 'legal tests' described above. Watch out for any blanket policies; local authorities must base their decision on the individual child and not on 'themes' such as the age of the child.

Case study: Challenging decisions

Cassius is 37 months and has been attending his Early Years setting for eight months. He accesses weekly Speech and Language Therapy and Music Therapy, and this advice informs the support provided in the setting, alongside high quality universal and targeted experiences. At the most recent Team Around the Family

(TAF) meeting it was agreed that as his progress has continued to be limited and due to the level of his needs, a request for EHC needs assessment would be made. The parent asked the setting SENDCo to complete the request. The local authority responded after four weeks with a refusal to assess. The parent was very upset, and after a tearful conversation with the SENDCo, she was determined to follow this up. The local authority explained that Cassius was too young for assessment and he needed to be in a setting for at least a year. The SENDCo knew this constituted a blanket approach rather than individual consideration and challenged the decision. Following a mediation meeting with the local authority, an EHC needs assessment was agreed.

How can I prepare for an EHC needs assessment request?

1. Visit your local authority's Local Offer website and make yourself familiar with the key procedures. Some local authorities have devised a flow chart or visual of their processes and timelines.

2. Download any request forms, key documents such as parent's guides or signposts. Many local authorities provide completed 'model' EHC needs assessment request forms. Save these in a desktop folder titled 'EHCP and assessment requests'.

3. Start to collate your observations (those recorded and those you store mentally). Ask colleagues for their observations and perspectives. At this stage include the parent as much as possible by asking for their observations from home. Try to 'co-produce' the assessment request with the parent and child and make sure they remain at the centre of the process, as they can often get lost under the weight of specialist reports, acronyms and 'systems'.

4. Talk through the process with the parent. Sarah Doyle has requested an EHCP assessment for her own child and explains, 'I always make sure I explain that whilst we do need to highlight the child's needs and this may seem the focus, we continue to recognise and celebrate their uniqueness, strengths and achievements.'

5. Make sure you have copies of any recent specialist reports (usually no older than 12 months) that can support your request

6. Check for any local authority contact details, including phone numbers and emails, in the event that you need to 'chase up'.

7. Review the request form or process so that you know what to expect. If anything is confusing or questionable, gain clarity or ask IPSEA whether it falls under the legal framework.

8. Write template emails for the 'chase up' so that you can send with more ease *if* timelines aren't adhered to.

9. Ask for absolute clarity on the conditions of the assessment request and check whether this is in accordance with the law – for example, the requirement to have particular specialist reports in place prior to assessment.

Top tips: What to include in an EHC needs assessment request

Firstly, remember that you are being asked for your knowledge of the child, not to have all the answers or to decide on the outcome.

- **Evidence of the child's developmental milestones (inchstones) and rate of progress:** Usually I would make it an absolute priority to send a staged development check. On occasion, I have sent two checks, including an earlier one to clearly show that the rate of progress is not as expected. Also highlight clearly if you are using an alternative development document – for example, the developmental journal – as milestones may be different to the normative ones laid out in our more common documents such as 'Development Matters' (DfE, 2020). It's useful to highlight a child's chronological age, and the current stage of development in the prime areas of learning, for quick reference.

- **Information about the nature, extent and context of the child's SEND:** It is absolutely crucial to clearly outline areas of need – for example, 'Joss is three years (42 months) and has a speech, language and communication condition. His broad areas of need are communication and language and social, emotional and mental health.' Straight away, a panel member can see his needs. You can then go on to provide clear and concise information about how his needs present in context. Be sure to include examples from different settings, including the home and nursery. Keep descriptions to bullet points which are easy to 'unpick' information from, and where possible make examples very specific – for example, the time in minutes that the child engages in attention builder activities.

- **Evidence of the action that has already been taken by the Early Years provider and parents to meet the child's needs:** Imagine that you are on the panel and you received the following: 'We have not yet done anything for this child as we have been stuck on a waiting list for a year, so we don't know what works because nobody has helped us.' There are two major issues with this real example. First, the requester has overlooked all the universal and targeted experiences, teaching and strategies that have likely been put in place, and second, there is an assumption that the specialists will provide the necessary action to progress. They may provide a therapy programme or set of strategies, but that alone does not secure progress. The panel want to see examples of action so that they can decide what may be needed in the future. Admitting to the success of your SEND support does not result in a child not getting help; it points a panel in the right direction. It also provides evidence that any progress has been the result of good quality SEND support which needs to continue. Equally, you may say what has been within your expertise and what has not, so that it further highlights the fact that the need cannot be met within universal or targeted support.

- **Evidence that, where progress has been made, it has only been as the result of much additional intervention and support, over and above that which is usually provided:** When I worked in a local authority, I once advised a setting to use a 'provision map' to monitor all the things that they were doing to support children with SEND (see the Companion resources for a template). After they screeched 'absolute no to more bloody paperwork', I realised that so many settings do not monitor their SEND provision spending – for example, the cost of covering a member of staff who goes out to SEND-based training, the additional hours spent on paperwork or Team Around the Child meetings, the additional resources, or calls made to services. We have become so accustomed to doing these things regardless that we can't then evidence the additional lengths to which we go to advocate for our children. But it is crucially important to document in some way what a child needs in order to progress. If you are able to state in your request that you have had to go far beyond your baseline budgets to support, it suggests to the panel that there is a cost to this child's intervention and it warrants an assessment of how much.

- **Evidence of a child's physical, emotional and social development and health needs, drawing on relevant evidence from clinicians and other health professionals, and what has been done to meet these by other agencies:** Gosh, the days of receiving returned requests because there was not enough specialist evidence! This is such an important aspect of an EHCP, but we need to be clear that conditions of an assessment cannot be entirely decided upon by a local authority. It needs to be a case-by-case decision in my professional opinion, rather than a one-rule-fits-all. If services are delayed – for example, educational psychology – you absolutely must ask what adjustments are being made to still be able to make a request. No child should be put at a disadvantage because of the larger failings of our SEND infrastructure.

Example

Below is an example of the ways in which you can outline the support and provision that you have given as a setting.

Analysis and summary of assessed needs
We intend to continue to work alongside specialists to ensure that strategies and interventions are effective. Due to Hattie's current rate of development, we predict that she has around a 28-month delay in communication and interaction and needs a high level of support in her next placement. This will include:

- a higher adult-to-child ratio with period of one-to-one support
- support and modelling from adults to complete self-care and learning tasks
- attention and listening support
- continued intensive therapy from speech and language therapy and occupational therapy
- toileting support
- family support, including transportation to and from school
- risk assessment and supportive behavioural approach
- opportunities for small-group work with peers.

Specialist reports

When I began collating specialist reports for an EHC Needs assessment, I would often worry that key information would be overlooked, particularly information that supported the plan. When it comes to submitting evidence, include the most recent reports and highlight the information that you clearly want the panel to see. This not only makes their job easier, but it also enables you to consider how it cross-references with your own assessments of the child. Where appropriate, directly quote specialists – for example, Sarah explained that 'a paediatrician wrote that he would support a request for EHC assessment, and this went straight into the first page of my request form (in bold)!' Although not strictly necessary, it can be good practice to contact specialists to gain permission for submitting their report as evidence.

Top tip: Don't duplicate your efforts

In my local authority role, I continually engaged with the powers that be to stop making settings carry out duplicate work – for example, having to write and rewrite information or transfer information to other forms. I think as a sector that we have to push back when we are entangled in bureaucracy.

For example, if you are completing a form that includes an 'All About Me' or section that you have already completed elsewhere, staple, attach or use it as an appendix. There is absolutely no reason whatsoever why you should be taking prolonged breaks from children to dabble in bureaucratic nonsense.

What does an EHCP/draft EHCP look like?

If the local authority agrees to assess, and following the assessment agree to a plan, the parent and the setting will receive a draft EHCP. There are 15 days to comment on the draft before it is finalised.

I have always asked to have a meeting with the specialists involved in the assessment, the parent (and child if appropriate) and the EHC case worker to discuss the 'drafting' of the plan before 'pen gets put to paper'. This gives the opportunity for everyone involved to share ideas and plan what the support might look like.

There is no national standard format for the EHCP. However, it must have certain sections that are clearly labelled. The sections are:

1. the views, interests and aspirations of you and your child

2. special educational needs (SEN)

3. health needs related to SEND

4. social care needs related to SEND

5. outcomes – how the extra help will benefit your child

6. special educational provision (support)

7. health provision

8. social care provision

9. placement – type and name of school or other institution (blank in the draft plan – link to info about draft plan)

10. personal budget arrangements

11. advice and information – a list of the information gathered during the EHC needs assessment.

The different sections may at first seem like a confusing alphabet soup. It can help to understand that there are three sections on needs (i.e. your child's difficulties) that are matched by corresponding provision (the help that your child will get) to meet those needs:

- 'Section 2: special educational needs' are met by 'Section 6: special educational provision'
- 'Section 3: health needs' are met by 'Section 7: health provision'
- 'Section 4: social care needs' are met by 'Section 8: social care provision'.

When we see lists like this, we can see a big body of work, but this should be more about collating evidence rather than doing it all in one big go.

Reviewing the draft

The advocacy and support of the Early Years setting doesn't stop at the request for assessment! Check if the parents would like to review the draft EHCP with you; this might provide some much-needed reassurance, as at first glance the document can look rather overwhelming. This is not to say you need to become an overnight expert of SEND law but it can help to collectively review the detail. Sarah explained that what she has found useful as an advocate and parent is to:

- Question: Are my child's strengths and abilities recognised and celebrated? Is there detail on *'how'* my child explores, plays, communicates, learns and is this information used to develop outcomes and strategies. Can I 'see' my child in this plan? This is my child's plan after all.
- Check the outcomes are positive/supportive/individualised/realistic/suitability challenging.
- Consider if the child and family have been consulted on the knowledge of what works best for them, and *how* the child can be supported – the concept of 'personalisation'.
- Develop the broader outcomes into shorter term 'steps' that will inform planning and support at the setting, and at home.
- Consider if the provision is suitable to support the outcomes (map these).
- Check that the provision is specified and quantified. For example, is there clarity on how often and for how long my child will receive a particular therapy/intervention, and what this will include? Look out for vague words such as 'should'; you are looking for certainties such as 'will'.
- Make sure there is written clarity, for example on the skills and experience required of adults supporting the child, on the training and professional development for practitioners and on what direct support my child needs and when. You may have to challenge the phrase 'it's an unwritten rule' (e.g. that the supporting adult(s) should be experienced in social communication differences).

Therefore, as a practitioner, you will want to align with the parent and ensure that there is a clear advocacy for a child-centred EHCP.

Parental self-efficacy

Parent's voice

To have to continually think about and report on your child on his worst days is soul-destroying.

During my psychology dissertation, I interviewed parents about their experiences of the SEND system. The above quote has stuck with me because it is so often expected of a parent to relive the experiences or challenges. I have completed lots of 'All About Me's with parents and, in truth, it has always felt quite tokenistic. In our discussions with parents, especially around the EHCP, we need celebratory discussions, rooted in ways forward. Northamptonshire County Council (n.d.) created a really good guide that gets practitioners to think more creatively about the child.

Step 1: Appreciate the child

A diagnosis is not a negative thing and will likely form part of the child's identity, so appreciate both the child and their identity markers. Take time to celebrate what the parent likes and admires about their child and give them the opportunity to talk about all the things they love and have learned about their child.

Step 2: Circle of connections

In her infamous TED Talk (see Chapter 1 Signposts and resources), the late Rita Pierson fiercely promoted the right for every child to have a champion – someone who believes in them and who insists that they become the best they can possibly be. A relationship circle can generate discussions about the important people and influences in a child's life.

Step 3: Communication is key

We have already covered the metaphor of the child's 'voice' but in understanding the child, we have to understand their preferred mode of communication and their personal communication dictionary.

Step 4: My way to a good day…

We all have good and bad days, and we should clearly outline to parents that discussions around those days that are not so good do not mean that the child is not good or loved.

The fact that we must sometimes focus on the bad days to understand exactly where support is most needed does not take away from the many good days that a child can have. It also allows us to be prepared.

Here are some questions that you could ask:

- If you had a magic wand and were going to create a really good day for your child, what would happen?
- What would they be doing?
- Who else would be there?

Ask a similar question for a bad day: What would you do if you wanted to make it a good day? This teases out what is important to and for them, and can be used to make changes by asking, 'What would it take to have more good days than bad days?'.

MY WAY TO A GOOD DAY...

IT IS NOT UNCOMMON TO HEAR PEOPLE SAY TO THINK OF THE CHILD ON THEIR "WORST DAY" AND THIS CAN FEEL QUITE UNCOMFORTABLE AND VERY DEFICIT-MINDED. THE PURPOSE OF THIS, HOWEVER, IS TO BE ABLE TO ESTABLISH WHAT HAPPENS WHEN THE CHILD IS NOT ADEQUATELY SUPPORTED. ALWAYS BEGIN THINKING ABOUT THE CHILD'S BEST DAYS AND THEN CONSIDER WHAT PUTS THIS AT RISK.

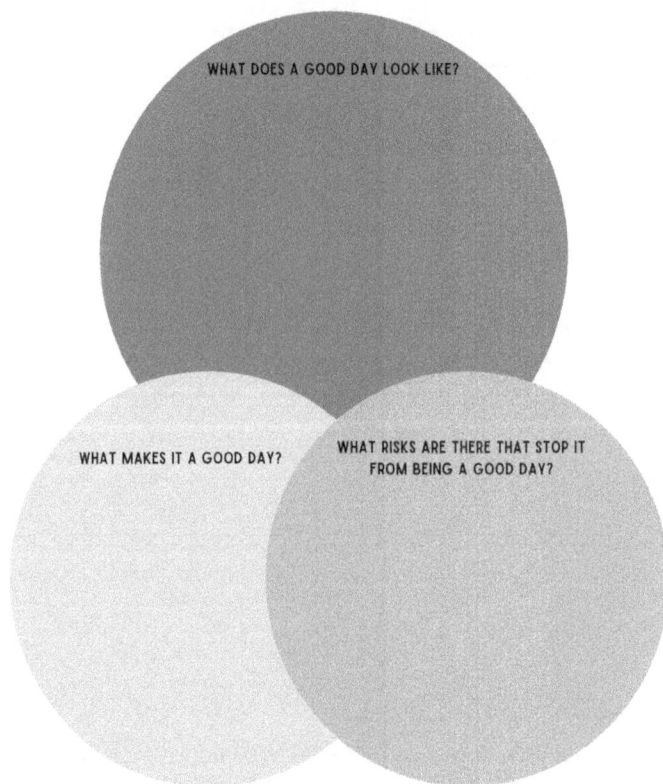

WHAT DOES A GOOD DAY LOOK LIKE?

WHAT MAKES IT A GOOD DAY?

WHAT RISKS ARE THERE THAT STOP IT FROM BEING A GOOD DAY?

Figure 11: *My way to a good day prompt*

It is not uncommon to hear people say to think of the child on their 'worst day' and this can feel quite uncomfortable and very deficit-minded. The purpose of this, however, is to be able to establish what happens when the child is not adequately supported. Always begin thinking about the child's best days and then consider what puts this at risk.

I was recently delivering some training to a group of practitioners, and we all agreed that describing children on their worst days feels like an uncomfortable practice. We discussed at length how we could reframe this, and we developed a framework for thinking about what a child needs to have a good day. We named this 'My way to a good day' (see Figure 11).

Step 5: Talents, qualities and skills

'People do not come in standard sizes or shapes, nor do their abilities and personalities. Understanding this basic truth is the key to seeing how the system is failing — and also how it can be transformed.' (Robinson, 2016, pg. 25)

The above quote by the late Ken Robinson highlights a significant point about the way in which our education system can narrow not only our perceptions of children but also the perceptions they may come to have about themselves. Parents of SEND children are so accustomed to hearing the ways in which their children don't fit into the system that we often overlook the uniqueness of children. When supporting children and families, our aim should be to highlight the talents, qualities and skills of children and to use this as a gateway for their learning.

Step 6: What is important to them and for them?

A fundamental person-centred thinking skill is to be able to separate what is important to someone from what is important for them:

- Important *to* is what really matters to the person from their perspective. Be mindful that with young children, you might be interpreting their actions and behaviours and deciding what they mean. It is important to have ways for children to express their perspectives, especially if they are non-speaking.
- Important *for* is the help and support that a person needs to stay healthy, safe and well. While this is clearly essential, families and professionals often put the main focus on *important for* and sometimes fail to ensure that there is an equal balance between the two.

Step 7: What are their aspirations?

We often ask young children 'What would you like to be when you grow up?', and we are often subject to lots of interesting answers full of awe and wonder. We ask this question as much for ourselves as the child, because we are affirming our belief that children should have the agency and autonomy to make a decision about their futures. These 'big' questions often make us view aspirations broadly, but the reality is that an aspiration has much more nuance to it. I remember my manager once telling me about working with one family whose child had a life-limiting condition, and whose care was pretty continuous. She asked about 'aspirations' and the parent simply answered, 'I just want to sit and watch a movie together.' The parent's capacity for quality time was spread so thinly across all the other tasks associated with parenting that she simply aspired for quality time.

The more and more conversations I have, the more I realise that an aspiration doesn't need to be rooted purely in those big life events. In discussions with a friend, she explained that the aspiration she had for her child was that he would make loyal friends, and she knew from observing her child that it was his aspiration too. Often with children who have SEND, parents can have anxiety about the degree of independence that their children can achieve, and one family shared that they were most keen to work on ensuring that their child could 'get around independently on transport'.

Something to look out for…

When an EHCP is agreed, the local authority will stipulate the name of the setting or school. It is important to ensure that this is correctly listed because it can create problems if the wrong setting is named. For example, if the plan is intended for implementation at your setting, you must be listed, or otherwise they could refuse allocation of funds.

Another thing to look out for…

In some scenarios, the funding is allocated after the plan's implementation. Check for clarity from the local authority as to when and how funding is spent, allocated and paid.

The EHCP is not forever

There have been numerous occasions where it hasn't been clear to the setting or the parent that the plan is not permanent. The EHCP must be monitored and reviewed within 6 months when a child is under 5, and every 12 months thereafter. In some cases, the plan does not continue, and in most, amendments are made to ensure that it remains relevant and up to date.

Support

If this is the first time you will have completed a statutory request, try not to panic. Ask your SENDCo whether they have a previous good example that you can look at and ask for your draft to be proofread by another person. You can also contact your local authority inclusion team and have a chat about the process.

Chapter summary

Being tuned into children

Developing your observational practice will be one of your greatest skills. Do not be driven by accountability measures of producing evidence; instead, observe to understand the child.

Observe, and not only for concerns

Check and challenge how you describe and document children's learning. Within SEND, this can be overly deficit-based and traces of learning can be missed. Remember, observation and documentation tell a story.

Get creative

Settings will often prescribe to one documentation system, but get creative and don't be shy to use novel ways of capturing children's learning. Pedagogical documentation should be fun, enjoyable, collaborative and meaningful.

Build SEND planning into your everyday practice

SEND support comes with too much paperwork. Practically consider how systems can be amalgamated or brought together. True inclusion brings things together.

Web of perspectives

The paperwork does not just come down to you! Gather lots of perspectives and share the load.

Practical paperwork

Review referrals and statutory requests and consider how they can be completed most practically. If there are nonsensical systems, duplication or bureaucracy, challenge these.

Signposts and resources

Leuven wellbeing and involvement scales (SICS)

Available at: www.kindengezin.be/img/sics-ziko-manual.pdf

National Strategies: 'Learning, playing and interacting'

Available at: www.keap.org.uk/documents/LearningPlayingInteracting.pdf

Froebel Trust: 'Valuing young children's signs of learning'

Available at: www.froebel.org.uk/research-library/valuing-young-childrens-signs-of-learning-observation-and-digital-documentation-of-play-in-early-years-classrooms

7 'All he does is line things up':
Keeping play at the heart of early intervention

Starting points

Read the following quote:

'Play must be the right of every child. Not a privilege. After all, when regarded as a privilege, it is granted to some and denied to others, creating further inequalities.' (Souto-Manning, 2020, pg. 785)

- Do you see play as a right?
- What is your understanding of play and what do you consider the key features to be?
- What do you consider your role to be when supporting play for children with SEND?

Introduction

Definition: Play-rich

Play richness acknowledges that play in early childhood is diverse, and has endless possibilities. It cannot be simply defined because it is so vast, and often falls out of the realms of what we see as conventional play. Play belongs to and is defined by the child.

It is odd to think that we would need a chapter that specifically addresses the *right* to play. Still, there has been a growing need for advocacy over the past decade due to an ever-increasing focus on standardising education and instructional-based teaching and intervention. While writing this very book, I had to be acutely aware of the major early education reforms that are in place in England from September 2021 (DfE, 2021a). These reforms have been met with a mixed response. On the one hand, they signify the government's commitment to reducing workload, and for placing greater trust in the knowledge and pedagogy of practitioners, and on the other hand, it has been argued that the reforms potentially create a narrowed view of child development and attainment (Fairchild & Kay, 2020). There are numerous risks when child development is narrowed down – for example, teaching may become more prescriptive and driven towards reaching normative developmental milestones, and we may knock the balance of child-initiated and adult-led off kilter. However, we might also see practitioners using the framework as a springboard for thinking more autonomously about child development, and not being contained by one guidance, but instead choosing to use what is right for our cohort of children. Dr Julian Grenier points out in a 2021 blog, 'no document or framework is perfect: sensible compromises have to be reached between different viewpoints. No-one will ever be completely happy with every aspect of the result' (para 31).

The concern that I do continue to hold about the EYFS framework, however, is that it is still in favour of the typically developing child, and continues to be underpinned by ableist thinking – for example, an emphasis on speaking as opposed to holistic forms of communication. While a framework needs to have structured elements to understand how and what children learn, there seems to be little opportunity to think diversely about the child's development, particularly if it falls outside the realms of 'typical'. If we as a sector are beholden to an ableist framework, we will, without doubt, see an impact on SEND. This includes children's autonomy in play and learning.

When supporting SEND, practitioners often want to learn about different techniques, strategies and intervention programmes, which is a crucial part of the support. Still, it is key to remember that play and child-led approaches remain at the core of what we do. Early intervention requires practitioners to provide individualised support that can be embedded within the child's everyday experiences. Yet, so often, the intervention work becomes separated, and this is where we see the loss and deprivation of play. This chapter will consider the role of play within SEND, and how intervention support fits within this.

Definition: Interventionist

A practitioner, parent or specialist who leads on and carries out SEND support.

Defining play

'It is both a tricky word and complicated concept to define.' (Scottish Government, 2014, pg. 28)

Defining play is not as straightforward as we may think, and when engaged in professional dialogue about play with practitioners, it always brings up a lot of contradictory and confusing thoughts such as the difference between play and being playful. Play is multi-layered, complex and takes on many different forms. For example, play is viewed through many different cultural lenses and so while play is a universal experience, it is experienced and valued in different ways. We have also observed our play change over time, and so it evolves providing each of us with unique play memories. Johnson & Dinger (2012) define play as being 'the important stuff' (pg. 1) in learning. It is still so common in education to see play being treated as a luxury, privilege or reward, as though it is something children should have to work for. Play is not something we can or should do in the Early Years, rather it is something we must do. Quite simply, it is essential for our healthy development (Murray, 2018) and this includes children with SEND. Assumptions can often be made that play is absent in children with SEND, but I would counter this view and encourage practitioners to develop their skills of interpretation, and to deconstruct their vision of what play should 'look' like. Alistair Bryce Clegg (2021) points out that play provides infinite variety, and all forms of play are equally as valuable as each other and children need as much of it as possible (para. 19). If we adopt this belief in our everyday practice, the possibilities of play and SEND can also become endless…

The features of play

To be active in our promotion of play, we must consider defining the key features. Here we will consider a combined definition from several scholars, including Peter Gray, whose book *Free to Learn* (2013) advocates play-filled lives. It is also important to recognise the increasing literature that demonstrates the impact of play on the developing brain. According to Liu et al. (2017), the defining features of each type of play have associations with different neural networks within the brain. This positively impacts on learning, as play supports reward processing, memory, thinking and cognition, and emotional regulation (Puschmann et al., 2013). Play prepares the brain for later academic and life learning, and so we should be mindful of these features as we embrace the role of play-rich practitioners.

> *'Adults are trained to think in terms of forming the unformed child, to socialising the savage toddler and forcing compliance in the obstinate young child.' (Plank, 2016, pg. 171)*

When we consider the defining features of play, we must also consider how we promote these for children with SEND. I have always felt torn by seeing early intervention work in practice, as it can often contradict the very defining features of play – for example, if we think of the number of times we hear the word 'outcomes' when talking about children with SEND or how often we need to provide measurable evidence of progress through SMART targets. The procedural aspects of SEND support can lead to prescriptive experiences being

Table 10: Combined features of play

Self-chosen and self-directed	Play belongs to the child and should therefore be chosen by the child. Peter Gray has described this as children doing what they want to do, as opposed to what they are obliged to do (Gray, 2008). Another important aspect of a child's play is that they can choose to quit, move on or redirect their play. The child is a free agent within their play, and though they may face challenges, there is an unquestionable engagement.
Imaginative	To be play, the behaviour must be distinct from serious, important, adult-regulated life (Trawick-Smith, 2019). The child's mind is not prohibited from engaging in awe, wonder and pretend play, and they are free to become lost within their imaginations. Within imaginative play, children can take on roles and act out scenarios, and they can imagine rules and ways of being (Bodrova & Leong, 2015). This is crucial for the development of pro-social behaviours because children practise real life in imaginary situations.
Intrinsically motivated	Play is a behaviour that must be motivated by children's own desires, interests, needs, feelings or curiosities (Trawick-Smith, 2019). The child is 'in the driving seat' of their play, and their engagement emerges from their own motivations to explore what excites or elicits interest (Liu et al., 2017). Through play, children show their inner selves to the outer world, and by following their lead, we allow children the space to become themselves (Bruce et al., 2020).
Active	According to Gray (2008), play without external pressure allows the child to engage in a relatively stress-free state, free of overwhelm. When children are active and in control of their play, they can become immersed with and interested in their ideas, and enter a state of flow (Csikszentmihalyi et al., 2014. They become active agents of their own play, and this cycle of positive reinforcement that play belongs to the child becomes a motivator to keep seeking information and action (Liu et al., 2017).
Process-orientated	In play, the child is motivated by being in the moment, rather than focusing on a specific outcome in their play (Gray, 2008). The child is engaging with ideas and possibilities and embraces the different directions of their process. Children will show pride in their products of play but will often be much more interested in telling you how they got there as opposed to their final creation (Trawick-Smith, 2019).
Emotionally meaningful	Play is personal and it elicits positive emotions and enables the child to work through all kinds of feelings (Trawick-Smith, 2019). Play can rarely exist without exhibiting some positive effect such as joy, enjoyment and fun (Huizinga, 1950; Chea et al., 2001). Emotions are interwoven with play and it can be a primer for powerful learning (Liu et al., 2017).
Socially interactive	Play is owned by the child but through play, children interact with the social world. Social interaction plays a remarkable role in shaping our brain and behavioural development (Bos et al., 2009). Through play, children observe, connect and collaborate with others to extend their network of play. Children depend on warm, responsive and stimulating interactions that cultivate trust and self-esteem. They initially depend on safe adults to reciprocate their interactions, and eventually begin to connect with peers. Supporting children's socially interactive play also includes valuing their play conflicts or engagement with difficult concepts, such as good vs bad (Bruce et al., 2020). Through play, children can also develop and practise empathy skills.

Table 10: Combined features of play (continued)

Mental rules	Contrary to understanding, play has rules, and these often take shape and structure in the child's mind (Gray, 2008). It is most common for children to assert rules in their pretend play. Children can test boundaries within their play and will engage in private speech (Berk & Meyers, 2013) or re-enactments of the things that they observe in the world around them. Through social play, children become better at self-regulation, as they practise rules without pressure (Diamond et al., 2007).

planned for children and essentially steering them away from their self-chosen play. Even play-based intervention programmes can become hijacked by a structured and adult-led dynamic. According to Sutton-Smith (1993), we can often have good intentions with these interventions. Still, they can easily lapse into 'didactic play bumblings' (pg. 5), which actually impede play behaviour. Social play is eventually diminished by too much adult interaction (File, 1994; Harper & Huie, 1998; Harper & McCluskey, 2003). So, while we may be able to say we reached a target, we must consider at what expense. This leaves us with the critical question of how we remain true to play in early intervention. A good starting point is to reposition our thinking from play-based intervention to play-richness. Play is at the heart of the Early Years and so we must promote the ways in which it threads itself through the very fabric of our pedagogy and provision. We must also promote play as the right of every child, and while differences and difficulties in development might emerge, the absolute last thing we should be reducing is access to true experiences of play. The approaches we take for children with SEND must be embedded within equitable play-rich foundations and we develop buildable practice that helps those children to thrive.

Why play is a crucial part of SEND support

'In play a child is always above his average age, above his daily behavior; in play it is as though he were a head taller than himself… in play it is as though the child were trying to jump above the level of his normal behavior.' (Vygotsky, 1967, pg. 16)

In 2015, the specialist visual, multi-sensory and D/deaf organisation Sense undertook a public inquiry into the provision of play opportunities for children aged nought to five with multiple needs in England and Wales. The inquiry found that disabled children have significantly fewer opportunities to access play settings and activities than their non-disabled peers (A toolkit for play settings in 'Making play inclusive', Sense, n.d.). This is particularly worrying when so much research highlights the specific benefits of play for children with SEND. In *Young Children's Play, Development, Disabilities and Diversity*, Jeffrey Trawick-Smith (2019) outlines several benefits of play for learning and points out that we must continue to advocate for play amid 'data-driven worlds' (pg. 16). Consider the benefits in relation to your own play-rich practices through the following activity.

Activity: Research, reflect and action

Research: According to Cohen and Uhry (2007), children speak more words and complex sentences when they are playing.

Research: Chang et al. (2018) found that children with autism and a variety of other disabilities would speak more often and use their most advanced language skills when at play.

Reflection: Do you note down the areas or play resources that children with SEND are most drawn to and do you plan for intervention support to take place in these areas? In what ways do you use resources or toys of interest to engage SEND learners' confidence in other areas of play?

Research: Roskos (2017) found that the use of reading and writing props across play led to children naturally incorporating literacy into their daily activities.

Reflection: How much access and ownership do children with SEND have over literacy props and resources? Do you use diverse resources to support children who have different forms of communication, for example, visual symbols or technology?

Research: According to Charlop et al. (2018), play enables children with disabilities to converse, persuade, explain and negotiate with peers.

Reflection: In what ways do practitioners utilise mixed aged and ability play, and how are all children engaged with intervention experiences? Remember that intervention approaches benefit all children's understanding of difference.

Research: Pretend play has been found to support the development of emotional self-regulation skills (Berk & Meyers, 2013), as children can engage in private speech, which supports them to process their emotional experiences.

Reflection: Do children have opportunities to move away from adults so that they can retreat, rest and recover?

The above activity should help you to consider the benefits of play for children with SEND and explore how SEND support can be utilised by the everyday play environment. When we explore the wealth of research about play, it can seem strange to immediately think of adult-led intervention programmes, especially as play-rich environments and warm, responsive play partners work for all children, including those with SEND. However, intervention programmes become relevant when we think of children who need to be taught particular skills through play. It is important that a setting strikes a good balance of play and intervention in the Early Years.

Activity: Play-rich observation

Rossetti (2001) noted that by eliciting, observing and describing the play of infants, toddlers and young children, one can gain significant insight into the child's overall development, which may provide information and direction for intervention efforts. Therefore, professionals who work with children need to become play experts and protagonists and know how to match this up appropriately to assessment, and intervention (as cited in Casby, 2003).

When observing a child with SEND, carry out a specific play-rich observation to assess for their current play skills. The following questions will help you to think about play, but they should also encourage you to consider whether you define types of play in conventional ways. Challenge your perceptions and definitions of play as you observe:

- Does the child initiate play or have specific interests?
- Will the child persist at a particular type of play?
- What happens if the child finds aspects of play difficult or frustrating?
- Does the child extend or scaffold up their play in any way?
- Does the child show any signs of using imagination or pretend play?
- Will the child combine play resources?
- What signs of emotion and feeling are presented throughout their play?
- Does the child invite or interact with others in their play?
- What types of communication, both verbal and non-verbal, are observed during play?
- Does the child seek reassurance or 'ask' for help during play?
- Are there aspects of play that seem unfamiliar to you and require more tuning in?

By referring to the features of play, you should be able to identify specific abilities and areas of need and can therefore plan specific opportunities for everyday play. It is also important to recognise that the play might not always make sense to you, but it likely makes sense to the child; our role is to develop our understanding of the various forms of play. It is also useful to remember that play is not a neatly packaged product but rather an ongoing process for the child and adult. By embracing that you are within the process of play, you can also engage in play detective work as you come to understand the unique motivations of each child.

There is another specific issue in education where teachers will exhaust themselves planning environments for children whom they have never even met. They might also already have their interventions mapped out. While a degree of preparedness is good, this can lead us to believe that children can be neatly organised into our own teaching agenda. To be a play partner is to relinquish a lot of control around strict teaching agendas. If play belongs to the child, they need opportunities to construct the spaces in which the play itself takes place. Children with SEND should benefit from adaptable environments that also leave room for their unique play blueprint. This applies to intervention too. The framework of an intervention programme is just that – a framework – but in many cases, the way it is carried out must be in rhythm with the child. The following case study demonstrates this well.

Case study: Beyond the bucket

Marica had recently attended a training course for supporting autistic children. This course aimed to increase attention through a structured programme of novel, exciting and fascinating sensory experiences. Marica had explained that the training was great and she felt it would make a difference to her practice. The first stage involved building suspense by taking out novelty items from a lidded bucket and showing these to the children, who looked on in utter fascination. The bucket belonged to Marica and only Marica could touch the items, which further engaged the children. As this intervention progressed, the setting had noticed that the attention of children was indeed increasing during the activity. Marica valued this intervention, but she began to feel frustration that this appeared to be the absolute go-to for every autistic child, and actually, she was often working on a myriad of specific needs. The intervention programme had become the dominant approach, not just in her setting but everywhere. She decided to look at the research for developing attention, and quickly discovered that such skills could be cultivated within and beyond the specific programme – for example, using attention-grabbers during routines and modelling play skills for children while encouraging them to find their own way of playing and paying attention. Marica expressed that as much as she valued the intervention, she became restricted by it, rather than using it as a springboard for developing her overall practice. Does she still use the bucket? Only when necessary, but she has also taken more steps to go beyond the bucket using both attention grabbers but focusing more intently on identifying what actually motivates children's attention. Marica also realised that attention looks different from child to child, and that the bucket prescribed to a 'one size fits all' approach.

The play-rich interventionist

While putting this chapter together, I engaged in numerous discussions with practitioners about their understanding of play and SEND. The responses had a lot of alignment, but what stood out most was that practitioners often have very little uninterrupted quality time with children to become fully immersed in understanding their play. If practitioners do not have time to make sense of children's play, many important play behaviours could be overlooked and therefore not adequately supported. This is where we may see practitioners focusing on surface play skills and who may end up simply looking for ways to 'fix' the child's play rather than to tune more deeply into it. For example, a colleague shared with me that she was supporting a child who seemed to stay in one play area, and they assumed he was not engaging in play because he wasn't accessing all the areas of continuous provision. Upon closer observation, they noticed that the reason he remained in this space was because he was fascinated by angles, edges and corners, and the shadow of the sun created an outline on the floor in which he could trace his fingers. It was also within this space that he could explore different blocks and bricks which had different edges. By leaning into this interest, the practitioners were able to build upon it rather than to assume it was simply a sign of a child reluctant to play. While we must integrate intervention approaches within these everyday experiences, I fully believe that more uninterrupted quality play time where a practitioner can be beside children in their play is a gateway for play-rich foundations for learning.

The play-rich interventionist:

- is not afraid to play
- knows that there is no optimal way to play and that there are infinite possibilities within play
- centres the child as competent, capable and the owner of their play
- recognises that forming a connection with a child may entail ups and downs, but that these are experienced on both parts, and it is a journey that practitioner and child go on together
- is not seeking compliance, conformity or to 'fix' the child, but rather uses the play and intervention as the springboard for learning, growth and optimal development
- looks for shared interests and intentions as the entry point for a play relationship
- sees the child as an individual within their own right, not simply tolerating the child, but deeply caring for and respecting them
- finds time to simply be with the child, enjoying the process of play and intervention, with no specific fixed agenda or outcome
- knows when to stand back and when to lean in to play, understanding that risk, rejection, resolution and patience are part of the learning process
- mirrors and models play skills and behaviours to empower the child
- communicates their availability to children, prioritises play and ensures that children feel valued and understood
- recognises when a child needs time away from play to rest and recharge
- reviews what works and what does not and adapts their practice to suit the different pace and needs of children.

Training in early intervention

While many settings will request training around specific needs, including intervention programmes, the reality is that they can quickly threaten personalisation. They can also place demands on practitioners' time. For example, I supported a setting that invested in an intervention programme and costly resources. Due to constraints, they could not deliver it in the way in which it should be delivered. Even worse news came when the person who had trained up in the role moved on to another setting. Settings should be mindful about this when deciding which intervention programmes to commission and should also think practically about how it can be delivered.

Similarly, I supported a school that used intervention programmes across the day, meaning that children with SEND were continually removed from their main environment, which again, resulted in play being interrupted and ended up creating more disruption to the routines and rhythms of the day. I often say as a golden rule that any interventions that take you out of the main environment must only do so if it is in the absolute best interests of the child. There have been many instances where this can work well, particularly if the child has quality time with a key person or can gain access to provision that cannot be provided within the main play spaces. For example, using large play equipment, sensory items or technology.

We often invest in intervention programmes because they offer a strong evidence base. This does not always mean that we should blindly believe that it will provide the answer to the child's needs. I am not against intervention programmes, but I do believe that there is a major gap in ensuring that we, as practitioners, utilise intervention, strategies and techniques to build on play rather than to take it away.

Playtime is happening all the time

Play partners

One of the most critical skills that a practitioner can develop in play is the ability to scaffold learning. This concept is often talked about but not always fully understood. The term originates from Vygotsky's notion of the zone of proximal development (1978). It describes the ways in which a skilful practitioner can help a child to construct and extend skills and knowledge. The practitioner offers responsive and tailored support so that the child can gain momentum and confidence in knowledge and skill-seeking, and is key for developing independent learning. Once this has occurred, the child assumes responsibility for that knowledge and can continue to seek new opportunities for learning (Van de Pol, 2010). For a child with SEND, the concept of scaffolding is crucial, and we may spend more time within the different zones, but the process remains the same. The other consideration for us as practitioners when supporting children's learning is that we may be acquiring new knowledge about alternative forms of learning. Therefore, we may also need to develop our confidence in engaging with new knowledge.

According to the National Strategies 'Learning, playing and interacting' good practice guide (DCSF, 2009b), skilful teaching requires practitioners to adopt a range of skills in the Early Years. Practitioners should consider the following.

Direct instruction, mirroring, modelling or demonstration

It is quite common for the practitioner to model how something could be used or provide instructions during play. It is common for practitioners to think that they should avoid direct instruction or teaching at all costs, but as with everything, there is a time and place for it. This is particularly beneficial in supporting children who may feel nervous about how to play.

The concept of 'presenting' activities and experiences for children is a common practice in Montessori settings. Activities are broken down step by step to support a child's sequential understanding, and time is given for the child to process how a resource or item may be played with (Davies, 2019). While we want to encourage creativity and divergent thinking, it is also good to show the possible ways to use a toy or resource so that the child gets the maximum benefits.

Providing assistance, support and guidance

We must support children to think for themselves, but they will need our help at times. By making ourselves available, we can begin to tune into the different ways in which a child may ask for help. A child with SEND may require hand-under-hand support, or they may non-verbally demonstrate that they need us. We should look for indicators of when a child might need help, and offer this in a supportive rather than invasive way.

Guided interaction

According to Rogers (1951, cited in Fisher, 2016), practitioners should view interactions as an opportunity to build bridges of knowledge from what the child already knows to what they can learn. Practitioners need to know which 'hooks' to attach interactions onto. This is especially important when supporting children with SEND because speaking may not be the preferred form of communication. It is here where visuals, objects of reference and holistic communication come in handy.

Participating in play

Play is something that practitioners should be thinking about a lot. Reflections on play must occur so that the environment and space are forever evolving. A play-rich practitioner will play alongside, nearby and with children so that they can gain a perspective of that play, and use opportunities to extend, inspire and ignite play curiosity. To be a play-rich practitioner, you must take time to play, as demonstrated in the following activity.

Activity: Playtime

One of the most crucial activities that practitioners should engage in is play within the Early Years environment. Often, we set up, plan out and design early environment spaces without ever actually playing in them ourselves. Plan time, for example during a team meeting, to play within the environment child-free. Ask yourself the following questions:

- Is it inviting and interesting?
- Do the spaces and resources engage me?
- Can I access resources and engage in key tasks independently?
- Does the layout make sense?
- Are there different spaces for different moods?
- Is it communication friendly?
- Is it sensory friendly?
- Are there any barriers that may get in the way of my play?

Case study: Playtime

During my last training session, I set playtime as a gap task and these are the things that practitioners reported back to me:

'I noticed that I am always repeating to children where things are located or how resources should be accessed, and when playing in the art corner, I noticed how chaotic and confusing it was. I had to keep stopping and looking for things, and it was so busy so quickly I became overwhelmed. Nothing had a "home". I hadn't even labelled anything.'

'The block corner was spacious but contained by shelving units, and I enjoyed being able to hide away and retreat while I was constructing. I felt uninterrupted.'

'It was immediately loud, the noise just bounced off every corner, and I noticed that everything was a hard surface. The acoustics just made the space seem so much louder, and I couldn't concentrate.'

'It was too busy with colours and all the things I might be interested in, such as artwork or images, I had to strain my neck to look up and see.'

'When I went over to the hand-washing sink, the images helped me to know what to do. I never realised how useful sequenced images could be, and there was a mirror so I could smile at myself.'

Teaching play skills

I am often asked what types of play skills we should be supporting in children with SEND, and this often depends on the strengths, interests, differences and needs of the child, but generally, children in the Early Years should be supported with the following:

- identifying specific interests
- showing willingness to initiate play, to explore and to sustain some attention in things that interest them
- trying to figure things out through exploration and risk-taking
- finding ways of seeking or 'asking' for help
- continuing to engage in forms of play even when problems arise
- developing some flexibility in thinking and play
- engaging with activities and experiences, and exhibiting enjoyment, concentration and focus
- making choices and decisions during play
- playing alongside, nearby and with peers and key people
- being able to effectively manage their own emotions during play
- being able to 'bounce back' when play is not going their way
- developing some understanding of the perspectives of other players.

Play intervention

According to Dunst and Trivette (2009), intervention can only be effective if the way in which we train and upskill interventionists is itself effective. Practitioners should not be simply instructed how to carry out an intervention, but they should also understand the benefits and impact on the child. According to Fletcher-Watson (2018), interventions can become problematic when they focus purely on correcting a child's deficits, and this can detract from the skill of building upon a child's interests and strengths to introduce new skills and learning. We should also consider how we measure the success of an intervention, and whether a neurotypical or normative set of outcomes is expected, as this is potentially incompatible with those children who will have lifelong learning differences – for example, a practitioner recently told me that they were using a communication intervention that focused on sitting still and listening as signs of attention. We discussed whether these were appropriate measures of success, and quickly established that there are huge variations in how children demonstrate the skill of attention. The practitioner shared an example of a child who would 'fidget' a lot but who could recall everything that occurred during the short session indicating that she was, in fact, engaged with the intervention activity. To suggest she had not met the outcomes of the intervention because she didn't remain still is an ableist mindset. Below are some additional considerations when thinking about how and if we use interventions within our Early Years spaces:

Is it child-led?: Interventions must have some flexibility to remain child-led and personalised. For many children with neurodevelopmental differences, the intervention can focus on 'fixing' their traits, but this should not be the main priority. Rather, the intervention should meet the child where they are at.

Child's voice: Fletcher-Watson (2018) makes the crucial point that we often measure the success of an intervention based on tests and measures that favour normative development. An intervention should actively seek to understand the views and perspectives of the child in receipt of that intervention. Settings should develop self-reporting practices so a child can indicate their feedback, and practitioners should tune-into signs of the intervention being supportive or stressful.

Consider the evidence-base, sustainability, purpose and format of the intervention: It is likely that local services have commissioned interventions and so you may be able to gain access to these within your local area. Check the evidence base, why the programme has been chosen and how it is delivered. I would also check how long the intervention is commissioned for, so that you can ensure regular access to training and upskilling.

Check whether it is play-rich and developmentally responsive: It is crucial that you check whether the intervention is suitable for the individual or group of children with whom you intend to use it, and for the Early Years, the key indicator is whether it is play-based and developmentally responsive. For example, does the intervention promote choices and exploration or does it cultivate social interaction?

Consider the feasibility of the intervention: Interventions often have a certain structure and design, and so you will need to consider whether you can actually commit to carrying out the intervention – for example, some programmes specify that the activities should be carried out at the same time every day or within the same environment. Is this feasible for your setting or are you likely to deliver it inconsistently? It is also useful to check the efficacy of the intervention – for example, if the child only demonstrates the skills within the intervention, and this does not translate into everyday skills, its success is actually limited.

Consider the training, skills and capacity for the intervention: How much commitment to training and upskilling is required for the intervention, and is this achievable? Is it possible to have all staff eventually trained up in the intervention?

How well will the intervention translate into everyday practice and across different environments? A significant issue with interventions is that they can appear separate from everyday experiences. How will you transfer the learning into the child's everyday routines, and have you considered how parents and carers will be upskilled?

Intervention programmes

There are many early intervention programmes available in the Early Years, and there are increasing resources to enable practitioners to review and decide upon the most appropriate intervention programmes, including those that are parent- and provider-led. The Early Intervention Foundation has an online guidebook where the evidence rating, cost-effectiveness and implementation can be considered. See guidebook.eif.org.uk. Programmes such as I CAN's Early Talk Boost can be reviewed, and short video clips can help a setting to decide whether they are worthwhile. It is important to consider how the skills promoted within these interventions fully benefit the child, and if they feel too adult-directed, it may be worth exploring other options. It is also vital to consider whether the skills within the intervention account for the diverse ways of learning.

Reimagining a definition of play for SEND

According to Eberle (2014), trying to functionally define play can result in us creating patrols and borders around play which can be limiting. He suggests that we should find comfort in accepting that play opens a vast open space of potential and can transcend in many ways. This idea of expanding our play borders could potentially allow us to think more broadly about the types and features of play and this could lead to more inclusive approaches for SEND. We tend to focus predominately on what we would describe as successful play, such as role playing or using our imagination, but is it only these forms of play that are to be favoured? This can be particularly difficult if we feed into stereotypes about conditions such as autism and thus believe children incapable of expressing these play attributes in their own ways. Whether or not to define play remains tricky, but what I believe we can do is begin to reimagine play, and to develop more curiosity about the diverse ways of playing. This could potentially lead us to a more play-rich pedagogy which welcomes all its players.

Top tips: Play

Uninterrupted play: When supporting children with SEND, we can often feel like we should be doing something more to direct their play. This can often come down to us not seeing value in their unique styles of exploration. Some children may engage in repetitive play, and we become focused on introducing new experiences, or other children may flit and we try to focus, but we should become comfortable with play that varies and is not always clear to us. The biggest thing to remember is that it doesn't need to make sense to us if it makes sense to the child.

Become a play detective: Contrary to what many practitioners believe, we do not always need to be centre stage in children's play. Often, we are using our detective skills to understand the play, so we may in fact spend time gathering evidence, engaging in curious conversations with others, and attempting to make sense of the play. This can take time and we have to trust that play is a process, not a product.

Follow the child's lead: We need to develop highly tuned-in observation skills when supporting children with SEND and we need to value the style of play. For example, rather than just seeing a child lining things up and not attributing any meaning, we should lean in and build on this play behaviour where appropriate, eventually extending it.

Interaction over invasion: Julie Fisher (2016) uses a great term about knowing when to 'meddle in the middle' with children at play. We should not invade children's play with our adult agendas – for example, focusing on numbers when the child is motivated by sensory experiences.

Mirroring and modelling play: We must value the play of the child and so mirroring is a crucial form of connecting. Respecting and valuing the child's play will lead to their curiosity in our play. It is only then that we should use modelling to further promote play. As a play partner, you can play in parallel or demonstrate through your own playing skills. Research has also found that video modelling can be highly effective for children with SEND – for example, filming block play and enabling the child to watch in order to learn.

Be distraction-aware: Play can be disrupted with distractions. Research has suggested that early childhood environments can be quite detrimental for attention skills because they can be overstimulating. Children with SEND may not be able to communicate that the swirling pom poms hanging from the ceiling keep invading their play or that the strip lighting is elevating their stress levels.

Zones of regulation: Children's play and engagement varies at different stimulation levels, and sometimes they wish to play in different spaces according to their mood – for example, retreating to a space of privacy where they may engage in private speech or engaging in relaxed play in a cosy corner.

Play is the intervention

Research has consistently found that by supporting play, you can help to support a wealth of skills. However, we can move into an instructional mode, and this can be overwhelming for the child. Try to meet the child where they are and embrace their play, even if it doesn't 'look' like what you are used to.

Make yourself available

Children need availability and uninterrupted time to play alongside a key person; having you physically near can make a huge difference. It can seem like there is always something more pressing to do but try not to take the most important resource away from the environment, which is YOU!

Interruption or interaction

At the same time, available doesn't mean always being immersed in the child's play. It might be that you are on hand to support, or you mirror, model and make yourself available for play.

Intervene for independence

Our purpose in early intervention is not to attach ourselves to the child but to ensure that we are facilitating independence.

Embrace routines and rhythms

Interventions or strategies often appear separate to the main curriculum. Still, we should consider how intervention programmes transfer into everyday practices.

Try not to take it outside

While there is a time and place for out-of-class interventions, they are not always ideal for children because they can interfere with meaningful social and emotional learning opportunities. It is crucial to think about a balance that is supportive and empowering to the child, and for interventions not to become a fragmented part of their early learning experience.

It doesn't have to make sense to you if it makes sense to the child

We often don't recognise play as play because it doesn't make sense to us or does not follow the usual pathway of progress. We should be mindful not to judge this as making no sense or having no meaning. Remember that all behaviour is communication, and that includes play-based behaviours.

'All he does is line things up'

Signposts and resources

LEGO Foundation: 'Learning through play: A review of the evidence'

Available at: www.legofoundation.com/media/1063/learning-through-play_web.pdf

LEGO Foundation: 'Neuroscience and learning through play: A review of the evidence'

Available at: www.legofoundation.com/media/1064/neuroscience-review_web.pdf

8 'How is she going to cope without me?': Developing wellbeing for all during transitions

Starting points

Transitions are a significant aspect of early childhood, and a time when children learn to manage the emotional and physical experiences of change. Transition can cause feelings of uncertainty. Think about how uncertainty makes you feel as an adult:

- What feelings does uncertainty evoke?
- What do you do to manage this uncertainty?
- How can others support you through uncertainty?

Introduction

Imagine that feeling you get when you have to shift gears from one thing to another. These can often be minor things, such as going from the weekend into the working week or going from socialising to relaxing. Or they can be more significant things such as moving home or transitioning to a new job. These experiences, even when positive, require us to be flexible, open-minded and resilient. We can often manage the changes within our life because we have become accustomed to them happening. We have had time to practice and predict scenarios. We can tune into our emotional dials to keep ourselves in check. We may also experience challenging transitions that leave us feeling disorientated and out of sorts. It is here that we rely on our prior positive experiences to know that change is inevitable and that we can navigate our way through.

As adults, we talk about how transitions impact us continuously, whether personal or professional; we are engaged in situational and emotional change experiences. This is demonstrated in the following case study.

Reflection: The new normal

For many of us during the Covid-19 pandemic, we have had to adjust to what many refer to as a 'new normal'. This time has been one of increased uncertainty due to the many transitions – for example, in and out of lockdowns. As restrictions have eased, there have been numerous situations where we have had to plan for transition – for example, when going to places such as shops. Previously, we knew the social rules and expectations but with new safety regulations, we have had to manage several changes. Think of the times you have walked into a shop, and suddenly been faced with those new systems, such as wearing face masks, navigating one-way systems, and not being able to pick things up freely as you browse. Now think of those things that made the transition easier such as the use of arrows on the floor to direct you, visual prompts and reminders, and shop assistants who offer a helping hand.

- Can you think of a similar example where you have had to manage a transition?
- What feelings did the transition ignite?
- How did you prepare yourself?
- How might you have felt if something didn't go to plan?

You may read this case study and find it an odd description for transition and an odd place to start when we are talking about SEND, but it is important for practitioners to recognise that the things they plan for when supporting young children are often the things that they have to support themselves with on a daily basis. Therefore, we are often much better equipped than we realise to engage in the ongoing, continuous and active process of transition for children.

Transition is not just about 'school readiness' (but it is an important step for children with SEND)

When I came to write this chapter, I started to read and absorb as much information about transition as possible. Still, I kept finding myself coming up against the same brick wall. Contrary to the definition of transition being a process rather than an event, there is often a dominant focus on the milestone event of going to 'big school'. While there is no denying that this is a significant time for young children, we must not forget that transitions occur across the Early Years, and indeed life phase. These can form the steady foundations for bigger milestones. Transitions are one of the golden threads that runs throughout a child's early experiences and provide us with lots of 'teachable moments' for children in which we can help them effectively manage change.

Defining transition

The definitions of transition are often linked to how children are prepared for school, often referred to as 'school readiness'. For this chapter, I have developed my own definition, which accounts for transition across the Early Years phase and for children with SEND:

- Transition is the psychological and situational process of experiencing different types of change, including daily rhythms, routines and milestone events.

- It is a process that is underpinned by a child's emotional capacity to manage both expected and unexpected change, separations from people and places, and requires the maintenance of trust and flexibility of mind.

- It is recognised as a continuous, ongoing and active process, which, if adequately supported by warm and responsive key people, can help maintain resilience, curiosity and a sense of belonging.

- Transitions that are inclusive do not focus on blanket approaches, rather, they focus on individual needs, and adaptations are implemented where appropriate. The diverse transitional needs of children are considered, and planned for, and should aim to empower the child.

Types of transition

Transition travels in different directions and is therefore broken down into three types.

Horizontal transitions

These refer to the everyday experiences that occur within and beyond the setting and can include the morning journey to the nursery or a childminder, moving from play to snack or from person (key person) to person (parent). These transitions present perfect 'teachable moments' for practitioners to cultivate trust, continuity and predictability. However, these transitions can often become chaotic because we don't tend to have much 'buffering time' to support a range of needs. I have completed countless observations of children becoming highly stressed during lunchtime transitions or indoors to outdoors. For children with SEND, it is these transitions that elicit stress, resistance and confusion. Refer to the case study below.

Case study: Consistent visuals

Asim has been attending nursery for six weeks. The setting planned a thorough and personalised transition because Asim has complex needs and requires additional support. They are told by parents that he uses a specific visual routine, and they provide symbol cards to support Asim when he changes from one activity to another – for example, playtime to snack time. His key person loses some of the visuals so begins using a selection from different programmes and a few photographs. Asim becomes highly stressed, as he does not understand the combination of symbols.

This case study is taken from a selection of real examples and could have easily been avoided if the significance of the visuals was understood. While other children may be able to distinguish between a photograph, line drawing, clip art or symbols, children with SEND often have visuals that support their unique needs. By focusing on the potential stressors of these daily transitions, we can work to reduce them, thus having more 'smooth running' experiences of routines and rhythms.

The conveyor belt routines

We must also develop respectful transitions because we can often fall into the habit of treating children as though they are on a conveyor belt in order to maintain caregiving routines such as nappy changes. Far too often I have observed children being swooped from behind as they are taken off for a nappy change or to a snack table. These invasions can be unsettling and scary to children, and no matter the age of a child, we must be at their level, not just physically but emotionally tuned into the possible discomfort of being taken from safe spaces. When interacting with children in this way, we must seek to do the following:

- Ask permission (Can I take you to change your nappy, please?).
- Give affirmation (I know you are still playing, so I can wait here a moment until you are ready).
- Tune in to verbal and non-verbal cues to ensure 'readiness' for the transition – for example, look for signs of consent such as reaching for you, nodding or leaning in.

Internal transitions

This transition refers to the movements between stage phases, such as a child moving from baby to toddler room. These transitions give us ample opportunity to practise for movements beyond the setting that benefit the adult and child. Mixing age groups is beneficial for children's development and can be used to introduce children to different types of play and spaces. For example, as a practitioner, I would often take small groups of children to other rooms to spend quality time with other children, and to get to know the other spaces within our nursery environment. When the time came for transition, I had taken away a little of the unknown.

Case study: Mirroring movements

When I worked as a nursery practitioner, I was often supporting children with transition into the pre-school room. I made a habit of taking children up to the room for short visits, but I also developed a system of mirroring experiences. For example, if I had a child that was attached to a certain toy or resource, I would also ask for that to be made available in the next room. I would also communicate to the next key person how the child used different spaces. The key person could then mirror those experiences for the child and could create some sparks of familiarity. I had one child who loved the cosy corner, and so for the first few weeks, that is where the morning handover took place, and it made a world of difference for the child to be able to settle.

Practitioners should also consider the role of attachment within transition – for example, the child going from one key person (secure base) to another, and how that separation may feel for the practitioner, child and family. It is also common for key person changes, and these also need to be managed sensitively. Children develop blueprints from the caregiving that we provide, and changes can threaten the consistency and continuity of their attachment. The use of additional staff can occur when there is a child with SEND, and the setting should consider who is most appropriate for carrying out the key person role.

Vertical transitions

The vertical transitions refer to the significant changes within a child's life. Although we immediately think of 'big school', children can actually be experiencing several vertical transitions at any one time. As practitioners, we should be mindful of this constant newness, and however exciting, it is also a demanding process. It can be made even more so when we place too much emphasis on the vertical transitions, as demonstrated in the following parent's voice.

Parent's voice

I am so fed up with hearing the words 'big school'. The pressure for me and my child is just too much. The anticipated excitement quickly turns to anxiety when I consider all these new big milestones my child will have to face, knowing that many of those 'big' experiences are going to be hugely challenging for us as a family. The scratchy material of his new school jumper, his refusal to get dressed in the morning, managing three children on the walk, knowing he likes to run off, the sensory overloads from the dinner hall. This may be big and exciting for many but for me, please can you make this moment smaller and more manageable?

As you can see from this example, vertical transitions, no matter what the context, can have a certain fragility to them if we aren't tuned into individual differences and experiences. Often the focus can be on new beginnings rather than endings, and in our haste to prepare children, we likely miss out on those key quality-time moments just to be in each other's presence acknowledging the magnitude of that transitional ending.

Practitioner's voice

Children with SEND can form strong bonds with those caring for them. Leaving for school or another setting can be a major upheaval. The impact is felt by the child, the family and the new setting. We get to know a child's quirks, their personality, preferences, facial expressions, gestures, etc. These cues, no matter how small, can be the difference between a child being happy and thriving or unsettled and misunderstood. We can write reports and send data to the setting but sometimes it's the unwritten information we store – that tacit knowledge we don't even realise we know.

Definition: School readiness

'A culmination of all the essential social, emotional, cognitive and autonomy building competences that have been developed during the child's early years.' (Peckham, 2017, pg. 2)

Secure relationships & key people

'Key Adults act as a "surrogate secure base" which can contain the inevitable anxiety engendered by the challenges of learning.' (Geddes, 2006, pg. 141)

At the heart of our Early Years framework is the key person, whose role is particularly important in ensuring children's emotional security. The key person model became a statutory requirement in the 2008 EYFS statutory framework (DCSF) and is underpinned by attachment theory (Bowlby & Ainsworth, 2013). Most practitioners have heard of the term 'attachment' or of John Bowlby, but the development of attachment-informed practices is still very much ongoing. It is particularly challenging to achieve in large settings. The key person continues to be confused with an administrative role – for example, assigning children to practitioners based on workload instead of bond.

According to Taggart (2013), key people have the potential to be 'agents of compassion' (para. 8), recognising that their availability and ability to meet needs provides the basis for a special relationship (cited in Prowle & Hodgkins, 2020). I am often asked, 'Is it OK to change a child's key person if they show a preference for another practitioner?' My answer is a resounding YES! The key person model should be informed by our desire for children to feel safe and secure, because these features of attachment provide a springboard for learning.

To 'deeply understand'

'Transition is potentially traumatic for young children, but in an emotionally supportive climate, where children experience a sense of being deeply understood, there should be a diminishment of psychological threat.' (Prowle & Hodgkins, 2020, pg. 4)

When it comes to allocating children with SEND to a key person, the 'old school' habit was to choose the setting's SENDCo, although it is rare for the setting to adopt this mindset nowadays. Still, it has always concerned me that these children often require the most consistency in a relationship, as their individual differences can make changes and transitions difficult. I have worked with practitioners before who have been cautious about being named key person to a child, even though the child has shown an emotional preference for that practitioner. Still, because of the anxiety associated with supporting children with SEND, practitioners can miss opportunities to develop a deeper understanding of children, including why differences aren't to be viewed with ambivalence. When I was a key person, I also felt this anxiety. It is important to remember that there are great rewards in supporting a child to belong and being committed to deeply understanding.

Lead with empathy, and you will lead the way…

'Much of today's popular advice ignores the world of emotions. Instead, it relies on child-rearing theories that address the children's behaviour but reject the feelings that underlie that behaviour.' (Gottman, 1997, pg. 16)

Prowle and Hodgkins (2020) discuss the role of empathy in transition, suggesting that empathy should show up in all our interactions and can act as a buffer to the unease of transition. They point out that this unease is felt by children, parents and practitioners. This is something that I often observe in practitioners, as they too worry about how the child will cope with change. The very title of this chapter, 'How is she going to cope without me?', is based on those many situations where practitioners reflect on the role that they have played in a child's life. As children move on, the practitioner has to confront that they will no longer be a physical presence. The legacy a practitioner leaves with a child is that they held that child in mind enough for the them to feel loved, safe and secure. That form of emotional presence has the potential to offer a long-lasting impact. Our desire is often that the next key person will take the trouble to work a child out in the way in which we have. Through informal chats, I hear the detailed investigations that key people carry out to deeply understand children. Despite these qualities being viewed as the naturally gifted talents of a caregiver, they are skills that must be developed. Through our continual demonstrations of care, we tap into the needs and perspectives of others.

Activity: Attachment

Imagine that you get a new job and you feel excited but nervous. Now note down all the things that could make your transition effective. Consider the following:
- How would you expect to be greeted on the first day, and who would you expect to meet?
- What types of experiences could help you to feel settled?
- How would you become familiar?
- What additional things could occur so that you feel like you belong?

Now consider the ways in which you build some of those experiences into your transitions within the setting.

In her book *Understanding Transition in the Early Years* (2017), Anne O'Connor provides a perfect analogy for thinking about attachment. She asks the reader to imagine that they are floating in space, attached only by a lifeline to a spaceship. This task allows us to think about the importance of being safe, secure and connected. O'Connor asks about how vital this lifeline is to us and what feelings it provokes. She asks the reader to imagine that the lifeline is suddenly cut, and we are left disconnected.

In this analogy, the spaceship signifies the safe spaces that children occupy – for example, the home or setting – and the lifeline is the attachment figure. Suppose we think of our role as practitioners. In that case, we have a huge responsibility for ensuring that children can thrive through their relationships. Though we may not be their lifetime attachment figure, we contribute to the child's trust in others. Our significance should never be underestimated. Developing attachment-informed practices can therefore go a long way in supporting children's wellbeing (Bayat, 2019).

Developing strong bonds with children requires minimal resources other than the adult. Below are some top tips for developing attachment-informed practices.

Top tips: Attachment aware

Being held in heart and mind: Transition can make children feel uncertain, and they may fear being forgotten. One of the most powerful things that we can do to help children feel secure is to tell them that we hold them in mind. Simple reminders of 'I'm thinking of you' or 'I will think of you' can be grounding for a child and essentially communicate that they exist and are important to us.

Hellos and goodbyes: Meaningful rituals for endings and beginnings can be hugely supportive for the child who is moving from known to unknown relationships. This shouldn't necessarily require a huge amount of planning, as it can become difficult to sustain and it may differ from child to child. One practitioner drew a heart on three pebbles and explained that she would keep one, the child could keep one and the other should be given to the new key person. This creates a transitional link.

The cycle of trust: The key person is often referred to as a secondary attachment figure or an attachment back-up, and so we can support a child's inner working model of trust by aiming to be warm, responsive and consistent. One of the ways in which we can develop trust is to be tuned into experiences that might cause stress for the child and seek to find ways to meet the child's needs. Once a child recognises that we can be trusted, they can focus on the busy tasks of play.

Being 'good enough': The psychoanalyst Donald Winnicott (1953) first suggested the idea of a 'good enough' mother when considering attachment and bonding. Through his observations of thousands of mother–child interactions, he concluded that the way to be good at caregiving was to be just that: good enough. Being perfect is neither possible nor desirable (O'Connor, 2017).

Be a springboard: It is important to recognise that we become attached to children, and sometimes we can also develop some dependence on that relationship. Viewing ourselves as a springboard is important because we essentially want our bond to lead to the child's growth. Koplow (2007) talks about the concept of being by a child's side but also letting them explore and take risks. An Early Years practitioner is a big presence in the beginning, and our emotional impact is enduring but sadly our physical presence is not. Part of our role is to set our children up with the emotional tools and skills for pastures new.

Transition and SEND

Practitioner's voice

It has taken me 18 months to establish a routine and rhythm that works for Sophie. Through trial and error, I have established that she thrives on the predictability and sameness of my childminder setting. While I know that a school-based setting will actually support this aspect of her personality, it is important for them to understand that her routine won't necessarily match their idea of a routine. My priority will be to share her routine booklet, which includes all the aspects of 'sameness' that she thrives on, such as having her favourite plate at lunch, being able to keep her smelly sock in her pocket at all times, her need to engage in trajectory play several times a day and her Now & Next board, which helps me to move her into new experiences.

Uncertainty

It is often assumed or taken for granted that children understand their immediate routines and rhythms. Often practitioners can become exasperated when a child becomes stressed or frustrated. Imagine all the first experiences that you have had where your feelings of uncertainty have made you feel stressed. Often it can come down to really simple things such as the first time we need to get a train to somewhere new or enter a building and navigate our way around. Think back to the earlier reflection about the global pandemic and the 'new normal'. We have become accustomed to different routines and rhythms. Think about how this uncertainty has made you feel and what we have relied on to feel safe. I bet that signs and visuals have helped, or the person explaining the step-by-step instructions, or the objects of reference, or pointers or emails sent beforehand. All these strategies work to reduce our uncertainty and stress, yet we often overlook the importance of doing this for children in systems that, to us, seem straightforward and self-explanatory.

While a degree of uncertainty is considered good for our learning, this applies to a child who has developed adequate self-regulation skills, communication and executive function. For a child who may have differences in these areas, uncertainty can cause significant stress (Herry et al., 2007). Transition is not always about preparing the child; rather, it is about being self-prepared as a supportive, responsive and tuned-in adult. If we start with ourselves, we can then work outwards to the environment, the practice, the partnerships and, eventually, our setting's culture.

Top tips: Transitions – prepare and provide

What to expect: When children are experiencing transitions, it can be unsettling. They have become accustomed to your environment, routines and key people. Practitioners should consider ways in which to support children in knowing what to expect. For example, video recordings can help children to process and understand what is to be expected, so a short show-round that can be sent to the parents means that they can help to prepare the child for a new environment.

Who to expect: The change in attachment figure is a significant emotional experience for a child, and it is important to have some familiarity with the person who will be their 'go-to'. Practitioner passports or accessing staff photos on websites can be useful to reduce stranger anxiety. Similarly, a video introduction can go a long way in helping a child to feel reassured. If the child uses a particular strategy such as Makaton, recording a short hello using key signs can be the beginning of a connection.

Familiarity and predictability: Children with SEND often need to have a good grasp of daily rhythms and routines, and this can help them to feel safe. Along with understanding the layout of the environment, it is also useful to share a typical daily routine. You might consider a child-friendly version and a more detailed routine for the parents, so that they can let you know of any challenges the child may experience. For example, a parent may notice that all the children join together at lunch, and this may be potentially overwhelming for a child with sensory processing differences. This type of information supports you to make decisions about reasonable adjustments.

Opportunities for independence: The environment and experiences that you plan within your Early Years setting should have opportunities for independence. For this to be equitable for all children, you will need to consider different ways of demonstrating independence. For example, photo routines are not easily processed by all children, and so you may need to consider line drawings or clearer visual cues.

Case study: Consistency in transition

The above tips focus on what you can do as a setting, but often practitioners are concerned about feeder settings or schools. Manzoor is the manager of a large nursery and has a high number of children with SEND. He knew that some of the ideas he used for transition would be useful for his feeder schools. He knew that they might not always have the time to meet, so at the beginning of each year, he set up a small 'Our Transitions' booklet with key practices and ideas. It was a gentle nudge to the school to perhaps adopt similar approaches for consistency. Over time, this avenue of communication provided a gateway for more collaborative working and discussions, and eventually, those partnerships were established in transition.

Timing transitions

A common tool for supporting internal transitions is the use of a 'Now & Next' board. We often target these strategies at children with SEND, but it can be a universal practice that can become more specific with individual needs. Whenever I mention visual support to practitioners, they often begin to think of Velcro®, laminators, symbols, boards and lots of preparation. While there is a time and place for this, 'Now & Next' can generally be pretty straightforward, and I often used a small A4 whiteboard and a whiteboard marker. Every practitioner should develop some confidence in line drawing because it can save a lot of time. I simply produced key line drawings that matched the visual programme that I was using. I would draw out what was happening now and next, as in Figure 12.

The use of a whiteboard enables you to be able to prepare children more efficiently for change and, matched with some non-verbal actions, can help a child to engage. When one task ends, you can move on and continue this rotation throughout the day (Figure 13).

There may be other visuals, but as a starting point for communicating changes, most practitioners can pick this up pretty quickly. It can also be useful to use props for starting and finishing – for example, sand timers to provide ample reminder of a change, or push-button lights. These types of items can also support reciprocal communication as children access resources independently. It is also crucial to remember that you need to often provide specific information for a child with SEND, and break this down. If you suggest that a change will happen, try to ensure that you do this in a timely manner.

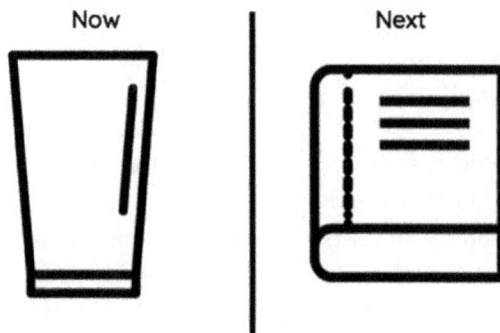

Figure 12: *Now and next*

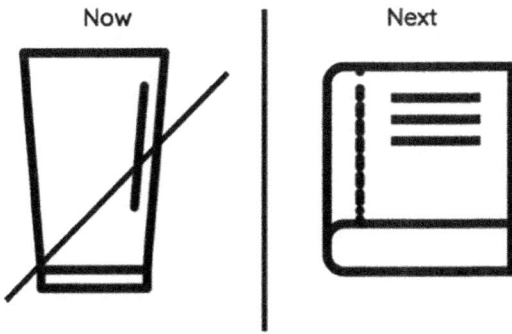

Figure 13: *Now and next in use*

Sequencing

Breaking information down into manageable chunks is one of the most helpful things that you can do when a child is dealing with change. Therefore, when we consider transition, we must consider the task-specific and event-specific experiences that may pose as stressors. It is usual for us to take pictures of environments or collect information about routines, but this may need to be broken down further for children with SEND.

Transitional objects

One of the most awful experiences that I had as a consultant was when I was supporting a child with significant emotional and behavioural difficulties. The child sought to connect but when his needs were not met, he would engage in behaviours that even I felt shocked to see in such a young child. It was one of those moments where I really felt confused about why the child was experiencing such intense reactions. During the visit, I noticed a rather large bear on the top of a shelf in the office and commented on it. The manager informed me that this was Berty and belonged to the child in question. When I asked why it was up on the shelf, I was told that it had been taken away from the child because it was too big. Berty, I found out, went everywhere with the child and provided his greatest source of comfort. So why would anyone take him away? The child hovered near the door, staring at Berty. At that exact moment, very early on in my consultancy career, I realised that our lack of training can lead to very harmful practices. While I knew that Berty would not be the solution to the child's emotional challenges, his removal from the child was clearly exacerbating his uncomfortable feelings. I have debated with many practitioners over the years about the importance of transitional objects, especially during transition itself. Yet they still seem to be something that we are desperate to wean children off. I do wonder what would happen if those same practitioners walked into my training space and I took their phones away from them – an item that holds significant emotional value – would they maybe reconsider the harmful impact of this practice? Children need their creature comforts, and we must value their role in supporting children through change and emotional regulation. While there may be moments where we need to protect the item from damage or loss, they should never be taken away as a punishment or considered an interference.

Transitional object vs. object of transition

According to Winnicott (1991), the child uses transitional objects as an extension of their 'secure base', usually the parent. The child will keep this item in close proximity to feel soothed, secured and held in mind via the object. These objects are incredibly valuable during change and transition processes and can support the child to feel connected when separated. According to Whalley (2017), an object of transition is an object that becomes emotionally significant or symbolic because of its reminder of the 'secure base', and these can vary from day to day. The object may be selected by a caregiver or the child, but helps the child to feel safe and secure.

Parent's voice

My child will pick up a random item each day, even if it's just a Lego® brick, and keep it in his pocket. It's his piece of home when he is away from home, I guess.

Empowering others through shared knowledge

When I am with practitioners who have deep bonds with children, I see them as possessing wisdom about that child. Still, so often, wisdom doesn't always get passed on or received in the way in which it should. In short, transition procedures can end up being a job to do, rather than a process to value. The way in which we transition information does not need to be limited by paperwork or prescribed questions. Instead, our focus should be on developing quality information-sharing and systems that recognise that transition is unique and varied. Practitioners often put pressure on themselves to have the smoothest-running transition. Still, the reality is that it can be a messy process. Remember, it doesn't need to be perfect; it needs to be 'good enough'.

Case study: The banana on the table

During one of my SEND leadership courses, we explored the child's voice in great depth. It is often that the greatest anecdotes come directly from the practitioners and parents about the importance of advocating 'voice'. Adam was three years old and had a settled relationship with his key person Clare, who had spent a long time building a firm and secure bond. During his diagnosis, Clare had marvelled at all the little things that served as forms of communication – the way that spinning meant that Adam needed the toilet, and snatching was simply a way to let peers know that he wanted to be included. During annual leave, Clare was careful to ensure that all transition information was clearly explained. While on her holiday, she received a phone call stating that Adam had become inconsolable during snack time for the past two days. They knew they were missing something but were not quite sure what. 'Oh!' Clare exclaimed, 'You need to ensure that a banana is in the middle of the table.' As odd as this sounds, Clare knew that Adam loved bananas and it had become a comfort to him because, as his Dad explained, there was always a full fruit bowl at home and the banana was his favourite fruit. Low and behold, the banana solved the issue.

As educators we become investigators, looking for clues and pointers. We often don't realise just how many communication mysteries we are solving every day.

While it will be unlikely for our children to start a sentence with, 'Well, my perspective is…', it doesn't mean that they are not communicating their voice to us every single day in a whole heap of ways. We, as practitioners, as advocates, provide a platform for that voice through our daily actions, behaviours, approaches and systems.

Case study: Child's 'voice'

Liz had been receiving transition forms from the childminder for the past few years. Often these consisted of a basic set of questions with some vague answers. For example:

Q. 'What is important to me?'

A. 'Trains and mummy.'

Liz found that the transitional information felt at times quite tokenistic and it did not necessarily empower her to build connections with the children.

Liz decided to give the childminder a quick call, and after a short while, she learned the following about what was **important** to the child:

Charlie displays lots of affection towards his parents and can sometimes struggle to separate from them in the morning. It is **important** for Charlie to be met where possible by familiar adults such as his key person. It helps if Charlie is met outside of the main environment, as noise and busy spaces can lead to him feeling overwhelmed. It is **important** for Charlie to have a transitional object, such as his Thomas train, as this provides comfort and helps him to settle.

It is **important** for Charlie to be understood. He is non-verbal and so his communication passport, which is attached to his backpack, will provide key indicators of his needs and wants. He also has a communication dictionary, as he will use different actions to indicate different needs – for example, spinning means that he is excited, and pulling at his waistband means that he needs the toilet.

It is **important** for Charlie to be with his peers. He can become confused if the other children do not acknowledge him, and he may sometimes take hold of them to say hello. Teaching his peers his main forms of communication helps him to connect with others.

Charlie loves to spin things and so it is **important** to have items in the environment that he can spin. It is also **important** to embed this interest into his play because it gives him the motivation to try new things.

As you can see from this case study, there is so much more that is important to the child, and a curious conversation led to information that could actually be utilised in practice. Feed the next educator's curiosity by asking yourself, 'What information will empower and equip the next educator so that my key child can thrive?'

Circles of connection

Children with SEND are often engaged with other services and specialists, and their interventions will have continued in some format during Covid-19 lockdowns. For example, assessments have taken place online in a virtual format, and practitioners have demonstrated key strategies for a home-based setting. Where possible, practitioners, should make contact with specialists to discuss the continuation and transition of strategies and techniques. Discuss whether there are new ways of delivering interventions and discuss the progress. The sharing of information will lead to greater knowledge about how to meet the child's needs. Liaise with specialists and parents so that you can build a clear picture in preparation for transition. In preparing for transition, consider the following:

- In-person or virtual supervision will be crucial during this time to gauge the emotional mindsets of practitioners. Identify specific anxieties around the return of children and consider how we prepare for the varying needs of children.

- View parents as co-educators and place a high value on their knowledge and expertise. Explore home routines and home learning, including the benefits and challenges. This will give you key starting points for the transition.

Reflection

We often think of the ways in which we help children to become ready for transitions, but in what ways do we make ourselves, as practitioners, ready? Transition is happening to us too, and our own emotional resilience can be impacted.

Top tips: Preparing yourself for transition

Anticipatory knowledge is power – Try to gather as much information as possible especially around care routines, comfort cues and the ways in which main needs are communicated. Ask whether there are particular toys, ways of playing or transitional resources which might be of support. Check the child's communication preferences. If the child has SEND, using a communication passport early on can help you to build a clear picture.

Quality time – Often we refer to transition as 'settling in' but it is also important to remember that it serves as an early opportunity for quality time. Ensure that you have uninterrupted time to focus on building a bond with the child, and tuning-in. Try to focus on being by the child's side and mirror their play as a way of connecting. Settling can often also be used to gather lots of information, and ask lots of questions, but ensure this quality time is relatively relaxed and non-demanding.

Give it time and repetition – If a child has SEND, acknowledge that it might take a bit longer for you to both feel settled with one another. It is not a failing on your part if the child resists coming into the setting or does not appear to feel comfortable with you. Try to remain consistent and repeat experiences that are positive for the

'How is she going to cope without me?'

child. Do not distract the child from their distress, rather acknowledge it, and sit with it. Often we think we need to eradicate the distress caused by transition, but the way to resolve it is to validate that it is indeed a difficult experience.

Access supervision support – One of the biggest breakdowns in transition for SEND is when a key person does not feel able to work through some of their own uncomfortable emotions when a child needs further support to transition. Request supervision support or ensure that there is time and space to talk through some of the barriers. Also celebrate the wins.

Transition is a psychological process, and change is situational... prepare for both

It is important to remember that the process of transition is rooted in belonging. When children's environments and key people change, this can impact on their psychological experiences of safety and security. Be attachment-informed in transition.

Transition is experience-orientated, not task-driven

Transition is part and parcel of every day, and if we manage the smaller transitions well, the bigger ones will be well prepared for.

Strengthen the transition lifeline

If we view the child as holding onto a transition lifeline, we can focus on ensuring that they remain strong as they progress. The best way to strengthen a transition lifeline is to provide high-quality information exchange. Think about the main headlines of information that you would want the next key person to know.

The concept of being 'held in mind'

When they are leaving you, whether it be for the day or for a next setting, you should let the child know that they are held in mind and that you think of them. This can provide children with a sense of safety and security.

Transitions affect everyone

Transitions are happening to all of us, and as a key person, you will also feel the emotion of separation. Take care of yourself during more significant transitions, and acknowledge your feelings.

Transition needs to be 'good enough', not perfect

Transition can be an unsettling process, and so we must acknowledge that 'good enough' is good enough. It is key for practitioners to keep communication open, to ask questions and to be open to problem-solving.

Transition is unique

While settings may have universal systems for supporting transitions, you must be flexible to the individual and family needs as a practitioner. It is highly likely for children with SEND that a child may need a specific type of support during the transition. Agree on the exchange of information early on so that you can be developing transitional resources over time.

Good transitions should be a springboard

A good transition should act as a springboard from one state to another. Children's wellbeing should be maintained and supported. While not all changes are good, all transitions can be.

'How is she going to cope without me?'

Signposts and resources

Transitions for children with SEND
Kinderly
Available at: www.youtube.com/watch?v=MrbUxwLud8c

Conclusion: Where do we go from here?

When I came to write this book, I realised pretty quickly that each chapter could be a book in itself. For so long, I have signposted practitioners to websites, resources, guides and strategies while fully knowing that they only scratch the surface of inclusion. It is an area in which we are forever evolving and learning. Even after 14 years, I unlearn, relearn and learn something new every day. At times, this can feel majorly overwhelming, and I always find myself saying, 'It seems like you can't do right for doing wrong in SEND.' This is absolutely OK, though. It is usually the most significant indicator that we are showing up every day for our children and families. The words at the start of this book about inclusion as a constant state of becoming rather than being (Nutbrown, 2013) stick with me throughout this role, as I realise that the Early Years is in a constant state of flux. Is it exhausting? Sure, but I have come to realise that, as a sector, we possess a wealth of knowledge, and I wanted this book to in some way capture our learning, both the good and challenging aspects.

This book could not have been written without the practitioners with whom I have worked over the years, the parents I remain in awe of as they navigate what sometimes feels like a battlefield, and the children who continue to show me their ways of learning beyond those normative expectations. For the practitioner, I want this book to have given you a toolkit of ideas and reflections and to help you feel sure of your competencies and skills. Throughout the book, I came back to the same point, time and time again: the fact that we do all this work under ever increasing pressures. Yet there are so many celebratory examples of children getting what they need because we refuse to back down. Therefore, this book is an ode to the rights of children for which we continually try to advocate.

My best advice going forward is that beyond what we must do, settings should develop their own unique inclusive pedagogy, and when the challenges threaten to overwhelm them, they should always return to those basic principles. For children to thrive, they need someone who believes in them, shows up for them every day and works with their potential. We are enough as a sector, but we deserve better in our role as advocates. It felt apt to end this book with a dialogue with a practitioner about their SEND experience – realising that, despite the complexities, providing support actually comes down to some basic principles…

Closing conversation: A dialogue on play, meeting children where they are and the power of an available adult

David has worked as a one-to-one support worker for two children with SEND. He has connected with both children through a shared love of video games, and our original discussion was a general exploration of his experiences of one-to-one but soon expanded into play, connection and our availability.

Kerry: You became a one-to-one support for a child. What did that mean to you and how did it come about?

David: I was in a primary school, working part time in our programme for socially marginalised two-year-olds and their families, and I needed extra work. They offered me the role of being a one-to-one in the afternoon for a boy in Year 2. He was one of those kids you heard stories about, running in corridors, hiding under tables, not really getting targeted support until this point. Sadly, I had no real training, and I had to wing lots of things with him as I was totally learning as I was going. I truly think we've got to a good place, but the hard truth is it took a lot of ups and downs and frustration on both our parts.

Kerry: What was the root of those frustrations?

David: I think I was frustrated because I didn't have a clear idea of my role. I knew little about autism and I didn't really know what my goals were with him each afternoon. In this vacuum it was honestly very hard not to fall at times into a cop or 'enforce compliance' mindset. So it became, 'You do this work,' (that neither of us cared about) 'and then you can play on the laptop.' He was fascinated by Mario Kart and enjoyed using technology but that wasn't valued as 'proper work'.

I played these games as a child, and our shared interest was the entry point into our relationship. I am convinced that what really turned the corner in our relationship, and his later ability to cope with and grow at school, was introducing him to the world of computer emulators.

Kerry: What is an emulator?

David: Emulators are computer programs that allow you to run and play video games on a computer. The important bit here was they also give you the opportunity to save your progress. For weeks, every transition away from playing a game was a 'battle'. Home-time is home-time and playing the games in the browser meant he could never save his progress. So, he might get close to beating XYZ level, and then he had to stop! As someone who played video games as a child, I could empathise with that frustration.

Once I set this up on the laptop, and he realised he could get further in the game, and return to the same spot the next time, the battles over home-time disappeared. It immediately made our relationship more secure, and looking back, I think it lessened a daily source of stress for him. This gave us both some more room for him to grow emotionally and academically.

Kerry: It does make you wonder how our children perceive our actions of care. Do they see the ways in which we are seeking to understand them, especially those children that may have the experience of rotating adults or different support staff? What purpose did the one-to-one have? It so often gets confused as just being someone continually attached to a child, and we hear terms such as 'Velcro® Vera' to describe the dependency that occurs in that relationship.

David: I was getting acclimated to the mostly unspoken feeling in the air that some kids 'get' to go on a laptop because no one knows how to deal with them in the school context. I didn't buy this fully, but I must have to a degree, and felt the pressure of assuming that other staff were judging me: 'Why can't David make him do any schoolwork?' No one said this ever, but it was in my head, and there is rarely enough time for colleagues in education to honestly talk and debrief with each other. A lot of assumptions fill this void. Anyway, I sincerely think that demonstrating enough care and respect for his interest in video games, by figuring out how to install and use an emulator, was a key part of the deepening of our relationship. Beforehand I think I must have been clearly demonstrating that I was only 'tolerating' him. I know I don't have much interest in having relationships with people who might 'tolerate' my interests in life; why would it be any different for this child? I learned a lot from this experience. He reminded me of the absolute importance of seeing each child as a full human and individual in their own right. The sad truth is that the crammed timetables and constant rushing around, trying to do a million things at once in the UK education system, makes achieving this a true challenge.

My recent experience of helping run a 'Covid bubble' for mostly nursery-aged children has further shown me the importance of educators – and children! – having some true time and space to simply be with each other. We had so many children, SEND or otherwise, who demonstrated so much in such a short amount of time.

Kerry: What do you think happened in the bubbles to make those differences?

David: We didn't do as much damn stuff! Our timetables were bare. There were fewer children. Us adults simply had less to do and this made it possible for us to truly respond in a different way. We were interacting more and deeper with them – as opposed to spending our time and energy conducing crowd control and trying to cram in a timetable.

Since there were fewer children – and fewer adults – I could set up the outdoor environment more how I wanted. There was a trapeze and a rope ladder. I let children engage in significantly supposedly 'riskier' play than I would have otherwise. The children had more time to organically play with each other and in the process develop physically, emotionally and socially. Children labelled as 'low' (we all absolutely have to kill this word in our thoughts and practice) or 'quiet', who had never spoken a word to an adult in nursery pre-Covid, were chatting up a storm with each other and with us. Children labelled 'difficult' ended up demonstrating empathy, patience, coping skills and all sorts of pro-social behaviour.

We had definite ups and downs, and it was hard work, but we clearly saw what is possible when us educators and children have a bit more space, time and freedom to just be with each other.

A Year 1 boy I had been supporting prior to Covid-19 was also with us. In this new context he was, for the first time I believe, showing a stronger interest in playing with and building relationships with peers. This was emotionally risky for him, and he did not take perceived rejection lightly. It was significant that he was willing to keep at it though. On some days it broke my heart as he tried to work through why his peers might not want to play, but I believe he felt safer to do it within the bubble. Some days I would just stand back, while being physically and emotionally present but also allowing them to practise all these friendship interactions. Other times I more directly intervened, suggesting phrases or ways he could successfully enter others' play. Or I modelled phrases and directly asked on his behalf. By the last week he was using so many of these tools for himself.

Kerry: It seems to me that lockdown has enabled adults to become more available to children. While we don't need to be fully immersed within their play, we can tune into it and be that secure base. The bubble has almost allowed us to actually spend time with children, and the children clearly are picking up on that availability.

David: Yeah, in the context of our little bubble, absolutely. Young children need present adults in their lives, and they have a keen sense of when we are actually present or not. To be clear, this doesn't mean they need us to be playmates or leaders of every activity, but they need to feel seen and understood. As educators, our time and energy are a truly precious resource, and I desperately want us educators to start demanding some say of how and where we spend it. Unfortunately, there is a culture of not wanting to say no and misguided martyrdom in education, and it appears 'normal' to run through our days like headless chickens trying to do everything we are expected to do in this stupid system. The children might not understand the system, but they definitely sense our lack of presence and our inability to hold a space where they can move at their pace, and this leads to all sorts of issues that increase our own stress and burnout. That sense of, 'Oh, I love working in Early Years, but it is full on, it's like herding cats.' Cats aren't meant to be herded.

We do a lot of things in Early Years that are not necessary. We have to start putting some boundaries on our time and energy. We simply have to start doing less so we can have the time and presence of mind needed to build real relationships with the children as well as our co-workers. Some of these tasks come from without, but we also put a lot of stuff on our shoulders, ironically in a way to buy us a bit of truly needed breathing time away from the children. To me, displays are the most common example of this. Why do we really, in our heart of hearts, put so much effort into them?

Kerry: How often do we choose the display over the child? I know as a practitioner; I personally couldn't handle being contained in a room for so many hours. High-quality play alongside children can only exist if we have the resources and capacity to be present… to be available… rather than, as you said, walking around with our heads cut off.

David: And to bring it back to my children with SEND, during this 'bubble', they were jumping over stupid passport targets and going in a much wider variety of directions than would have been possible during a typical pre-Covid day. Play is how children are genetically hard-wired to seek out the experiences and relationships they need for their holistic development. This is no different for SEND children. We need to fully learn and accept this fact if we ever want to stop running ourselves ragged.

Honestly, I get that 'atypical' children can make many educators feel unsure or uncomfortable. With a proper lack of training and education, many of us assume our job is to get them to 'act normal'. If we – educators but also setting leaders – don't truly understand their behaviours, it makes perfect sense why we are in this state of currently drowning under all these ineffective interventions.

Kerry: It is so true… within SEND, we have become so burdened by procedural systems and prescribed interventions that play almost seems like a segregated aspect. If we see a 'typically developing' child interested in something, we build our teaching around it, but if we see a child unusually fascinated by something, it suddenly becomes an indicator of a delay, and we intervene. In fact, most of the interventions we see directly contradict the definition of play.

Companion resources

There are numerous recommendations throughout this book and the following companion resources have been developed to support you in your ongoing practice. Please visit www.eyfs4me.com and use the password 'SENDGUIDE' to access the following:

Acronym dictionary – This resource can be used to create a list of acronyms and their meanings. This can be a particularly helpful tool for parents.

Celebratory profile – This framework for thinking can be used to capture a child's strengths, interests, differences and needs, and provides a holistic way to planning the right support.

Inclusion monitoring form – This resource provides the setting with a format for monitoring those children who may need SEND support. It is ideal for the SENDCo to ensure that they have a good overview of the settings needs.

Local Offer board example – This visual gives you an idea of how a local offer board could work within your setting.

Local Offer questionnaire – This short questionnaire will support you to think about what you currently offer a setting for SEND children and families.

Meeting agenda – This format can be used when planning meetings with parents and specialists and will help you to ensure that everyone is on the same page when discussing the child's needs.

Observation schedule – This format can be used to support joint observations and discussions about children's development.

Play passport – This passport contains numerous ways to capture a child's unique way of playing and communicating.

Play-rich SEND toolkit – This short guide will support you to set up your own SEND toolkit and provides a suggested structure for developing an accessible and practical set of strategies, techniques and approaches.

Referral checklist – A short handy guide that can be used to support your referral processes and requests for statutory assessments.

SENDCO/Practitioner passport – This resource can be used to develop profiles of your staff for parents. It is great for transitions, and key person allocation.

Transition headlines – This format is useful for capturing key information about a child when they are transitioning from one setting to another.

References

Allred, K. and Hancock, C. (2012). 'On death and disability: reframing educators' perceptions of parental response to disability'. *Disability Studies Quarterly*, 32, (4).

Athey, C. (1990). *Extending Thought in Young Children: A Parent Teacher Partnership*. London: Paul Chapman.

Athey, C. (1991). *Extending thought in young children: A parent-teacher partnership*. Sage.

Aynsley-Green, A. (2018). *The British Betrayal of Childhood: Challenging Uncomfortable Truths and Bringing About Change*. Routledge.

Bayat, M. (2019). *Addressing Challenging Behaviors and Mental Health Issues in Early Childhood*. Routledge.

Bercow, J. (2018). *Bercow: Ten Years On: An independent review of provision for children and young people with speech, language and communication needs in England* [online]. Available at: www.bercow10yearson.com/wp-content/uploads/2018/03/337644-ICAN-Bercow-Report-WEB.pdf

Berk, L. E., & Meyers, A. B. (2013). The Role of Make-Believe Play in the Development of Executive Function: Status of Research and Future Directions. *American Journal of Play*. 6(1), 98-110.

Bodrova, E., & Leong, D. J. (2015). Vygotskian and Post-Vygotskian Views on Children's Play. *American Journal of Play*. 7(3), 371-388.

Bos, K. J., Fox, N., Zeanah, C. H., & Nelson, C. A. (2009). Effects of early psychosocial deprivation on the development of memory and executive function. *Frontiers in behavioral neuroscience*. 3, 16.

Bowlby, J. (1951). Maternal care and mental health. *World Health Organization Monograph* (Serial No. 2).

Bowlby, J., & Ainsworth, M. (2013). The origins of attachment theory. *Attachment theory: Social, Developmental, and Clinical Perspectives*. 45, 759-775.

Brown, B. (2018). *Dare to Lead: Brave Work. Tough Conversations. Whole Hearts*. Vermilion.

Brown, B. (2019). 'Are People Doing The Best They Can?' | Brené Brown & Russell Brand [online]. *Youtube*. Available at: https://www.youtube.com/watch?v=w5TkA7d7eTw

Bruce, T., McNair, L., & Whinnett, J. eds. (2020). *Putting Storytelling at the Heart of Early Childhood Practice: A Reflective Guide for Early Years Practitioners*. Routledge.

Bryce-Clegg, A. (2016). Gender Schema, Your Space and You!. *ABC Does* [blog]. 6 February 2016. Available at: https://abcdoes.com/abc-does-a-blog/2016/02/06/gender-schema-your-space-and-you/

Bubb, S. and Earley, P. (2013). The use of training days: finding time for teachers' professional development. *Educational Research*. 55, (3), 236–248.

Cameron, C., & Moss, P. eds. (2020). *Transforming Early childhood education: Towards a Democratic Education*. UCL Press.

Canning, N. (2007). Children's empowerment in play. *European Early Childhood Education Research Journal*. 15(2), 227-236.

Casby, M. W. (2003). Developmental assessment of play: A model for early intervention. *Communication Disorders Quarterly*. 24(4), 175-183.

Castro-Kemp, S., Palikara, O. and Grande, C. (2019). Status quo and inequalities of the statutory provision for young children in England, 40 years on from Warnock. *Frontiers in Education*. 4, 76.

Chang, Y. C., Shih, W., Landa, R., Kaiser, A., & Kasari, C. (2018). Symbolic play in school-aged minimally verbal children with autism spectrum disorder. *Journal of autism and developmental disorders*. 48(5), 1436-1445.

Charlop, M. H., Lang, R., & Rispoli, M. (2018). *Play and Social Skills for Children with Autism Spectrum Disorder*. Springer International Publishing.

Cheah, C. S., Nelson, L. J., & Rubin, K. H. (2001). Nonsocial play as a risk factor in social and emotional development. In A. Göncü & E. L. Klein (eds.), *Children in play, story, and school* (pp. 39–71). The Guilford Press.

Chilvers, D. (2020). Development Does Matter…. *Watch Me Grow* [online]. 15 March 2020. Available at: https://watchmegrow.uk/2020/03/development-does-matter/

Christakis, E. (2017). *The Importance of Being Little: What Young Children Really Need from Grownups*. Penguin.

Cohen, L., & Uhry, J. (2007). Young children's discourse strategies during block play: A Bakhtinian approach. *Journal of Research in Childhood Education*. 21(3), 302-315.

Council for Disabled Children (2013). *How to use the early years developmental journal* [online]. Available at: https://councilfordisabledchildren.org.uk/sites/default/files/uploads/files/merged-school-years-developmental-journal.pdf

Council for Disabled Children (2015a). *SEN and disability in the early years toolkit* [online]. Available at: https://councilfordisabledchildren.org.uk/help-resources/resources/sen-and-disability-early-years-toolkit

Council for Disabled Children (2015b). *Disabled Children and the Equality Act 2010* [online]. Available at: https://councilfordisabledchildren.org.uk/sites/default/files/uploads/files/equality-act-early-years_online.pdf

Crutchley, R. ed. (2017). *Special Needs in the Early Years: Partnership and Participation*. Sage.

Csikszentmihalyi, M., Abuhamdeh, S., & Nakamura, J. (2014). Flow. In: *Flow and the Foundations of Positive Psychology* (pp. 227-238). Springer, Dordrecht.

Dahlberg, G., Moss, P. and Pence, A. R. (1999). *Beyond Quality in Early Childhood Education and Care: Postmodern Perspectives*. Psychology Press.

Davies, S. (2019). *The Montessori Toddler: A Parent's Guide to Raising a Curious and Responsible Human Being*. Workman Publishing.

Department for Children, Schools and Families (DCSF) (2008). *The Early Years Foundation Stage Statutory Framework* [online]. Available at: https://earlyyearsmatters.co.uk/wp-content/uploads/2011/01/Statutory-Framework-for-the-Early-Years-Foundation-Stage-EYM.pdf

Department for Children, Schools and Families (DCSF) (2009a). *Achievement for all* [online]. Available at: https://dera.ioe.ac.uk/2401/1/sen_afa_guide_00782.pdf

Department for Children, Schools and Families (DCSF) (2009b). *Learning, playing and interacting: good practice in the Early Years Foundation Stage* [online]. Available at: www.foundationyears.org.uk/wp-content/uploads/2011/10/Learning_Playing_Interacting.pdf

Department for Education (DfE) (2014a). *Integrated review at age 2: implementation study* [online]. Available at: www.gov.uk/government/publications/integrated-review-at-age-2-implementation-study

Department for Education (DfE) (2014b). *Early years: guide to the 0 to 25 SEND code of practice* [online]. Available at: https://assets.publishing.service.gov.uk/government/uploads/system/uploads/attachment_data/file/350685/Early_Years_Guide_to_SEND_Code_of_Practice_-_02Sept14.pdf

Department for Education (DfE) (2017a). *Study of Early Education and Development (SEED): meeting the needs of children with special educational needs and disabilities in the early years* [online]. Available at: https://assets.publishing.service.gov.uk/government/uploads/system/uploads/attachment_data/file/586240/SEED_Meeting_the_needs_of_children_with_SEND_in_the_early_years_-_RR554.pdf

Department for Education (DfE) (2017b). *SEN support: a rapid evidence assessment* [online]. Available at: https://assets.publishing.service.gov.uk/government/uploads/system/uploads/attachment_data/file/628630/DfE_SEN_Support_REA_Report.pdf

Department for Education (DfE) (2018a), 'Working Together to Safeguard Children', https://assets.publishing.service.gov.uk/government/uploads/system/uploads/attachment_data/file/942454/Working_together_to_safeguard_children_inter_agency_guidance.pdf

Department for Education (DfE) (2018b). *What to expect, when?* [online]. Available at: www.foundationyears.org.uk/wp-content/uploads/2019/01/What-to-Expect-When-2018.pdf

Department for Education (DfE) (2019). *Education inspection framework (EIF)* [online]. Available at: www.gov.uk/government/publications/education-inspection-framework

Department for Education (DfE) (2020). *Early Years Foundation Stage reforms* [online]. Available at: https://assets.publishing.service.gov.uk/government/uploads/system/uploads/attachment_data/file/8968 7 2/EYFS_reforms_consultation_-_government_response.pdf

Department for Education (DfE) (2021a). *Changes to the Early Years Foundation Stage (EYFS) framework* [online]. Available at: www.gov.uk/government/publications/changes-to-the-early-years-foundation-stage-eyfs-framework/changes-to-the-early-years-foundation-stage-eyfs-framework

Department for Education (DfE) (2021b). *Special educational needs and disability: an analysis and summary of data sources* [online]. Available at: https://assets.publishing.service.gov.uk/government/uploads/system/uploads/attachment_data/file/985162/Special_educational_needs_Publication_May21_final.pdf

Department for Education (DfE) (2021c). *Statutory framework for the early years foundation stage: Setting the standards for learning, development and care for children from birth to five* [online]. Available at: https://assets.publishing.service.gov.uk/government/uploads/system/uploads/attachment_data/file/974907/EYFS_framework_-_March_2021.pdf

Department for Education (DfE) (2021d). *Development Matters: Non-statutory curriculum guidance for the early years foundation stage* [online]. Available at: https://assets.publishing.service.gov.uk/government/uploads/system/uploads/attachment_data/file/1007446/6.7534_DfE_Development_Matters_Report_and_illustrations_web__2_.pdf

Department for Education (DfE) and Department of Health (DoH) (2015). *Special educational needs and disability code of practice: 0 to 25 years* [online]. Available at: https://assets.publishing.service.gov.uk/government/uploads/system/uploads/attachment_data/file/398815/SEND_Code_of_Practice_January_2015.pdf

Department for Education and Skills (DfES) (2001). *Special educational needs code of practice* [online]. Available at: https://assets.publishing.service.gov.uk/government/uploads/system/uploads/attachment_data/file/273877/special_educational_needs_code_of_practice.pdf

Department for Education and Skills (DfES) (2003). *Keeping Children Safe* [online]. Available at: https://www.gov.uk/government/publications/government-response-to-the-victoria-climbie-inquiry-report-and-joint-chief-inspectors-report-safeguarding-children

Diamond, A., Barnett, W. S., Thomas, J., & Munro, S. (2007). Preschool program improves cognitive control. Science (New York, NY), 318(5855), 1387.

Dobson, J. and Melrose, A. (eds) (2020). *Working with Children, Families and Young People: Professional Dilemmas, Perspectives and Solutions*. Routledge.

Dodd-Nufrio, A. T. (2011). Reggio Emilia, Maria Montessori, and John Dewey: Dispelling teachers' misconceptions and understanding theoretical foundations. *Early Childhood Education Journal*. 39(4), 235-237.

Duffy, S. (2011), *Citizensip & Professional Gift Models*. Centre for Welfare Reform.

Dunst, C. J. and Trivette, C. M. (2009). Capacity-building family-systems intervention practices. *Journal of Family Social Work*. 12, (2), 119–143.

Early Education (2012). Development matters in the Early Years Foundation Stage (EYFS) [online]. Available at: www.foundationyears.org.uk/files/2012/03/Development-Matters-FINAL-PRINT-AMENDED.pdf

Early Intervention Foundation (n.d.). *What is early intervention?* [online]. Available at: https://www.eif.org.uk/why-it-matters/what-is-early-intervention

Eberle, S. G. (2014). The Elements of Play Toward a Philosophy and a Definition of Play. *American Journal of Play*. 6(2).

Education Scotland (2020). *Realising the ambition: being me* [online]. Available at: https://education.gov.scot/media/3bjpr3wa/realisingtheambition.pdf

Ephgrave, A. (2020). *Planning in the Moment with Two and Three Year Olds: Child-Initiated Play in Action*. Routledge.

European Agency for Special Needs and Inclusive Education (2017). *Inclusive Early Childhood Education: Literature Review*. (F. Bellour, P. Bartolo and M. Kyriazopoulou, eds.). Odense, Denmark. Available at: https://core.ac.uk/download/pdf/155235595.pdf

Fairchild, N. & Kay, L. (2020). *The early years foundation stage (2021): Challenges and opportunities* [online]. Available at: https://www.bera.ac.uk/blog/the-early-years-foundation-stage-2021-challenges-and-opportunities

Family Action Network (FAN) (2014). *The Essential Conversation: What Parents and Teachers Can Learn From Each Other* [online]. Available at: https://www.familyactionnetwork.net/events/the-essential-conversation-what-parents-and-teachers-can-learn-from-each-other/

Fatherhood Institute (2007). Ten top tips for father-inclusive practice. *Fatherhood Institute* [online]. Available at: http://www.fatherhoodinstitute.org/2007/ten-top-tips-for-father-inclusive-practice/

File, N. (1994). Children's play, teacher–child interactions, and teacher beliefs in integrated early childhood programs. *Early Childhood Research Quarterly*. 9, 223–240.

Fisher, J. (2016). *Interacting or Interfering? Improving Interactions in the Early Years*. Maidenhead: Open University Press.

Fletcher-Watson, S. (2018). Is early autism intervention compatible with neurodiversity?. *DART* [online]. 21 June 2018. Available at: https://dart.ed.ac.uk/intervention-neurodiversity/

Flewitt, R., & Cowan, K. (2020). *Guidance for practitioners on digital documentation*. Froebel Trust. Available at: https://www.froebel.org.uk/uploads/documents/guidance-for-practitioners-on-digital-documentation.pdf

Garboden Murray, C. (2021). *Illuminating Care: The Pedagogy and Practice of Care in Early Childhood Communities*. Exchange Press.

Geddes, H. (2006). *Attachment in the Classroom*. London: Worth.

Gershensen, S. (2015). The alarming effect of racial mismatch on teacher expectations [online]. Available at: https://www.brookings.edu/blog/brown-center-chalkboard/2015/08/18/the-alarming-effect-of-racial-mismatch-on-teacher-expectations/

Goldstein, H. (2006). *Toward inclusive schools for all children: Developing a synergistic social learning curriculum*. Austin, TX: Pro-Ed.

Gottman, J. M., Katz, L. F., & Hooven, C. (1997). *Meta-emotion: How families communicate emotionally*. Lawrence Erlbaum Associates, Inc.

Gray, P. (2008), The Value of Play I: The Definition of Play Gives Insights. *Psychology Today* [online]. Available at: https://www.psychologytoday.com/gb/blog/freedom-learn/200811/the-value-play-i-the-definition-play-gives-insights

Gray, P. (2013). *Free to Learn: Why Unleashing the Instinct to Play Will Make Our Children Happier, More Self-Reliant, and Better Students for Life*. Basic Books.

Greenfield, P. M. and Suzuki, L. K. (1998). Culture and human development: implications for parenting, education, pediatrics and mental health. In: W. Damon, I. E. Sigel and K. A. Renninger (eds) (1998). *Handbook of Child Psychology: Child Psychology in Practice*. John Wiley & Sons Inc., pp. 1059–1109.

Grenier, J. (2021). *The EYFS reforms: Priorities, opportunities and myths* [online]. Available at: https://www.headteacher-update.com/best-practice-article/the-eyfs-reforms-priorities-opportunities-and-myths-development-matters-birth-to-five-matters-dr-julian-grenier-reception-communication-skills/236813/

Harper, L. V., & Huie, K. S. (1998). Free play use of space by preschoolers from diverse backgrounds: Factors influencing activity choices. *Merrill-Palmer Quarterly*. 44, 423–446.

Harper, L. V., & McCluskey, K. S. (2003). Teacher–child and child–child interactions in inclusive preschool settings: Do adults inhibit peer interactions?. *Early childhood research quarterly*. 18(2), 163-184.

Heiskanen, N., Alasuutari, M., & Vehkakoski, T. (2018). Positioning children with special educational needs in early childhood education and care documents. *British Journal of Sociology of Education*. 39(6), 827-843.

Herry, C., Bach, D. R., Esposito, F., Di Salle, F., Perrig, W. J., Scheffler, K., Lüthi, A. and Seifritz, E. (2007). Processing of temporal unpredictability in human and animal amygdala. *Journal of Neuroscience*. 27, (22), 5958–5966.

Hodgkins, A. (2019). Advanced empathy in the early years – a risky strength?. *New Zealand International Research in Early Childhood Education*. 22, (1), 46.

House of Commons Education Committee (2019). *Special educational needs and disabilities First Report of Session 2019* [online]. Available at: https://publications.parliament.uk/pa/cm201919/cmselect/cmeduc/20/20.pdf

Howard, J. (1998), *Families*. Transaction Publishers.

Hughes, T. (1995) 'A March Calf'. In: *A March Calf: Collected Animal Poems Vol 3*. Faber & Faber.

Huizinga, J. (1950). *Homo ludens, a study of the play-element in culture*. Roy.

Institute for Health Visiting (2020). *Health visiting during COVID 19: Unpacking redeployment decisions and support for health visitors' wellbeing* [online]. Available at: https://ihv.org.uk/wp-content/uploads/2020/04/Health-visiting-during-COVID19-Unpacking-redevelopment-decisions-report-FINAL-VERSION-17.4.20.pdf

Jacobson, T. (2008). *'Don't Get So Upset!' Help Young Children Manage Their Feelings by Understanding Your Own*. Readleaf Press.

Johnson, J. A. & Dinger, D. (2012). *Let Them Play: An Early Learning (UN)curriculum)*. Redleaf Press.

Koplow, L. (2007). *Unsmiling Faces: How Preschools Can Heal*. Teachers College Press.

Lane, J. (2008). *Young Children and Racial Justice: Taking Action for Racial Equality in the Early Years – Understanding the Past, Thinking About the Present, Planning for the Future*. Jessica Kingsley Publishers.

Langsted, O. (1994). Looking at quality from the child's perspective. In: Moss, P. & Pence, A. (1994), *Valuing quality in early childhood services: New approaches to defining quality*. Sage Publications.

Lawrence-Lightfoot, S. L. (2004). *The Essential Conversation: What Parents and Teachers Can Learn from Each Other*. Ballantine Books.

Lindon, J., Beckley, P. and Lindon, L. (2016). *Leadership in Early Years: Linking Theory and Practice* (2nd edn). Hachette UK.

Liu, C., Solis, S. L., Jensen, H., Hopkins, E. J., Neale, D., Zosh, J. M., Hirsh-Pasek, K., & Whitebread, D. (2017). *Neuroscience and learning through play: a review of the evidence* [Research summary]. The LEGO Foundation, DK.

Long, S., Souto-Manning, M. and Vasquez, V. (eds) (2016). *Courageous Leadership in Early Childhood Education: Taking a Stand for Social Justice*. Teachers College Press.

Longfield, A. (2019). *We need to talk: Access to speech and language therapy* [online]. Available at: https://www.childrenscommissioner.gov.uk/wp-content/uploads/2019/06/cco-we-need-to-talk-june-2019.pdf

Loreman, T. (2011). *Love as Pedagogy*. Springer Science & Business Media.

Love, B. (2014). Hip hop, grit, and academic success [online]. *Youtube*. Available at: https://www.youtube.com/watch?v=tkZqPMzgvzg

Mahoney, G. and Wiggers, B. (2007). The role of parents in early intervention: implications for social work. *Children & Schools*. 29, (1), 7–15.

Malaguzzi, L. (1994). Your image of the child: Where teaching begins. *Child Care Information Exchange*. 52-54.

Malaguzzi, R. (n.d.). *100 languages* [online]. Available at: www.reggiochildren.it/en/reggio-emilia-approach/100-linguaggi-en

McCoy, S. and Banks, J. (2012). Simply academic? Why children with special educational needs don't like school. *European Journal of Special Needs Education*. 27, (1), 81–97.

McNiff, J. (2014) *Writing and Doing Action Research*. Sage.

Meggitt, C., Manning-Morton, J. and Bruce, T. (2016). *Child Care and Education* (6th edn). Hodder Education.

Miller, D. and Brown, J. (2014). *We have the right to be safe: Protecting disabled children from abuse* [online]. NSPCC. Available at: https://library.nspcc.org.uk/HeritageScripts/Hapi.dll/search2?CookieCheck=44354.5502978472&searchTerm0=C5234

Murray, J. (2018). The play's the thing. *International Journal of Early Years Education*. 26:4, 335-339, DOI: 10.1080/09669760.2018.1527278

Murthy, V. H. (2020), *Together: Loneliness, Health and What Happens When We Find Connection*. Profile Books.

NASEN (2020). *Identifying Special Educational Needs In The Early Years* [online]. Available at: https://www.eymatters.co.uk/wp-content/uploads/2020/07/Identifying-special-educational-needs-in-the-early-years.pdf

Neaum, S. (2017). *What Comes Before Phonics?*. Learning Matters.

Nicholson, N. and Palaiologou, I. (2016). Early years foundation stage progress check at the age of two for early intervention in relation to speech and language difficulties in England: the voices of the team around the child. *Early Child Development and Care*, 186, (12), 2009–2021.

Northamptonshire County Council (n.d.). *Completing the 'All about Me' Section of EHC Plans: A guide for parents* [online]. Available at: https://www.northamptonshire.gov.uk/councilservices/children-families-education/SEND/ehc/Documents/EHC%20Plans%20Booklet%20web.pdf

NSPCC (2020). *Safeguarding children with special educational needs and disabilities (SEND)* [online]. Available at: https://learning.nspcc.org.uk/safeguarding-child-protection-schools/safeguarding-children-with-special-educational-needs-and-disabilities-send

Nutbrown, C. (1996) *Respectful Educators – Capable Learners: Children's Rights and Early Education*. Paul Chapman Publishing.

Nutbrown, C., Clough, P. and Atherton, F. (2013), *Inclusion in the Early Years*. SAGE Publications Limited.

O'Connor, A. (2017). *Understanding Transitions in The Early Years: Supporting Change Through Attachment and Resilience*. Routledge.

Ofsted (2010). *SEND review* [online]. Available at: www.gov.uk/government/publications/special-educational-needs-and-disability-review

Ofsted (2017). *Local area SEND inspections: one year on* [online]. Available at: https://assets. publishing.service.gov.uk/government/uploads/system/uploads/attachment_data/ file/652694/local_area_SEND_inspections_one__year__on.pdf

Ofsted (2021). *Early years inspection handbook for Ofsted registered provision* [online]. Available at: www.gov.uk/government/publications/early-years-inspection-handbook-eif/ early-years-inspection-handbook-for-ofsted-registered-provision

Page, J. (2014). Developing professional love in early childhood settings. In: Harrison, L. & Sumison, J. eds. (2014.) *Lived Spaces of Infant-Toddler Education and Care* (pp. 119-130). Springer.

Palikara, O., Castro, S., Gaona, C., & Eirinaki, V. (2019). Professionals' views on the new policy for special educational needs in England: ideology versus implementation. *European Journal of Special Needs Education*, 34(1), 83-97.

Peckham, K. (2017). Supporting effective school readiness in all children. *Journal of Health Visiting*, 5, (7), 342–345.

Pen Green Centre for Children and Families & Charnwood Nursery School (2018). *A celebratory approach to SEND assessment in the early years* [online]. Available at: www.pengreen.org/ wp-content/uploads/2018/05/A-Celebratory-Approach-to-SEND-Assessment-in-Early-Years-1.pdf

Pen Green Centre for Children and their Families (n.d.). Planning [online]. Available at: www. pengreen.org/holistic-approach-send-assessment-early-years-section-3/planning

Perry, P. (2019). *The Book You Wish Your Parents Had Read (and Your Children Will be Glad that You Did)*. Penguin.

Plank, E. (2016). *Discovering the Culture of Childhood*. Redleaf Press.

Prowle, A. and Hodgkins, A. (2020). *Making a Difference with Children, Young People and Families: Re-imagining the Role of the Practitioner*. Red Globe Press.

Puschmann, S., Brechmann, A., & Thiel, C. M. (2013). Learning-dependent plasticity in human auditory cortex during appetitive operant conditioning. *Human Brain Mapping*, 34(11), 2841.

Robinson, K., & Aronica, L. (2016). *Creative schools: The grassroots revolution that's transforming education*. Penguin.

Rodd, J. (2012). *Leadership in Early Childhood* [3rd ed]. McGraw-Hill Education.

Roger, C. R. (1951). *Client-centered therapy: Its current practice, implications and theory*. Houghton Mifflin.

Romanou, E. and Belton, E. (2020) *Isolated and struggling: social isolation and the risk of child maltreatment, in lockdown and beyond*. London: NSPCC.

Roskos, K. A., & Christie, J. F. (2000). *Play and literacy in early childhood: Research from multiple perspectives*. Lawrence Erlbaum Associates Publishers.

Rossetti, L. M. (2001). *Communication intervention: Birth to three*. Cengage Learning.

Rudoe, N. (2014). School exclusion and educational inclusion of pregnant young women. *Ethnography and Education*, 9, (1), 66–80.

Scottish Government (2014). *Building the Ambition*. Edinburgh: Crown. Available at: https://learn. sssc.uk.com/apps/development/bta.pdf

Sense (n.d.). *Making play inclusive* [online]. Available at: www.sense.org.uk/get-support/ support-for-children/play-toolkits

Shanker, S. (2016). *What is self-reg?* [infographic]. Available at: https://self-reg.ca/wp-content/uploads/2021/05/Infographic-What_Is_Self_Reg2021.pdf

Sibthorp, K. and Nicoll, T. (2014). *Making it Personal A Family Guide to Personalisation, Personal Budgets and Education, Health and Care Plans* [online]. Available at: https://www.preparingforadulthood.org.uk/SiteAssets/Downloads/ho3syw4n636379745638956594.pdf

Snyder, P., Hemmeter, M. L., Meeker, K. A., Kinder, K., Pasia, C. and McLaughlin, T. (2012). Characterizing key features of the early childhood professional development literature. *Infants & Young Children*, 25, (3), 188–212.

Souto-Manning, M. (2017). Is play a privilege or a right? And what's our responsibility? On the role of play for equity in early childhood education. *Early Child Development and Care*, 187:5-6, 785-787

Stelmach, B. (2004). The Essential Conversation: What Parents and Teachers Can Learn From Each Other by Sara Lawrence-Lightfoot. *Alberta Journal of Educational Research*, 50(2).

Sutton-Smith, B. (1993). Dilemmas in adult play with children. *Parent-child play: Descriptions and implications*, 15-40.

Taggart, G. (2013). *The importance of empathy* [article]. Available at: https://www.nurseryworld.co.uk/Opinion/article/the-importance-of-empathy

Taylor, E. W. (2017). Transformative learning theory. In: A. Laros, T. Fuhr and E. W. Taylor (eds) *Transformative Learning Meets Bildung: An International Exchange*. Brill Sense. pp. 17–29.

Trawick-Smith, J. (2019). *Young Children's Play: Development, Disabilities, and Diversity*. Routledge.

UK Government (2004). *Children Act 2004* [online]. Available at: www.legislation.gov.uk/ukpga/2004/31/contents

UK Government (2006). *Childcare Act 2006* [online]. Available at: www.legislation.gov.uk/ukpga/2006/21/pdfs/ukpga_20060021_en.pdf

UK Government (2010). *Equality Act 2010* [online]. Available at: www.legislation.gov.uk/ukpga/2010/15/contents

UK Government (2014). *Children and Families Act 2014* [online]. Available at: www.legislation.gov.uk/ukpga/2014/6/contents/enacted

Van de Pol, J., Volman, M., & Beishuizen, J. (2010). Scaffolding in teacher–student interaction: A decade of research. *Educational Psychology Review*, 22(3), 271-296.

Vygotsky, L. S. (1978). Socio-cultural theory. *Mind in society*, 6, 52-58.

Whalley, M. (2015). *Working with children 0-3: Building a creative workforce* [Powerpoint presentation]. Early Years Scotland's National Conference, 3 October. Available at: https://earlyyearsscotland.org/Media/Docs/Conference/Presentations/Scotland%200-3.pdf

Whalley, M. (ed) (2017). *Involving Parents in Their Children's Learning: A Knowledge-Sharing Approach*. Sage.

Whalley, M., John, K., Whitaker, P., Klavins, E., Parker, C. and Vaggers, J. (2018). *Democratising Leadership in the Early Years: A Systemic Approach*. Routledge.

Winnicott, D. W. (1953). Symptom Tolerance in Pædiatrics: President's Address. *Proceedings of the Royal Society of Medicine*. 1953;46(8):675-684. doi:10.1177/003591575304600816.

Winnicott, D. W. (1991). *Playing and Reality*. Psychology Press.

Wright, C. Y., Darko, N., Standen, P. J. and Patel, T. G. (2010). RETRACTED: visual research methods: using cameras to empower socially excluded black youth. *Sociology*, 44, (3), 541–558.

Index